The Political Christopher Nolan

POLITICS, LITERATURE, & FILM

Series Editor: Lee Trepanier, Samford University

The Politics, Literature, & Film series is an interdisciplinary examination of the intersection of politics with literature and/or film. The series is receptive to works that use a variety of methodological approaches, focus on any period from antiquity to the present, and situate their analysis in national, comparative, or global contexts. Politics, Literature, & Film seeks to be truly interdisciplinary by including authors from all the social sciences and humanities, such as political science, sociology, psychology, literature, philosophy, history, religious studies, and law. The series is open to both American and non-American literature and film. By putting forth bold and innovative ideas that appeal to a broad range of interests, the series aims to enrich our conversations about literature, film, and their relationship to politics.

Advisory Board

Recent Titles

Irony, Liberalism, and Fantasy in the Films of Christopher by Jesse Russell
Magic in Early Modern England: Literature, Politics, and Supernatural Power by Andrew Moore
Philosophical Perspective on Film by Pedro Blas Gonzalez
Between Empire and Republic: America in the Colonial Canadian Imagination by Oana Godeanu-Kenworthy

The Political Christopher Nolan

Liberalism and the Anglo-American Vision

Jesse Russell

LEXINGTON BOOKS
Lanham • Boulder • New York • London

Published by Lexington Books
An imprint of The Rowman & Littlefield Publishing Group, Inc.
4501 Forbes Boulevard, Suite 200, Lanham, Maryland 20706
www.rowman.com

86-90 Paul Street, London, EC2A 4NE

British Library Cataloguing in Publication Information Available

Library of Congress Cataloging-in-Publication Data

Names: Russell, Jesse, 1982- author. Title: The political Christopher Nolan : liberalism and the Anglo-American vision / Jesse Russell.
Description: Lanham : Lexington Books, [2023] | Series: Politics, literature, & film | Includes bibliographical references.
Identifiers: LCCN 2023002813 (print) | LCCN 2023002814 (ebook) | ISBN 9781666906196 (cloth) | ISBN 9781666906202 (ebook)
Subjects: LCSH: Nolan, Christopher, 1970---Criticism and interpretation. | Neoliberalism in motion pictures. | Politics in motion pictures.
Classification: LCC PN1998.3.N65 R77 2023 (print) | LCC PN1998.3.N65 (ebook) | DDC 791.4302/33092–dc23/eng/20230227
LC record available at https://lccn.loc.gov/2023002813
LC ebook record available at https://lccn.loc.gov/2023002814

™ The paper used in this publication meets the minimum requirements of American National Standard for Information Sciences—Permanence of Paper for Printed Library Materials, ANSI/NISO Z39.48-1992.

For my dad, who taught me about movies.

Contents

Introduction

THE END OF HISTORY (AGAIN)

In 1989, Japanese American political scientist Francis Fukuyama published his monumental essay, "The End of History?" in *National Interest*.[1] This text, trumpeting the "triumph of the [American liberal capitalist] West" over the reactionary past, would later form a bestselling book titled *The End of History and the Last Man*. Drawing from Russian philosopher Alexandre Kojève's reading of the work of G. W. Hegel, Fukuyama's central thesis is that human history has reached its climax in American liberal democratic capitalism with the defeat of democratic capitalism's principle rival, Soviet Communism, at the end of the Cold War.[2] Throughout much of the 1990s, Fukuyama's thesis seemed largely validated. America appeared to boom under the Bill Clinton presidency, entering the odd twilight era between the electronic age and the digital age when the future seemed to promise unlimited wealth and freedom. America, at this time at least, faced very few serious rivals. Great Britain, headed by Tony Blair, was undergoing the rage of "cool Britannia" in which wealth and personal freedoms expanded. Prior to the advent of Vladimir Putin in 2000, Russia seemed poised to enter the American system, and NATO as well as the European Union, which likewise promised a liberal utopia of wealth and liberty, was in the process of engulfing Eastern Europe. Although shaken by colonialism, the Global South was not a threat to the United States so much as an opportunity for forging economic and political bounds (which some have called *neocolonialism*). The big threat to America was the enormous stretch of land and a host of people known as the Islamic world.

While it is well known that much of early twenty-first-century American culture was focused on depicting Muslims as enemies to the free world, American neoliberal cultural propaganda against Islam actually began in the 1990s. As if in preparation for the War on Terror, Americans battled Islamic terrorists on big screens in films such as Lewis Teague's 1990 *Navy Seals*, which has been identified as the first major film of the 1990s to present

Islamic terrorists as a serious threat to America. Muslims served as the villains in the 1951 *Sirocco* and other earlier works but, for obvious reasons, during the Cold War, Islam was not projected as the principal threat to the United States. As the Cold War ended, however, there was a need for a new national enemy. In the '90s, *Navy Seals* was accompanied by James Cameron's 1994 *True Lies*, Edward Zwick's 1998 *The Siege*, and Wolfgang Peterson's *Air Force One* (1997).[3] With the seeming demise of the Soviet Union, these films presented a new enemy for post–Cold War America. With much of the world folding into the wider neoliberal system, the Islamic world seemed to be the primary outlier who needed to be brought into the fold. This is not to argue that there were not genuine Islamic terrorists at this time who committed deeply unethical acts. However, as a host of critics have noted, the principal message of these films was that the Arab world was a chaotic threat to world peace that needed to be neutralized through American military might. These films were accompanied by various sci-fi movies of the 1990s that presented fears of an invasion of the United States by a militant Other, such as, most notably, *Independence Day* (1996).[4]

Islamic terrorism—whether explicitly presented or figured as extraterrestrial threat—was not the only obstacle to the end of history. The 1990s saw the rise of a host of dissident and radical movements from the left but especially the right as well. As the Cold War ended, the alliance of social conservatives, fiscal conservatives, and war hawks that formed the Reagan era began to dissolve, and various rightwing figures challenged the new Republican Party represented by George H. W. Bush and later Newt Gingrich and Bob Dole. White nationalist David Duke successfully won a Louisiana house seat in 1989 and ran very competitive campaigns for a Louisiana national senate in 1990 as well as the Louisiana governor's seat in 1991. Catholic traditionalist and paleoconservative Patrick Buchanan also ran two powerful presidential campaigns in 1992 and 1996.

At the grassroots level, a host of militia movements and low-level right-wing organizations sprung up across the country in response to Bill Clinton's electoral victories in 1992 and 1996. With right-wing populist anger simmering below the surface and exploding into national media with events like the Oklahoma City Bombing, it was necessary for American films to present homegrown right-wing resistance to Clintonian liberalism as a marginal pathology. Films such as *Falling Down* (1993) and *American History X* (1998) accomplished this by presenting the angry white male as a mental health pathology that either needed to be reformed, retired, or, in the case of *Falling Down*'s Michael Douglas's character William Foster, executed for his own good. As right-wing populism as well as various terrorist organizations grew in Europe as well, the old European enemies of America as well—especially Germany and Russia—made the appearance in films as rogue agents or mercenaries who still carried the Nazi or Soviet brutal and totalitarian ethos into the late twentieth century. For the most part, these threats could be handled by James Bond or Harrison Ford or whatever other superhero fit the bill. There were also World War II films such as Stephen Spielberg's 1993 *Schindler's List* and *Saving Private Ryan* (1998), which represented one of the most important narratives of the American Century: the triumph of liberal and tolerant America over cruel and totalitarian Germany. During the chaos, upheaval, and "spin" of the 1990s, there never was a sense that American neoliberalism would seriously be challenged from within or without, and there was a general feeling that the world was, indeed, living at the "end of history."

That optimism collapsed on the morning of September 11, 2001 (9/11). The advent of 9/11 was a profound event that shook the notion of American global supremacy. At the same time, it was an event that paradoxically and simultaneously reaffirmed American global rule and galvanized American culture in the service of American military and cultural supremacy. It is a truism that every film released after 9/11 for at least a decade is about 9/11. Works such as Terrence McSweeney's *The War on Terror and American Film: 9/11* and Scott Laderman and Tim Gruenewald's collection of essays, *Imperial Benevolence: U.S. Foreign Policy and American Popular Culture Since 9/11*, as well as Dan Hassler-Forest's *Capitalist Superheroes: Caped Crusaders in the Neoliberal Age* document how American films, even those that are not specifically nationalistic, nonetheless have endorsed American foreign policy as well as neoliberalism. Throughout a host of films—ranging from Michael Bay's *Transformers* series (2007–present) to *The Avengers* series (2007–present), as well as a host of more serious films such as Kathryn Bigelow's *The Hurt Locker* (2008) and *Zero Dark Thirty* (2012)—there is constant thread: the world of liberal capitalist humanism led by the United States is, despite its flaws, fundamentally good. The reactionary, fundamentalist, and radical threats to this regime, whatever their attractiveness, are fundamentally dangerous and only can offer worse evils than those faults in American liberalism that these groups criticize.

September 11 further helped to create what Mark Fisher has called "lost futures" or anticipated positive futures that were dreamed of—especially during the 1990s—but never came to fruition. Fisher explains that "the 21st century is oppressed by a crushing sense of finitude and exhaustion. It doesn't feel like the future. Or, alternatively, it doesn't feel as if the 21st century has started yet."[5] Fisher argues that the West, and perhaps the wider world, is culturally exhausted and cannot produce new art anymore. Thus, if the bulk of twenty-first-century culture appears almost entirely derivative from the past, then it is because it is. Fisher further explains that the emergence of the digital age has "altered the texture of everyday experience beyond all recognition.

Yet, perhaps *because* of this, there's an increasing sense that culture has lost the ability to grasp and articulate the present. Or it could be that, in one very important sense, there is no present to grasp and articulate anymore."[6] The twenty-first century is defined by its sense of unreality, for the past is made present and the future is immanentized on digital platforms, but it is not really present. The mind can only be fooled for so long—although, it can certainly be fooled.

Among the number of filmmakers who have risen to prominence in the twenty-first century, Anglo-American director Christopher Nolan stands at the precipitous nodal point between the attempt for Anglo-American neoliberalism to establish itself as the dominant intellectual system while it is aggressively challenged from within and without as well as the new normal of the digital age in which the divide between fiction and reality has been completely obliterated. Beginning with his 1998 *Following* to his 2020 *Tenet*, Nolan's films have navigated the transition from the end of history through the 9/11 era to the new post-Trumpian COVID era. Nolan's films are principally known for their mind-bending narrative and intellectual puzzles they present and do not usually inspire political debates. However, at the same time, there has been much critical attention drawn to the political implications of his *Dark Knight* trilogy. Much of this debate has focused on the degree to which Nolan supports the political order of Gotham vis-à-vis the revolutionary forces seeing to undermine it. Despite Nolan's seemingly sympathetic portraits of his villains such as Ra's al Ghul, Joker, and Bane (among others), the *Dark Knight* trilogy ultimately affirms the order of Gotham, which stands as representative of the twenty-first-century (Anglo-)American world order. This affirmation of American neoliberalism is, in fact, a persistent theme of Nolan's work—even in his most "artistic" or "aesthetic" works.

Nolan's first major studio film, *Memento* (2000), is very much a film about the later twentieth century. Its focus is upon the life and mind of one key character: Leonard Shelby (played by Australian actor Guy Pearce), an insurance investigator who appears to have anterograde amnesia (the inability to make new memories) and is ostensibly tracking his wife's murderer. However, as the film progresses, the viewer is left uncertain what really happened, and Nolan ends the film with the possibility that Leonard is traveling about murdering random men to give meaning to his banal and unhappy late twentieth-century bourgeois life. Receding backwards from its "ending," *Memento* is a deep exploration of human consciousness and the meaning of human acts. However, the end of the film is basically a Nietzschean post-ironic affirmation of the will to live and create meaning in one's life. At the same time, *Memento* explores the ironic predicament of post–Cold War American life. For many in the West and Far East in the late twentieth and early twenty-first centuries, every comfort and desire appeared to have been fulfilled, leaving postmodern humans unhappy and unsatisfied, seeking meaning in alternative, ludic lifestyles. Drawing from Nietzsche, in his *End of History and the Last Man*, Francis Fukuyama chronicles this paradox. Humans living in liberal democracy are (ideally at least) affirmed in their dignity and worth, but many humans feel stifled by the mediocrity that this egalitarian system engenders. In *Memento*, Leonard Shelby has the Gen X dream of a beautiful wife and an affluent job, but such a life is stifling and mediocre, and he must create a new self that gives meaning to existence. However, in *Memento*, it is precisely the comfort and stability provided by the American Century that enables one to pursue an innovative life, becoming the (at least apparent) director and actor of one's own life.

The first film of what would become Christopher Nolan's *Dark Knight* trilogy, *Batman Begins*, uniquely tells the story of Bruce Wayne's development into the caped crusader. The film is thus, like *Memento*, about the life of one man. However, it is also a bigger story about Bruce Wayne–Batman's struggle against the League of Shadows, a mysterious ancient order headed by Ra's al Ghul. As a result, *Batman Begins* is story about the Old World Order and the new. The League of Shadows has a strongly Eurasian Old World feel. Associated with magic and mystery, the members of the league practice martial arts and speak in European accents and dwell in the Himalayan mounts. In contrast, the young and fit and very American Bruce Wayne is a symbol of the future of the new world. He is further a humanist and "liberal," attempting to avoid directly killing anyone. He thus stands in contrast to Ra's al Ghul and the League of Shadows, who use lethal violence liberally. Batman's (temporary) triumph (with possible and surprising echoes of the second Iraq War) in the film is representative of triumph of American liberalism over the old world and the need for this new order to be both just and humane.

Very likely echoing the War on Terror, which was then ramping up at the end of the Bush era and the beginning of the Obama era, *The Dark Knight* and *The Dark Knight Rises* are both exceptionally dark and represent a realpolitik assessment of the need for the liberal order to occasionally use the "iron fist" when dealing with especially dangerous enemies, who in the films are represented by the Joker and Bane. In *The Dark Knight*, the Joker is a deeply primal and archetypal character who represents the recurrent temptation of evil, to which Batman and the people of Gotham (and the people of the world) are drawn. Although temporarily needing to use harsh methods with Joker, Batman eventually returns to a more humane approach at the end of the film.

In *The Dark Knight Rises*, Bane represents a less primal force than Joker: an unchained populist rebellion against the establishment such as potentially was present in the Occupy Wallstreet movement and Tea Party of the "real world." Bane's movement, which is a spinoff of the old order of the League of

Shadows, is representative of twenty-first-century challenges to the American world order. Employing brute force to defeat Bane, Bruce Wayne ultimately sacrifices himself for Gotham, faking his own death. He is later found by Alfred in Florence, Italy, while Joseph Gordon Levitt's Robin continues the perennial struggle against political and moral chaos. Bruce Wayne's retirement with Selina Kyle, or Catwoman, in a foreign and exotic country is made possible because of the vigilance of Batman and Robin and the American security state as well as the capitalist liberal imperium over America (here represented by The Wayne Corporation and Gotham City).

Christopher Nolan's seventh major studio film, *Inception*, is, in a certain sense, a return to the cerebral musing of *Memento*. However, in *Inception*, Nolan crafts a film with a much larger budget and with much larger expectations. With the success of *The Dark Knight*, Nolan had cut his teeth on the making of a blockbuster and, in *Inception*, was able to weave a deep exploration of human consciousness with an international thriller headlined by Leonardo DiCaprio. The plot of *Inception* is structured around Dom Cobb, a thief with a penchant for psychology who has developed the ability to enter dreams and manipulate the minds of others. Like *Memento*, *Inception* is a movie about the mind, but it is also a film about the new global world order in which billionaires travel the world emmeshed in espionage, bending nature, the law, and even the mind to their will. Despite some small criticism, *Inception*, however, is not an indictment of (American) global capitalism. It is rather, on one level, an homage to its power. Framed for the murder of his wife, Cobb is attempting to get back to Los Angeles, California, for a *nostos* or homecoming with his children. At the end of the film, we are left wondering if Cobb truly made it home. At this point, Nolan's puckish and ironic exploration of consciousness, reality, and art returns, for the final scene of the movie is a three-layered illusion. If he is no longer dreaming, then even this reality is a "brief candle," and the homecoming is unreal. If he is still dreaming, it does not matter, for his dreams are experienced as being as (un-)real as physical reality. Finally, *Inception* is a movie, and Cobb's journey is ironically an illusion experienced as something real by the audience. Again, all this musing is made possible for Nolan, the audience, and the characters (and actors) in the film because of the global capitalist, liberal order that the film subtly fetes.

Christopher Nolan's *Interstellar* famously began as a Steven Spielberg film about a future space race between the United States and China. This space race, of course, would have been won by the United States whose astronaut Joseph Cooper would have saved the world. The Spielberg vision, however, was eventually lost as Spielberg's DreamWorks studio was purchased from Paramount by Disney. Christopher Nolan, however, having been gifted the script crafted by his brother Jonah, added another element to the *Interstellar* script: the story of the love between a father and daughter. While some critics have complained that the two narratives conflict, and *Interstellar* should have been two or perhaps even three different films, the narrative of Cooper's relationship with his daughter Murph is integrally tied to the salvific space mission in the film. In Christopher Nolan's *Interstellar*, Joseph Cooper and his daughter Murph save humanity from extinction by helping humanity escape from a dying earth. Their efforts, however, clash with those of Dr. Mann and the elder Dr. Brand, who hold an aggressive selfish and violent vision of human survival. In contrast to the brutal utilitarianism of Dr. Mann and the older Dr. Brand, Dr. Amelia Brand teaches Cooper a new impetus for success: love. Acting as a gravitational force, love can guide humans to each other, and, in *Inception*, love ultimately saves not only the Cooper family, but the whole human race. There is a clear political message to the film as well. As illustrated in films such as *The Right Stuff* (1983), the first era of American space flight as well as American military-industrial success was marked by an aggressive will to power and willingness to sacrifice individuals for sake of defeating America's enemies. The new era hoped for by the Nolan brothers is one in which love for humanity, which is expressed through love for one's family, will drive forward a new era of exploration and scientific achievement. Nonetheless, while love will be the driving force of a new America that will save the world, as the imagery and plot of *Interstellar* suggest, it will be America that will emerge as the dominant force in space, which the nation will colonize.

Christopher Nolan's *Tenet* is a film that, except for *Interstellar* (and perhaps his early *Following* [1998]) places the greatest intellectual strain on the viewer and sits uneasily in Nolan's canon. Although clearly set in the twenty-first century and deeply affected by twenty-first-century politics, Nolan attempts to frame the film on top of the Cold War tension on which so many twentieth-century thrillers were based. The story is deeply emmeshed with theoretical speculations about time travel and a murky and unresolved espionage plot. Although ironically set almost entirely in Europe (with forays to India), the film is Nolan's first to feature a person of color in its title role. John David Washington plays a character simply known as "the Protagonist," who is attempting to save the world from destruction at the hands of a dying Ukrainian arms merchant while, at the same time, helping the Ukrainian's estranged wife, Kat. *Tenet* is deeply post-Trumpian. John David Washington's Protagonist is one of many historic black American characters who have come to prominence in the third decade of the twenty-first century. *Twilight*'s Robert Pattison presents the petit and sensitive post–Arnold Schwarzenegger action hero, and the brutal and ambitious Ukrainian arms dealer, played by Kenneth Branagh, serves as a figure for the menacing East. The film further has an immense global cast, including two prominent Hindi actors, representing not only Christopher Nolan's popularity in India, but the new multipolar world. However, in the end, it is John David Washington, the new face of post-millennial America, who saves the day, thus asserting, once again, the need for American preeminence to not only to rescue the world, but to hold the very fabric of time in place.

While I do make mention of *Following* and treat *Insomnia* in my conclusion on Nolan and truth, I do purposely omit one of Nolan's most explicitly political films: *Dunkirk*. The 2017 film, released during the era of the election of President Donald Trump and the Brexit referendum, would seem to be a perfect fit for a book on Christopher Nolan and Anglo-American imperialism. The film quiet clearly showcases the bravery of British soldiers in the face of seeming defeat at the hands of totalitarian Germany. However, *Dunkirk*, while dealing with the psychology of war and employing some cinematic "tricks," is not the same sort of film as Nolan's other works, which deal with the question of how humans form and manipulate their own realities. Nonetheless, *Dunkirk* is a film that deserves continued scholarly analysis.

Ultimately, Christopher Nolan's films are not simply reducible to pure propaganda. They should not be read as advertisements for the US military, intelligence agencies or the Department of Defense.[7] Nonetheless, Nolan's films present Anglo-American liberalism as being the most feasible vehicle for the good life the characters in his films desire (but perhaps never find). This order this threatened by the reactionary past of the "Old World," which demands adherence to a strict moral code and violent suppression of dissident. However, Nolan feels as though this Old World must be suppressed and tamed and integrated into the new and increasingly diverse Western liberal imperium. The radical left further makes legitimate criticism of capitalism in the unequal distribution of wealth. Nonetheless, again, Nolan holds that such criticism must spurn the liberal system to improve itself, and this system should not be destroyed in toto. As imperfect and flawed as Anglo-American liberalism is, in his films, Christopher Nolan ultimately depicts America as the last, best hope for the world.

NOTES

1. Fukuyama, "The End of History."
2. Fukuyama, *The End of History and the Last Man*.
3. Ramji, "From Navy Seals to The Siege: Getting to Know the Muslim Terrorist, Hollywood Style."
4. Michael C. Frank, "Alien Terrorists: Public Discourse on 9/11 and the American Science Fiction Film."
5. Fisher, *Ghosts of My Life*, 8.

6. Fisher, *Ghosts of My Life*, 9.

7. For the relationship between Hollywood and the CIA, see Boyd-Barrett, Herrera, and Baumann; Serdouk; Hajjar; and Willmetts.

Chapter 1

The Twilight of the American Century in Christopher Nolan's *Memento*

Christopher Nolan's first major studio film, *Memento* (2000), is a movie very much about the later twentieth century and the 1990s specifically. Its focuses upon the life of Leonard Shelby (played by Australian actor Guy Pearce), an insurance investigator who appears to have anterograde amnesia (the inability to make new memories) and who is ostensibly tracking his wife's murderer. However, as the film progresses, the viewer is left uncertain what really happened, and Nolan ends *Memento* with the possibility that Leonard is simply traveling about murdering random men to give meaning to his banal and unhappy late twentieth-century bourgeois life. Receding backwards from its "ending," *Memento* is an exploration of human consciousness and the meaning of human acts. However, the end of the film is basically a Nietzschean post-ironic affirmation of the will to live and create meaning in one's life. At the same time, *Memento* explores the ironic predicament of post–Cold War American life. As Francis Fukuyama notes in *The End of History and the Last Man*, at the "end of history," for many in the West and the Far East, every comfort and desire was fulfilled, leaving postmodern humans unhappy and unsatisfied, seeking meaning in alternative, ludic lifestyles. However, in Nolan's vision, it is precisely the comfort and stability provided by the American Century that enables one to pursue an innovative life, becoming the (at least apparent) director and actor of one's own life.

In 1992, Francis Fukuyama published his now classic tome: *The End of History and the Last Man*. In this work, Fukuyama trumpeted the triumph of (Anglo-American) liberal capitalism over Soviet Marxism. Indeed, for many (but not all) Americans and other Westerners, the 1990s had the feeling of an Indian Summer in which the benefits of American capitalism could be harvested by the middle and upper classes. However, the end of history did not produce the deep and abiding happiness for which many sought. A host of counter cultural rebellions, ranging from gangster rap to grunge and techno attempted to upend the social order, but were, in fact, repackaged and sold to the masses by capitalism. In *The End of History*, Fukuyama notes that, in his original *National Interest* piece, he identified the problems present in capitalism as being the result of the "incomplete implementation of the twin principals of liberty and equality on which modern democracy is founded, rather than flaws in the principles themselves."[1] Fukuyama also notes that liberal capitalism was integrally linked with and empowered by the tremendous technology of the electronic age, stating, "Technology makes possible the limitless accumulation of wealth, and thus the satisfaction of an ever-expanding set of human desires."[2] The key problem here is that once these desires were satisfied, members of liberal democracies wanted something more. The world became increasingly monotonous and boring as Fukuyama further notes, "This process guarantees an increasing homogenization of all human societies, regardless of their historical origins or cultural inheritances."[3] In a world in which everyone was the same and equal, there was no escape from the boredom. It had achieved total dominance. Drawing from Nietzsche, Fukuyama further argues that "Liberal democracy produced 'men without chests,' composed of desire and reason but lacking *thymos* [spiritedness], clever at finding new ways to satisfy a host of petty wants through the calculation of long-term self-interest."[4] Liberal democracy's last men ultimately lost their identity and ceased to be human.

Some Marxist critics have emphasized the role that capitalism has played in suffocating not only human achievement, but cultural production. The late post-Marxist thinker Mark Fisher has commented that the twenty-first century is stuck in a creative feedback loop in which the culture of the 1980s and 1990s are continually re-presented in variant form. Fischer writes in *Capitalist Realism* that there is a "sense of exhaustion, of cultural and political sterility" in the twenty-first century.[5] It seems that late and what now could be called "post-capitalism" has run out of creative energy. Fisher identifies the 2008 economic crash as the point at which neoliberalism was deprived of its "confident forward momentum."[6] Fisher further explains that within the twenty-first century, despite the crisis of neoliberalism after the 2008 market crisis, there was no alternative, and "neoliberalism is still politically inevitable."[7] Ultimately, as Fisher writes, capitalist realism can be described as the belief that there is no alternative to capitalism. The realization of this presents depression and anxiety for those who dreamt of alternative or variant modernities from that of liberal democratic capitalism. Not only is there no way to escape from the supposed nightmare of capitalism, but it is also impossible to imagine a world in which capitalism is not the exclusive economic and cultural system. However, as the twenty-first century has progressed, other scholars have taken alternative views. Following the trajectory of Fisher (who himself is following that of Frederic Jameson), the contemporary Slovenian Marxist Slavoj Žižek likewise has herald the anticipated end of capitalism in works such as *Living in the End Times* (2010) and, more recently, *Surplus Enjoyment: A Guide for the Non-Perplexed* (2022). However, while in the third decade of the twenty-first century, pandemics, political chaos, and ecological disasters do seem to place real strains on capitalism, in the heady, pre-9/11 days of the turn of the last century, things were, at least for many, a lot more stable and boring. It is in this world of the twilight of the "end of history" that the film *Memento* is set.

Christopher Nolan's 2000 *Memento*, although having been released at the beginning of the twenty-first century, is deeply transgressive work that is simultaneously entirely dependent—both in its production as well as in the narrative of its plot—upon the stability and structure of the American Century. As Claire Molloy notes, the film *Memento* itself is a "product of reterritorializing affiliations between global mainstreams and local substreams facilitated by the neo-liberal climate within which such constellations could occur."[8] It is a quintessentially postmodern film, and much of *Memento* has to do with how we as viewers perceive media and how media gives (self-constructed) meaning to the life of Leonard Shelby. The film begins with a polaroid picture of murdered Teddy, which is developing in reverse. Leonardo is shaking the polaroid. It is slowly getting more and more unclear. We realize something is wrong. We proceed backward from the violence effect to the cause. It is very postmodern: the image takes precedence over the act. James Mottram calls *Memento*, a postmodern fable filmed in the information age" in which the "hero is a renegade gumshoe, an amateur private eye strangely (yet aptly) dependent on handwritten notes and fading Polaroids—the latter flashed like a detective's badge; both a symbol of his quest and an assured definition of self. The distinct lack of electronic paraphernalia—buts, camcorders, tape-players, computers, cell-phones—indicates just how out of step Leonard is. Just as the tattoo reads 'Never Answer the Phone,' so Leonard is marooned from modern technology."[9]

The film then commences with Leonard Shelby saying, "So where are you? You are in some motel room." He awakens to find himself in a transient state. This is a very Heideggerian-existentialist trope. He is thrown amidst things over which he has no or little control and which he himself did not make. Toth argues that the bulk of Leonards' stops along his journey are "temporary, interstitial spaces . . . ," a point that Nolan himself commented on as being tied to Leonard's identity crisis.[10] However, we later see that this "thrownness" is not entirely accurate. Leonard has built much of the world that he inhabits and exercise a tremendous but deceptively ignorant control over his day-to-day existence. There is an especially curious observation if Leonard is faking the whole thing and hiding in another place. He has abandoned his comfortable home and lucrative job for a transient anxious life. The "never-had-it-so-good" life of the twentieth century was not enough for Leonard. He became a man without a chest immersed in the desperate world of "capitalist realism." To break free from this world, he creates the fiction that he is a heroic quester looking to avenge his wife's mother, and it is at least possible that he is making up his amnesia as well.

This state of amnesia is ironically advantageous for Leonard, for it creates struggle in his life that he otherwise would not have. It also gives Leonard the ability never to truly reach his goal, for, once he has reached it, he forgets that he has. Finally, it identifies him as the quintessential postmodern subject lost in a frantic state, alienated from the world, other humans, and from God. Later in conversation with Burt, the hotel clerk, Leonard explains his experience is like "waking. Like you always just woke up" (*Memento* 2000). There is no sense of time in the film. Leonard is "off the clock" as he explains, "It feels like it's the first time you've been there but. . . . Perhaps you've been there for a week, three months. It's kind of hard to say. I don't know. It's just an anonymous room" (*Memento* 2000). This point is key, for he is alone. He craves anonymity as much as he craves identity. This sense of transience and lack of time is certainly one of the defining qualities of the digital age, but it also was the defining quality of late capitalism and postmodernity. Leonard's sense of time is articulated when he states when he is with Carrie-Ann Moss's Natalie:

> I don't even know how long she's been gone. It's like I've woken up in bed and she's not here because she's gone to the bathroom or something. But somehow I just know that she'll never come back to bed. I lie here, not knowing how long I've been alone. If I could just reach out and touch her side of the bed I could know that it was cold, but I can't. I have no idea when she left. . . . I know I can't have her back, but I want to be able to let her go. I don't want to wake up every morning thinking she's still here then realizing that she's not. I want time to pass, but it won't. How can I heal if I can't feel time? (*Memento* 2000)

Leonard is unable to experience time and is trapped in an endless repetition of the same events. However, unlike most postmodern men and women, Leonard himself is the architect of this time loop. He has deliberately placed himself out of time in order to escape the monotony of his existence as an insurance claims investigator. However, at the same time, the wealth and stability of the late twentieth century makes both distorted and illusory lives possible. Leonard worked to achieve success and that world of success and wealth and freedom has enabled him to live his life as a hunter of alleged criminals.

Like virtually every Nolan film, *Memento* is a film about deception—both the deception of the audience as well as the (self-)deception of the characters on-screen. Alone and confused, Leonard initially appears as sympathetic character whose alleged condition is being manipulated by those around him. Joe Pantoliano's seemingly corrupt police officer, Teddy, appears to enjoy torturing Leonard, calling him "Lenny" when Leonard tells him that he hates being called this. Leonard tells him, "It's Leonard . . . like I told you before" (*Memento* 2000). In response, Teddy states, "Did you? I musta forgot. I'm Teddy" (*Memento* 2000). Leonard lies to himself, but others in the film lie to him. Teddy also frequently tries to commandeer Leonard's car. Teddy tries to pawn his older 1970s style cop car on Leonard, telling him, "This is your car" (*Memento* 2000). Leonard jokes with Teddy that he "[s]houldn't make fun of somebody's handicap" (*Memento* 2000). Leonard curiously responds with the loaded, "You're in a playful mood" (*Memento* 2000). Teddy responds, "Just trying to have a little fun" (*Memento* 2000). This point is key, for despite Teddy's apparent corruption, Leonard's ludism and playfulness is enacted in the murder of human beings as part of an elaborate fantasy. He is (mostly) a nicer guy than Teddy; however, deep down inside he is a brutal killer that Teddy does not seem to be. Teddy is a police officer who found meaning in his life tracking criminals (as well as, it appears, committing crimes himself). Leonard is trying to give meaning to his postmodern late capitalist life by murdering the alleged killer of his wife. However, he ends up killing numerous men in the process. He has attempted to transcend postmodernity with barbarism. Teddy has attempted to do so as a crooked cop.

There are, however, other characters in the movie who seem (somewhat content) in postmodernity but who, nonetheless, play tricks on Leonard. The Discount Inn's front desk clerk Burt plays a trick on Leonard when Leonard asks him to hold his calls. Burt asks, "You don't know?" (*Memento* 2000). Leonard responds, "I think I may have. I'm not good on the phone" (*Memento* 2000). Burt confirms, "You said you like to look people in the eye when you talk to them. Don't you remember?" (*Memento* 2000). Leonard responds, "That's the thing. I have this condition" (*Memento* 2000). Burt facetiously questions Leonard, and Leonard explains his condition: "I have no short-term memory. I know who I am and all about myself, but since my injury I can't make any new memories. Everything fades. If we talk for too long, I'll forget how we started. I don't know if we've ever met before, and the next time I see you I won't remember this conversation. So if I seem strange or rude, that's probably . . . " (*Memento* 2000). Realizing that Burt has heard this before, Leonard states, "I've told you this before, haven't I?" (*Memento* 2000). Burt explains more sympathetically, "I don't mean to mess with you. It's just so weird. You don't remember me at all, and we talked a bunch of times" (*Memento* 2000). This point is especially ironic when viewed from the ending of the film in which it is suggested that Leonard has intentionally created this condition for himself to give meaning and purpose for his life. Burt is thus correct in identifying that Leonard should remember him, and Leonard is duplicitously acting. Burt, however, exploits Leonard, renting him another room because "[b]usiness is slow," and his boss instructed him to do so. Leonard tells Burt, "Well, at least you're being honest about ripping me off" (*Memento* 2000). To which Burt responds, "Well, you're not gonna remember anyway" (*Memento* 2000). And Leonard, in return, comments, "You don't have to be that honest, Burt" (*Memento* 2000). Looking at this scene as it is, we see humorous banter and sympathize with Leonard. However, looking at this scene from the end of the film in which it is revealed that the biggest and most deadly liar in the film is Leonard, Burt's honesty does not quite seem as cruel. Moreover, Burt is just a member of the lumpenproletariat who works a minimum wage job and plays a prank on a customer to make the Discount Inn more money. Burt is lethargic, obese, and bored, but he seems somewhat content in the film, reading his book behind the front desk plexiglass (a perhaps not too subtle reminder of 1990s Los Angeles violence). Burt engages in mild forms of lying and deception, but Leonard's deception is much more profound and egregious.

There are several hints throughout *Memento* that Leonard is lying about key elements of his narrative (and possibly lying about the whole narrative itself). Perhaps most importantly, Leonard's depiction of his wife is fictitious. Throughout the film, he speaks admirably of his wife, but Leonard informs Natalie that his wife could him Lenny, and he "hated it" (*Memento* 2000). This stands in contrast to his comment to Natalie about the small impressions he experiences of his wife's love: "You can just feel the details. The bits and pieces you didn't bother to put into words. And you can feel extreme moments even if you don't want to. You put these together and you get the feel of the person, enough to know how much you miss them, and how much you hate the person who took them away" (*Memento* 2000). These small impressions, including pinching his wife, may be illusion as we find out later in the film when Teddy suggests the image of Leonard giving his Leonard's diabetic wife insulin. There are other points at which Leonard may be exaggerating the goodness of his wife and the quality of his wife and his relationship. After being goaded by her, Leonard tells Natalie that his wife "was beautiful. To me she was perfect" (*Memento* 2000). The "to me" is carefully placed in the dialogue, hinting that Nolan is noting that Leonard's picture of his wife is precisely that: an image he has crafted for himself. Commenting on this scene, Toth argues that "Natalie's words carry a warning to the viewer to be wary of the stories Leonard robotically rehearses about his wife."[11]

Leonard also is driven by the lie that he must kill someone to avenge his wife's death. As we slowly learn throughout the film, Leonard is looking for an enemy and creating prompts on his polaroids such as "DON'T LISTEN TO HIS LIES," "HE IS THE ONE," and "KILL HIM" (*Memento* 2000). At one point, Natalie asks Leonard, "When you find this guy, this John G., what are you going to do?" (*Memento* 2000). Leonard simply responds, "Kill him" (*Memento* 2000). He has created an automated response for himself that allows him to justify his desire to kill. Elsewhere, he comments, "I've finally found him. How long have I been looking?" (*Memento* 2000). He has been spending his entire life looking for someone to kill; he hid it behind his insurance claims investigations, but now, in perfect honesty, he has made the purpose of his life is to kill. As he explains to himself, "Me? I gotta reason" (*Memento* 2000). In Jungian terms, Leonard's shadow self is a killer. This is what hid behind the insurance investigator, who is the man without a chest. During the diner scene, when Teddy tells him, "You're living." Leonard responds, "Only for revenge." This is the new "Uber mensch" or "superman" who Leonard has become, allegedly transcending good and evil by killing alleged criminals. When he accosts Teddy, who is very likely not the real John G. (if there even is one) at the end of the film, Leonard shouts at him: "YOU PAY FOR WHAT YOU DID! YOU BEG FORGIVENESS, THEN YOU PAY!" (*Memento* 2000). He positions himself as a god who demands restitution from Teddy and gives himself sway over the life and death of another person. The postmodern Leonard had no reason to live, so he gave himself a desire to kill constructed from lies.

However, in the same scene, Teddy unmasks the lies driving Leonard: "You don't have a clue, you freak" (*Memento* 2000). Leonard tries to force his will on the situation and reality, perhaps deliberately blocking Teddy's comments out by ordering him: "Beg my forgiveness! Beg my wife's forgiveness before I blow your brains out!" (*Memento* 2000). Teddy, however, wears on Leonard, telling him, "Leonard, you don't have a clue what's going on. You don't even know my name" (*Memento* 2000). Perhaps letting down his mask, Leonard responds, "Teddy!" (*Memento* 2000). Teddy, however, retorts, "You read it off your [expletive delete] photo. You don't know me, you don't even know who you are" (*Memento* 2000). Leonard responds with his facticity, like reading from his license: "I'm Leonard Shelby, I'm from San Francisco and I'm . . . " (*Memento* 2000). Teddy, retorts, "That's who you were, you don't know who you are" (*Memento* 2000). Teddy wants to show him what he has become, telling him, "Lemme take you down in the basement and show you what you've become. C'mon, Lenny—we'll take a look down there together. Then you'll know. You'll know what you really are" (*Memento* 2000). The real Leonard is a killer who has been unleashed. We might suspect that there are more bodies down in the basement than just Jimmy Grant's.

In this reading, Leonard is a killer who was lulled by the "big sleep" of the American Century Leonard kills Teddy because he doesn't want to face the truth of who he is. The paraphernalia or facticity of everyday life hides not only what Leonard has become, but perhaps who he always was: the killer hidden behind the insurance investigator.

The identities of Leonard Shelby the insurance claim investigator and Leonard Shelby the victim are thus intertwined. Leonard's ambiguous identity is revealed in one of the black and white scenes in which he states, "You know, you know who you are, and you know kind of all about yourself. But just for day-to-day stuff, notes are really useful" (*Memento* 2000). It is not true; he does not see the killer inside himself, and the notes are, in fact, a distraction from the truth. Leonard's seeming projection, Sammy Jankis, serves as a character of Leonard in contrast to which Leonard appears nobler. As Leonard explains, "Sammy Jankis had the same problem, but he really had no system. He wrote himself a ridiculous amount of notes, but he'd get them all mixed up. You really do need a system. If . . . If you're going to make it work" (*Memento* 2000). Leonard has just such a system, which serves as an image of some sort of ideological structure, which might hide the truth. Leonard elsewhere states, "You really need a system if you are going to make it work. You kind of learn to trust your own handwriting. That becomes an important part of your life. You write yourself notes" (*Memento* 2000). Leonard, like the postmodern subject, orders his life with paraphernalia that hide the truth from him. Natalie comments on how difficult this is in the diner scene: "Must be tough living life according to a few scraps of paper" (*Memento* 2000). Leonard responds, "It is tough. Almost impossible" (*Memento* 2000). This shaping of the incoherence of life with a narrative is not a new concept in film. However, Nolan adds a deeper lay in revealing that the incoherence of his life is something Leonard created to give more meaning to it.

It is not simply Leonard who lies to himself. Many people lie to Leonard, as he himself says: "And you have to be wary of other people writing stuff for you that is not gonna to make sense or is going to lead you astray. . . . I guess people try and take advantage of somebody with this condition" (*Memento* 2000). This is a profound line that points to the "everyman" character of Leonard, who serves as a figure for the postmodern self. With the shaking up of the certainty of narratives in the postmodern era, it is easy for people to be led astray. Teddy, in fact, does try to help him, ironically telling him, "Leonard, you need to be very careful" (*Memento* 2000). When Leonard asks "Why?," Teddy responds, "Well, the other day you made it sound like you thought somebody might be trying to set you up. Get you to kill the wrong guy" (*Memento* 2000). This language is very ironic—especially as we draw near the end of the film in which it is revealed that Leonard set himself up to kill the wrong guy. Leonard responds with the misleading, "Yeah, well I go on facts, not recommendations, okay? Teddy tells Leonard, Lenny, you can't trust a man's life to your little notes and pictures" (*Memento* 2000). Teddy tells him Your notes might be unreliable" (*Memento* 2000). Leonard responds, "Memory's unreliable . . . No, really. Memory's not perfect. It's not even that good. Ask the police, eyewitness testimony is unreliable. The cops don't catch a killer by sitting around remembering stuff. They collect facts, make notes, draw conclusions. Facts, not memories: that's how you investigate. I know, it's what I used to do" (*Memento* 2000). The key element that Leonard is leaving out is the reality that facts can be manipulated, and it is not simply facts that matter but the perception of facts.

Leonard and Natalie have a similar discussion about "facts" at her apartment. Natalie tricks Leonard, telling him, "Leonard, you decided to help me. Trust yourself" (*Memento* 2000). She explains, "You can question everything, you can never know anything for sure" (*Memento* 2000). Leonard responds, "There are things you know for sure." He further states, "I know the feel of the world. I know how this wood will sound when I knock. I know how this glass will feel when I pick it up. Certainties" (*Memento* 2000). Leonard explains that because of his wife's death, "the present is trivia, which I can scribble down as notes" (*Memento* 2000). His wife, whether she is dead or not, becomes a defied ideal in contrast to which everything is trivia. Postmodernity—and perhaps even the modernity that antedated it—is at least partially defined by the accumulation of trivial manufactured goods, images, and, in the twenty-first century, digital content. These material and information give the appearance of disposable stuff. All the data of the twentieth century—including the data which insurance investigators such as Leonard dealt with daily—are, for most people, boring trivia. His new life as a detective and killer is much more exciting. Leonard may have more than one mask or narrative he has made for himself. There is another: Sammy Jankis.

Sammy Jankis is another projection that serves to shape the narrative of Leonard's own life. Leonard puts "remember Sammy Jankis" on his hand as the most prominent tattoo because it is the most important lie (*Memento* 2000). Leonard himself explains, "I guess I tell people about Sammy Jankis to help them understand. Sammy's story helps me understand my own situation" (*Memento* 2000). Sammy is a scapegoat for Leonard as Leonard explains, "Sammy Jankis wrote himself endless notes. But he'd get mixed up. I've got a more graceful solution to the memory problem. I'm disciplined and organized. I use habit and routine to make my life possible. Sammy had no drive. No reason to make it work" (*Memento* 2000). If Leonard is the real Sammy, then Leonard here gives us a vision into his own empty life without the narrative of his wife's death and his pursuit of vengeance.

Leonard explains that he had met Sammy through his work as an insurance investigator. He notes, "I met Sammy through work. Insurance. I was an investigator. I'd investigate the claims to see which ones were phony. I had to see though people's [expletive delete]. It was useful because now it's my life. When I meet someone, I don't even know if I've met them before. I have to look in their eyes and just figure them out. My job taught me that the best way to find out what someone knew was to let them talk" (*Memento* 2000). This passage is interesting, for Leonard reveals that he is continuing to do as a murderer what he did as an insurance investigator. There is some link between his pursuit of happiness as a white-collar worker and his life as a serial killer. He refers to Sammy's case as "the strangest case ever," which indicates that it was some sort of ground zero that triggered him (*Memento* 2000). It was some sort of event that shaped him and changed his life. Whatever the truth of the case, Leonard reveals that his aggression and dogged service to his insurance agency ended up destroying the Jankis couple but earning him a promotion. He explains that after he proved that Sammy did not have a physical condition he was promoted and Sammy's wife entered a downward spiral:

> His wife got stuck with the bills, and I got a big promotion." He further explains how Sammy's wife was destroyed: Sammy's wife was crippled by the cost of supporting him and fighting the company's decision—but it wasn't the money that got to her. I never said that Sammy was faking. Just that his problem was mental, not physical. But she . . . she couldn't understand. She looks into his eyes and sees the same person. And if it's not a physical problem. So good old Leonard Shelby from the insurance company gives her the seed of doubt, just like he gave it to the doctors. (*Memento* 2000)

This seed of doubt is key, for it is something that Leonard gets rid of in himself. Even in the Sammy Jankis case, he assures himself of his own innocence: "But I never said that Sammy was faking. I never said that" (*Memento* 2000). Even when he was an insurance investigator, he was, at least one level, practicing a form of self-deception, and this self-deception principally was used to coverup the sadism in Leonard.

This sadism and cruelty infect many of the characters in the film and manifests itself through their lying and manipulation, in the case of Leonard, murder; it is also present in the story of Sammy Jankis's wife. Leonard tells the story of how Sammy Jankis's wife would desperately and perhaps sadistically try to get him back: "It had got to the point where she'd get Sammy to hide food all around the house, then stop feeding him to see if his hunger would make him remember where he'd hidden the stuff. She wasn't a cruel person; she just wanted her old Sammy back" (*Memento* 2000). We then see the point where the rapacious and aggressive Leonard Shelby manifests himself in telling Mrs. Jankis that he husband's condition was psychological. They banter back and forth and, finally, Mrs. Jankis says:

> Mr. Shelby, try and understand. When I look into Sammy's eyes, I don't see some vegetable, I see the same old Sammy. What do you think it's like for me to suspect that he's imagining this whole problem? That if I could just say the right thing he'd snap out of it and be back to normal? If I knew that my old Sammy was truly gone, then I could say goodbye and start loving this new Sammy. As long as I have doubt, I can't say goodbye and move on. (*Memento* 2000)

Mrs. Jankis is trying to find the truth from Leonard. She further tells him, "I want you to forget the company you work for thirty seconds and tell me if you really think that Sammy is faking his condition. I need to know what you honestly believe" (*Memento* 2000). Leonard responds somewhat facetiously, "I believe that Sammy should be physically capable of making new memories" (*Memento* 2000). Mrs. Jankis responds with "Thank you" (*Memento* 2000). Revealing his lack of empathy, Leonard says, "She seemed to leave happy. I thought I'd helped her. I thought she just needed some kind of answer. I didn't think it was important to her what the answer was, just that she had one to believe" (*Memento* 2000). Leonard thinks he can carelessly construct other's reality for them, but his off the cuff (semi-)nihilism has catastrophic consequences. Moreover, even at this point in his life, he is aware of how words and suggestions can shape reality. In this sense, his life as a killer is an extension of his life as an insurance agency. His attempt to transcend the boredom of late capitalism, postmodernity, the end of history, and/or capitalist realism is merely a continuation of the same self-deception and self-creation present in the late twentieth century. Leonard continues to attempt to shape his reality with illusion. There is thus a sense in the film that even Leonard's attempt to live a (premodern?) life of the "knight errant" is still itself a postmodern phenomenon—one of the key elements to his new life is the Jaguar he stole from Jimmy Grants as well as Jimmy's suit and money, so capitalism, in a certain sense, remains an essential part of Leonard's life.

Teddy tells the truth about Natalie to Leonard, but Leonard, perhaps intentionally, rejects it. Teddy is right to say that Natalie is "bad news" because she is involved in drug trafficking (*Memento* 2000). Teddy is further right to say, "She's gonna use you. To protect herself" (*Memento* 2000). However, as even Leonard himself is aware, Teddy himself is trying to use him. This is one of the ironies of *Memento*: everyone knows that they are using each other, but Leonard as a symbol of everyman, can block out this reality—at least for a while. Teddy further warns Leonard that people are going to start asking questions. Leonard provides a lie as an answer: I have money. . . . My wife's death. I used to work in insurance, we were well covered" (*Memento*

2000). After Teddy mocks him, he asks him, "You haven't got a clue, have you? You don't even know who you are?" (*Memento* 2000). This then turns to one of the key conversations that provides one of the keys to understanding the film. Leonard responds that he does know who he is: "Yes, I do. I don't have amnesia. I remember everything about myself up until the incident. I'm Leonard Shelby, I'm from San Fran . . . " (*Memento* 2000). Teddy tells him, "That's who you were, Lenny. You don't know who you are, who you've become since the incident. You're wandering around, playing detective . . . and you don't even know how long ago it was" (*Memento* 2000). Teddy tells him, "Maybe you need to apply some of your investigative skills to yourself" (*Memento* 2000). This is another key to the film: Leonard lacks introspection to see who he really is; however, this introspection is deliberately obscured by Leonard while he was an insurance investigator as well as a killer. To know himself is to know himself as a potential killer as well as a man living an incredibly prosperous but nonetheless boring and unsatisfying life.

There are several points in the film at which it appears Leonard's self-deception cracks, and the audience learns that Leonard may realize that he is lying to himself. Perhaps, the most pathetic scene in the film is perhaps the scene in which Natalie recognizes that Leonard is completely delusion—even though she continues to manipulate him. She asks him—perhaps rhetorically: "If you've got all this information, how come the police haven't found him for you?" (*Memento* 2000). Leonard responds that the police are not looking for John G. However, Leonard retorts that "They're not looking for him" (*Memento* 2000). When Natalie asks why not, Leonard responds strangely, "They don't think he exists" (*Memento* 2000). Leonard further explains, "There had to be a second man. I was struck from behind, I remember. It's about the last thing I do remember. But the police didn't believe me" (*Memento* 2000). Natalie asks, "How did they explain what you remembered? The gun and stuff?" (*Memento* 2000). Leonard gives the odd response, "John G. was clever. He took the dead man's gun and replaced it with the sap that he'd hit me with. He left my gun and left the getaway car. He gave the police a complete package. They found a sap with my blood on it in the dead man's hand, and they only found my gun. They didn't need to look for anyone else. I was the only guy who disagreed with the facts, and I had brain damage" (*Memento* 2000). The idea of an evil demon manipulator behind the scenes had earlier been addressed by Descartes as well as Bryan Singer in *The Usual Suspects*. Just as Leonard creates an idol to die for, so too does he create a devil to torment himself. This does not mean that Nolan is necessarily critiquing religion per se. There is a profound scene in which Leonard makes a confession, revealing, as Cobb does in *Inception*, that the postmodern self cannot escape from a guilty conscience. Leonard has a near confession scene when he is speaking to what we assume is Teddy on the phone acting as Officer Gammel: "What do you want? I know you're a cop, but what do you want? Did I do something wrong? No, but I can't remember things I do. I don't know what I just did. Maybe I did something wrong, did I do something wrong? I dunno—something bad. Maybe I did something bad" (*Memento* 2000). Despite the effort to eradicate ethics, the postmodern self seems still irrevocably drawn to some authentic ethical structure. There is a point at which humans crave genuine rules outside their own making.

This desire for an ethical core in the film is complimented by the desire of many of the characters in the film to abandon the capitalist ethic. As Leonard says of Mrs. Jankis, "She wasn't interested in the money. She just needed to understand his problem" (*Memento* 2000). This language obviously refers to Leonard himself who desired something more than his bourgeois existence. Even Natalie does not build her life around financial exchanges. When Leonard asks her "Do I owe you?," Natalie responds, "I wasn't helping you for money" (*Memento* 2000). Leonard later compliments her, saying, "It's great that you would . . . that you're helping me like this . . . " (*Memento* 2000). Natalie responds, "I'm helping you because you helped me" (*Memento* 2000). Natalie is driven by self-preservation, but she is also driven by revenge; her values may be evil, but they are outside the values of the marketplace. Leonard as well specifically states that he is not killing for money when Natalie asks Leonard to kill Dodd for money. Leonard responds, "What do you think I am?! I'm not gonna kill someone for money" (*Memento* 2000). Natalie responds, "What then? Love? What would you kill for? For your wife, right?" (*Memento* 2000). Leonard states, "That's different" (*Memento* 2000). Natalie says, "Not to me! I wasn't [expletive delete] married to her!" (*Memento* 2000). There are two key elements to this conversation. Leonard is motivated by something more than money, but, as Natalie notes, and Leonard notes elsewhere the value of Leonard's wife is relative of Leonard himself. He values her because of her relationship to him. Near the film's end, even Jimmy tries to reduce Leonard to bargaining about money, telling Leonard: "Look, there's two hundred grand stashed in the car. Just take it!" (*Memento* 2000). Leonard is offended and asks, "You think you can bargain with me?!" (*Memento* 2000). Jimmy reassures him, "Take the money and walk away!" (*Memento* 2000). Leonard responds, "I don't want your [expletive deleted] money!" (*Memento* 2000). Like Natalie, Jimmy then confusedly asks what it is Leonard wants, ""What?! What do you want from me?!" (*Memento* 2000). Leonard responds, "I want my [expletive deleted] life back!" (*Memento* 2000). Leonard like many heroes and villains in Nolan's films, attempts to live for something more than money—except that living here is revenge. However, once they adopt a more adventurous role, they often question whether the new life of adventure is worth it and often pine for their simpler lives. As Mottram notes, "A hero looking to avenge his wife, he is both chivalrous (helping Natalie) and savage (killing both Jimmy and Teddy). He is a man able to change his identity at will."[12] Leonard is, on one level, a superman capable of great things; in the film, however, he chooses great evil.

The ending of the film reveals its core and causes the reader to reevaluate the impression they had previously formed of Leonard. While in the abandon building where Leonard kills Jimmy, Teddy notes to Leonard that the Sammy Jankis "Gets better every time you tell it" (*Memento* 2000). The story of Sammy Jankis, like the story of Leonard himself, the stories of the majority of the characters in the film, as well as the audiences themselves, is a fictional narrative meant to hide boredom and pain and to give meaning to life. Critics have commented on the importance of the lie in Nolan's puzzle films. Todd McGowan argues, "Nolan's exploration of the false—exposes where the truth of the spectator's desire resides."[13] Ní Fhlainn writes that Christopher Nolan "Nolan's continue successes will then ultimately rest on the spin games and puzzles forms with which he tantalizes his audience; he know we want to be visually dazzled, but fundamentally, his auteur style rests on our continued culture desire to be fooled."[14] As Teddy himself tells Leonard, "So you lie to yourself to be happy. Nothing wrong with that—we all do. Who cares if there's a few little things you'd rather not remember?" (*Memento* 2000). Teddy hits a cord with Leonard suggesting that Lenny's wife was a diabetic who survived the assault. She did not believe his condition. When Leonard protests, "Like you've told yourself. Over and over. Conditioning yourself to believe, learning through repetition" (*Memento* 2000). When Leonard protests, Teddy reveals a curious comment, "Sammy was a con man. A faker" (*Memento* 2000). Teddy further tells Leonard that he "exposed" Sammy "for what he was: a fraud" (*Memento* 2000). This is curious, for if Lenny is a Sammy, then he is the fraud. Leonard further tells him: "You think I don't know my own wife? What the [expletive delete] is wrong with you?" (*Memento* 2000). Teddy says, "I guess I can only make you remember the things you want to be true, huh? Like ol' Jimmy down there" (*Memento* 2000). Leonard tells Teddy that "he's not the right guy!" Teddy, however, explains, "He was to you. Come on, you got your revenge—just enjoy it while you still remember. What difference does it make whether he was your guy or not?" (*Memento* 2000). Leonard responds, "It makes all the difference" (*Memento* 2000). Teddy reminds him, "Why? You're never going to know" (*Memento* 2000). Leonard and Teddy then banter back and forth over whether it will matter. Leonard returns, "Yes, I will" (*Memento* 2000). Teddy is also a nihilist, but Leonard is tormented nihilist trying to give meaning to his life. Leonard's comments seem feeble and pathetic as he tries to give order and coherence to his life. However, at the same time, it is very likely that he has made this situation itself.

Teddy explains that he thought that Leonard would remember killing the man. He said that he helped Leonard kill the real John G. Leonard didn't remember, so Teddy helped him in his quest to find another one. The reality or "why" of the question didn't matter. John G was just "some guy," as Teddy says, "some guy. Does it even matter who? I stopped asking myself why a long time ago. No reason, no conspiracy; just bad [expletive delete] luck. A couple of junkies, too strung out to realize that your wife didn't live alone" (*Memento* 2000). Teddy notes how happy Leonard was when he killed John G and said that he gave Leonard a "reason to live," and Leonard was "more than happy to help" (*Memento* 2000). As Teddy further tells him, "You lie to yourself! You don't want the truth. So you make up your own truth. Look at your police file. It was complete when I gave it to you. Who took the 12 pages out?" (*Memento* 2000). Teddy knows that Leonard is making up puzzles, as he tells Leonard, Leonard is creating a puzzle he "won't ever solve" (*Memento* 2000). This scene, like much of the film's ending, transforms the rest of the film's meaning. Leonard earlier had said to Teddy on the phone: "Yeah, and there's pages missing . . . I guess I've been trying to log them all. The police gave me the report themselves. I dealt with them a lot in my insurance job, and I had friends in the department. They must have figured that if I saw the facts of the case, then I would stop believing that we needed to find John G" (*Memento* 2000). If what Teddy is saying is true, then Leonard here is lying to him on the phone and lying to himself.

Teddy seems to think that Leonard does have some sort of condition and cannot fully interiorize what he has done. Noting that he must live with the guilt and dread of what they have done, Teddy tells Leonard, "You just wander around playing detective. You're living a dream, kid. A dead wife to pine for and a sense of purpose to your life. A romantic quest . . . " (*Memento* 2000). However, there is more to Leonard than simply creating a romantic quest. There is a deep and vicious violence in Leonard. When Leonard threatens Teddy, he states, "You're not a killer, Lenny. That's why you're so good at it" (*Memento* 2000). This is a confusing line because earlier in the film Teddy had suggested that Leonard had become a killer. Maybe he always had been one. As Novak writes, "Clearly, this little game of hide-and-seek (and find-and-kill) is for Teddy and Leonard a practiced bit of business."[15] The audience does not exactly know what to believe, and Nolan's point may be, as it is with *Inception*, that it does not matter because it's just a movie, anyway.

While critics have debated the veracity of Teddy's stories, they seem ratified by Leonard's tossing of Teddy's car keys in the bushes. Leonard here is deliberately hiding the keys to Teddy's car, but he is also deliberately hiding the keys to his life, namely that he is murdering men and constructing a fantasy to justify it. Leonard is intentionally making himself lost, as he tells Burt, "Hi I'm checked in here, but I think I've misplaced my key" (*Memento* 2000).

At the end of the film, this key image is further verified when Leonardo burns the photo of Jimmy Grants while saying, "I'm not a killer. I'm just someone who wanted to make things right" (*Memento* 2000). He is lying as he is deliberately destroying the evidence that would alleviate his alleged quest to find his wife's killers. He further admits to himself, "Can I just let myself forgot what you've told me?" (*Memento* 2000). He then writes the critical "DON'T BELIEVE HIS LIES" on the back of Teddy's polaroid, showing that he is really creating puzzles for himself to solve (*Memento* 2000). Leonard then shows his cruelty and malice when he says, "Can I just forget what you've made me do?" (*Memento* 2000). "You think I just want another puzzle to solve? Another John G to look for? You're a John G. You can be my John G." as he writes Teddy's license plate down (*Memento* 2000). He adds, "Do I lie to myself to be happy? In your case, Teddy . . . yes, I will" (*Memento* 2000). Leonard, in effect, ratifies everything Teddy has said. Tracking down the alleged killer of his allegedly dead wife, that is, murdering other humans under the illusion of justice gives his life meaning and purpose. If it is true that Leonard killed his wife or that she is still alive, then, as Toth suggests, "Leonard horrifically revises history, disavowing his own violence against his wife and killing various innocent people to avenge the crime he actually committed."[16]

There is further the weird reality that Leonard is stealing the clothes and cars of the men whom he kills like a parasite. He is wearing a flannel shirt and driving a truck and then switches to the suit and jaguar of a drug dealer. When he takes Jimmy's car, Teddy says, "Hey! Hey, that's not your car!" (*Memento* 2000). Leonard responds, "It is now" (*Memento* 2000). When Leonard warns him about the fact that he just killed the owner of the car, Leonard states, "I'd rather be mistaken for a dead guy" (*Memento* 2000). This is a curious scene, for in it, Leonard adopts the role of the man he previously killed like some sort of alien seeking a host. He is, in fact, shopping for, or, better, stealing identities. He can travel around California killing people with punishment from the law. He lives one version of the American dream as an action hero and vigilante. This entire life, however, is funded and enabled by capitalism, which further provided the basis for Leonard's life as an insurance fraud investigator and then, ironically, through Jimmy Grant's money, the life of a killer.

Leonard's final words, although clever and frequently quoted on the internet, are thus ultimately hollow and facetious. He states, "I have to believe in the world outside my own mind. I have to believe that my actions still have meaning, even if I can't remember them. I have to believe that when my eyes are closed, the world's still here" (*Memento* 2000). This is a very Cartesian problem of whether the world exists outside our mind. However, it is not the mind but the will that drives Leonard. He chooses to create a world in his mind that is out of sync with the real "extramental" world. The connection between this statement and Leonard's will is emphasized in the lines: "Do I believe the world's still here. Is it still out there? Yeah. We all need mirrors to remind ourselves who we are. I'm no different" (*Memento* 2000). This is deceptive, for the outside world is something that Leonard chooses to believe in and from which he takes and manipulates as the ultimate consumer exercising his will to power and fantasies on the population around him. The wealth of his previous life proved to be boring, but the same wealth and late capitalist system that bored him also provides the structure in which he can live out his fantasies.

Neither *Memento* nor any of Nolan's later films are propaganda for the Anglo-American world order, although many of them can easily be read (and deconstructed) as such. On one level, Leonard Shelby stands as a figure of the Gen Xer who was able to achieve the good life for which his forefathers and mothers had labored. His wealth and stability as well as the security of a bourgeois life grant him power and prestige. Nolan's Gen X style, surprisingly, has drawn little notice from critics, although Pete Deakin identifies Nolan as a Generation X auteur who was born "into anxieties circumventing 'greed is good' yuppie idealisms, 'ornamental culture' . . . the so-called feminization of labour. . . . and, largely by inflection of the former, most importantly a period in which later fervent charges are made toward a certain 'crisis of masculinity.'"[17] Nolan's *Memento* is film about this crisis, but it is also a film structured around the violence that humans often carry with them but hide beneath various (postmodern and postmillennial) facades provided by the wealth. Ironically, it is precisely this wealth power and prestige that bores Shelby and prompts him to engage in his act of ludic world-creation. This world-creation is not essentially transgressive of the neoliberal system; in fact, it implicitly endorses it.

NOTES

1. Fukuyama, *The End of History and the Last Man*, xi.
2. Fukuyama, *The End of History and the Last Man*, xiv.
3. Fukuyama, *The End of History and the Last Man*, xiv.
4. Fukuyama, *The End of History and the Last Man*, xxii.
5. Fisher, *Capitalist Realism*, 7.
6. Fisher, *Capitalist Realism*, 78.
7. Fisher, "How to Kill a Zombie."
8. Molloy, Memento, 25.
9. Mottram, The Making of Memento, 41.
10. Toth, "Memento's Posmodern Noir Fantasy," 77.

11. Toth, "Memento's Postmodern Noir Fantasy," 81.

12. Mottram, The Making of Memento, 45.

13. McGowan, "Stumbling over the Superhero," 165.

14. Ní Fhlainn, "You keep telling yourself what you know, but what do you believe?" 160–61.

15. Novak, "It's Like Waking," 34.

16. Toth, "Memento's Postmodern Noir Fantasy," 81.

17. Deakin, "Men in Crisis," 87.

Chapter 2

Batman Begins and the Taming of the Orient

Edward Said's *Orientalism* is one of the most important critical works of the later twentieth century. In his magnum opus, the Palestinian scholar notes the way Western modernity has categorized and commodified the East since antiquity. In recent years, critical and popular attention has returned once again to the concept of Orientalism.[1] In the wake of Donald Trump's election to the presidency of the United States, in much of Western media, the process of critical self-reflection and self-criticism has radically accelerated, attempting to combat a rise in alleged extremism and nationalism.[2] Moreover, during the post-Trump era, there has been a marked break from the Bush- and even Obama-era films of the War on Terror. These films usually (but not always) included a cast that orbited around either an individual white American or his or her family in combat with a suspiciously Eastern or Orientalized Other.[3] If a white American was not cast, then a white-presenting or wisecracking historic black American (such as Will Smith) or other person of color was granted the center stage in defending Anglo-America or Western values in face of what was often a stand in for the Taliban, ISIS, or the Chinese Communist Party. The dominant theme of these films is that the old world of reactionary and radical ideology may seek to seduce and/or destroy the American people, and thus Americans must be vigilant against the siren song of fascism, communism, and religious fundamentalism.

Within his *Batman Begins* (2005), released just two years into the Iraq War and four years after the *annus horribilis* of 2001, Christopher Nolan depicts the development and maturation of Bruce Wayne into Batman in a gritty, realistic world, but he also depicts a Batman as the defender of the city of Gotham and the Anglo-American world order. *Batman Begins* curiously stands almost as an amalgamation of the other top films of 2005. Like *Star Wars II: Revenge of the Sith* and *The Chronicles of Narnia: The Lion, the Witch and the Wardrobe*, *Batman Begins* is a "nostalgia" film that runs on a twentieth-century mythology crafted prior to the trauma and uncertainty of 9/11. Like *Mr. & Mrs. Smith*, *Jarhead*, *King of Heaven*, and *War of the Worlds*, *Batman Begins* is also a film about 9/11, the War on Terror, and the emerging American security state. Finally, like *Fantastic Four* and *Sin City*, *Batman Begins* is a superhero movie and is thus a film about America.

This is not to suggest that Gotham is an idealized vision of America; it is, rather, as Tom Shone writes, "a city rife with corruption" and is modeled, as Nolan himself tells Shone, on the 1973 Al Pacino film about police corruption, *Serpico*, a film that Nolan has described as "a horror movie set in the real world."[4] Gotham as an icon of America is rotten, and it must be reformed; at the same time, it is necessary for Batman to protect this imperfect Gotham from its Orientalized enemies.

Like many superheroes, Batman himself has become an icon for America itself. Michael Caine (who plays the sagacious Alfred in Nolan's *Dark Knight* trilogy) famously stated that while America thinks of itself as Superman, the world thinks of America as the tormented and morally ambiguous Batman.[5] Terrence McSweeney, in *The "War on Terror" And American Film*, likewise argues that, although Superman "has historically been considered as the pre-eminent personification of American ethics and values," it is rather "Batman, especially in his new millennial incarnation," who "more readily encompasses the complicated and polarized post-9/11 American psyche," which, according to McSweeney, "may be one of the reasons for the phenomenal success of Christopher Nolan's interpretation of the character in the decade after the attacks on 11 September 2001."[6] Batman is an icon of a brutal and tormented America striving to affect justice in the world. To affect this justice, in *Batman Begins*, Bruce Wayne/Batman must tame and subdue the Old World of Eurasia in order for Gotham (as a symbol of America) to flourish.

On one level, *Batman Begins* is a work deeply receptive to an Orientalist reading. Edward Said's *Orientalism*, released in 1978, is a watershed text that acutely diagnoses the Western colonial project from antiquity to the twentieth century. Drawing from the toolkit of postmodernism and critical theory, Said presents the phenomenon of Western colonial effort as being, fundamentally, an act of will to power or a "kind of *authority* over the Orient within Western culture."[7] Thus, drawing from German (post-)idealism, Said argues that Orientalism is among those "distinctive objects are made by the mind, and that these objects, while appearing to exist objectively, have only a fictional reality."[8] Orientalism, ultimately, according to Said, sprung from "a fairly constant sense of confrontation felt by Westerners dealing with the East," thus creating a "willed imaginative and geographic division made between East and West, and lived through during many centuries."[9] Orientalism is "fundamentally a political doctrine willed over the Orient because the Orient was weaker than the West, which elided the Orient's difference with its weakness."[10] Orientalism is not a cool and detached posture; rather, it is "all aggression, activity, judgement, will-to-truth, and knowledge."[11] Rather than liberal humanism being an ameliorating force of Western dominance over the East (as, we will see, is suggested in *Batman Begins*), it is a genus of which Orientalism is a compartment, which itself "*retards* the process of enlarged and enlarging meaning through which true understand can be attained."[12] Said points out that Westerners viewed the merger of East and West being joined together as an "apocalypse."[13] *Batman Begins* is about the merger of East and West, but it is principally about the dominance of the West over the East as well as the wider "Old World" of Europe.

Upon its release, as Will Brooker notes, *Batman Begins* represented a marked change in the representation of the Dark Knight from the campiness of Joel Shumaker's much-hated *Batman Forever* (1995) and *Batman and Robin* (1997), and to hard-edged graphic novels such as *The Long Halloween* (1996–1997), "The Man who Falls" 1989, Frank Miller's *The Dark Knight Returns* (1987), as well as Miller and David Mazzuchelli's *Year One* (1987), and Jeph Loeb and Jim Lee's *Hush* (2003).[14] Thus, Brooker argues Batman has resuscitated the "gritty violent vigilante" in contrast to the "camp Batman."[15] Nonetheless, within Nolan's work, "there remains no single source; these are multiple contradictory 'originals' of equal status circulating on their own distinct orbits, rather than a central, luminous urtext and its satellites."[16] The key point here is that Nolan is utilizing the Batman mythos not only for his aesthetic work, but also for his greater political program. Batman is raw material for a distinct (albeit complicated) ethos; just as the (Orientalized) Old World is a standing reserve for the new world, so too is the Batman mythos a resource for Nolan's political vision. *Batman Begins* is also very much a post-9/11 film. As Dan Hassler-Forest argues, *Batman Begins* "focuses instead on a sustained investigation of trauma and its defining role in the post-9/11 superhero narrative."[17] This narrative typically features the "new 'troubled superhero' of the post-9/11 era" who "consistently suffers through the psychological consequences of traumatic experience."[18]

On one level, *Batman Begins* is also very much an heir of Frank Miller's 1986 series *The Dark Knight Returns*. While *The Dark Knight Returns* is unquestionably as "dark," "gritty," and (perhaps) even "reactionary," as critics label it as being, the comic series, like Tim Burton's (sadly forgotten) *Batman* (1989), is also intensely satirical of the postmodern decadence of the late '80s and the post–Iran Contra Reagan administration. In *The Dark Knight Returns*, Superman is the at-times-buffoonish representative of American military superpower, which is, like a loyal gold retriever, faithful to the wisecracking President Reagan. In contrast, *The Dark Knight Returns*'s Batman is a (violent and delusion) enforcer of "street justice," who, by the end of the series, becomes the leader of a strange gang of vigilantes who will wage a guerilla war against the establishment bolstered by Superman. In contrast, as we will see, *Batman Begins*, is a film that offers only mild criticism of the newly emergent twenty-first-century Bush-era American security state and military industrial establishment. With his muscular physique, armor, and martial arts training, *Batman Begins*'s Batman, who is placed at the service of the American military establishment, is as much like Susan Jeffords's "hard bodied" heroes of Reagan-era action films as he is an heir to the Batman of Frank Miller's *The Dark Knight Returns*.

Batman Begins commences with a traumatic dream in which Bruce Wayne remembers his childhood encounter with frightening bats in a well near Wayne Manor. Bruce awakens and opens his eyes to find himself in a Chinese prison cell with a longhaired East Asian man who asks in broken English, "Did you have dream?" (*Batman Begins* 2005). After Bruce responds with the one word, "Nightmare," the Asian man asks, "Worse than this place?" (*Batman Begins* 2005). The answer to that rhetorical question is then given by the large, angry Asian man with a shaved head who stares at him as well as the armed Chinese Communist Party guards who greet him with unhappy stares. Shone identifies that place as a "a dank brick jail in a far-off, unidentified part of the world."[19] However, it is clearly the East. The Old World of Asia is a despotic prison full of barking German shepherds (a common "bad guy" dog in American films). As in films like *Blade Runner* and *Lost in Translation*, Bruce's encounter with East Asian language and Asian otherness emphasizes his sense of isolation and alienation—despite the helpful long-haired wiseman, who tells him that they are going to fight him until they kill him. The sense here is that Bruce is a foreign Western and European pest amid menacing danger.

The first moment where we get a strong sense that Bruce's encounter with the Asian Other is not simply or exclusively an encounter with the racial Other is when he begins his fight with the large bald man. The man tells him, "You are in hell, little man, and I am the devil" (*Batman Begins* 2005). Bruce responds with "You're not the devil. You're practice" (*Batman Begins* 2005). This is a key to understanding the cultural and even spiritual dynamics of the film. The tall man frames the prison in almost supernatural terms. It is a hell, and the tall man has a tremendous power over Bruce like a devil. However, Bruce disenchants this fear as he will do for his fear of bats as well as the trauma resulting from his parents' death, which is associated with the bats and demons that young Bruce Wayne saw in the opera *Mefistofele* the night of his parents' death.[20] An outrageous brawl ensues in which Bruce fights the menacing forces with physical violence, temporarily succeeding. However, if he were to remain in prison, eventually the raw power of his rivals would triumph over him. He cannot defeat his fears or the menace of not simply the

East, but the Old World in general on his own. He must learn the arts and spirituality of the Old World but ultimately overcome and dominate it via Western rationality and technology.

Bruce is initiated into the arts of the Old World (and especially the East) by, Ra's Al Ghul, a man with an Arab-sounding name and with a "Fu Manchu" moustache played by an Irish actor.[21] Curiously, the Orientalized Bane and Talia al Ghul in *The Dark Knight* Rises are played by the English Tom Hardy and the French Marion Cottillard, respectively. In *Batman Begins*, Liam Neeson's Ra's al Gul, or "Henry Ducard," encounters Bruce in his cell and offers him the opportunity to be initiated into the arts of the East via a "path." Ducard notes that Bruce was "exploring the criminal fraternity," but now has become "truly lost." With Bruce's journey to the East, Shone explains that Nolan goes "slumming" and unpicks "the knot of class, wealth, and entitlement that had hobbled previous adaptions" and "fills his Bruce Wayne with self-loathing"; Bruce accepts this roughness with "his pampered existence."[22] Nolan himself describes the Orientalist path nonchalantly, "We'll travel the world; there's going to be this huge Himalayan monastery and it's going to blow up."[23] However, this path is not simply, a tour of the East, as Ducard explains in the film; it is a path of a man who "shares his [Bruce's] hatred of evil and wishes to serve true justice" (*Batman Begins* 2005). Bruce suggests that, like he himself, the League of Shadows is made of "vigilantes." However, Ducard responds, "A vigilante is just a man lost in the scramble for his own gratification. He can be destroyed or locked up. But if you make yourself more than just a man . . . if you devote yourself to an ideal . . . and if they can't stop you . . . then you become something else entirely" (*Batman Begins* 2005). Ducard explains that this "something else" is a "Legend" (*Batman Begins* 2005). Ducard reveals that he has the power to release Bruce Wayne as he tells him, providing him with a choice. The scene here is key, for Bruce will be able to become more human than human by becoming and icon. He can either continue brawling, go home and luxuriate, or become this legend by climbing the mountain.

Bruce's subsequent climb up the mountain is a profound symbol of his physical, spiritual, and moral strength. The house of the League of Shadows appears as a Buddhist monastery, but as we are introduced to the League, we see that its members are drawn from a host of diverse peoples, and, although it draws from Eastern martial arts and Western and Eastern psychology, the League is truly a global phenomenon. The Orientalized East is merely a reservoir from which the League can draw wisdom and skills. As he explains to Ra's, Bruce also wants to utilize the League itself appropriation of the East and to "obtain the means to fight injustice" as well as "To turn fear . . . against those who prey on the fearful" (*Batman Begins* 2005). Ducard tells him that to "manipulate the fears in others," he must learn to master his own (*Batman*

Begins 2005). Bruce must encounter his own death, as Ducard tells him, "And make no mistake, here you face death" (*Batman Begins* 2005). Ducard then shouts out a litany of Eastern martial arts skills that, it is implied, Ducard will teach Bruce. Ducard's diagnosis is that Bruce is afraid. The process that Bruce undergoes is the hero's journey and a quest for self-transformation. However, Bruce is, as is remarked throughout the film, a symbol for Gotham itself. Tom Shone identifies the apprenticeship by Ducard as being unique to *Batman Begins* and a preparation of the "moral ambivalence into the sage from the get-go and making that ambivalence concrete by giving Bruce a place, or series of places, that represents his riven self."[24]

Ducard does teach Bruce and leads him to certain truths about his anger and guilty. However, Bruce does not ultimately submit to the League of Shadows due to their brutality. Ducard trains Bruce to function as a ninja and martial artists, but it is important to note that Bruce appropriates them for his own use just like the League does. Bruce's use of the league is ultimately in the service of Gotham and the Anglo-American order that Gotham represents. This does not mean that Batman is without flaws or without selfish ambition. During the training scene, Bruce first gets a taste of what justice is for the League of Shadows when Ducard shows him the Chinese farmer in the cage who murdered his brother. Bruce's questioning of what will happen to the man is an important scene, for it demonstrates the compassion and concern for the Other that Batman will (very imperfectly) have throughout the film. Ducard explains that the man will receive "Justice," and, anticipating Bruce's response, Ducard states, "Crime cannot be tolerated. Criminals thrive on the indulgence of society's understanding" (*Batman Begins* 2005). The point here is that the brutal Old World violence of the league of shadows is radically different from Bruce's new world (Anglo)-American humanism. This harsh justice will again appear in *The Dark Knight Rises* with Bane's revolutionary takeover of Gotham in which he metes out what appears to be excessive punishment on the wealthy.

Hassler-Forest notes that it is precisely Bruce's trauma that makes him susceptible to the kind of ideological radicalization associated with Islamic terrorism: "The disillusioned and disoriented Bruce Wayne of *Batman Begins* is easily taken in by villain Ducard's League of Shadows, which provides him with an ideological perspective that seems to suit his personal agenda, along with a paternal authority figure to replace the loss of his actual father."[25] Bruce's training, Hassler-Forest argues, "makes him an effective unit in a terrorist organization ben on maintaining order in the world by punish societies it deems overly decadent and/or corrupt."[26] However, Hassler-Forest specifically notes the training narrative as forming a "clear process of 'othering'" that makes the League of Shadows an Orientalized Al-Qaida-like threat to the West.[27] This is a unique form of training in which Batman "frames the character's beginning from a specifically foreign context, as if the Batman franchise in the age of globalization has been contaminated by the evil association with the Far East."[28] Hassler-Forest argues that Ducard "first inflects the kind of pitiless regimen on Wayne that is associated with radical terrorist groups, all the while quietly intoning the League's radical 'warrior code.'"[29] Further describing his training, Dan Hassler-Forest argues, "Like so many other Western subjects in the long history of Orientalist discourse, Bruce Wayne is temporarily seduced by the attraction of this form of alterity which obviously preys upon his feelings of trauma and alienation."[30] However, like many of these Western heroes, Bruce overcomes the East and appropriates its teaching for the sake of the Anglo-Americanized West.

Batman receives the deepest and most secret teaching of Ducard and the League of Shadows during the sword fight on the frozen lake. In this scene, Ducard, perhaps with some irony, says that Bruce's father's weakness caused his own death. There is some truth to this statement, although Bruce responds that he would have stopped Joe Chill because Bruce has had "training." Grant Gearhart also refers to the "failed humanitarian efforts" of Thomas Wayne, which carry with them a sense of "futility."[31] However, Ducard responds that, "Training is nothing! Will is everything! The will to act" (*Batman Begins* 2005). After Bruce fails to notice the literal thin ice on which he is treading, Ducard further elaborates to him that he is "stronger" than Thomas Wayne because of the "rage," "impossible anger strangling the grief" inside him—ice, interestingly, will play a role in *The Dark Knight Rises* as a means of executing the enemies of Bane after he takes over Gotham (*Batman Begins* 2005). Ducard reveals that he himself "wasn't always here in the mountains" (*Batman Begins* 2005). He once "had a wife," who was his "great love" but was "taken" from him (*Batman Begins* 2005). Ducard's lesson from this is that "there are those who must be fought without hesitation, without pity" (*Batman Begins* 2005). Bruce's anger gives him "great power," but he must not let it destroy him (*Batman Begins* 2005). Ducard notes that it was revenge that enabled him to be freed from his anger. Bruce however, comments that it is no help to him because, as we discover in a flashback, Joe Chill is dead. This scene is critical, for much of what Ducard tells Bruce is true. He must act against his enemies without hesitation, and, in a certain sense, this willfulness is more important than training. But it is the foundation on which the training is built. This training is not enough, however, for it must be accompanied and armed by Western liberalism and Western technology and put in the service of the West.

Many critics have failed to realize that Ducard/Ra's al Ghul is not Bruce's only teacher. As is revealed in another flashback, after watching the murder of Joe Chill, Bruce is instructed by Rachel about a deeper and more humanistic sense of just that must compliment the strength he learns from the League of Shadows. Rachel explains to him "Justice is about harmony. Revenge is about you making yourself feel better" (*Batman Begins* 2005). However, when Rachel continues stating "It's why we have an impartial system," a young Bruce responds, "Your system if broken" (*Batman Begins* 2005). Rachel then shows him the underbelly of Gotham, including the poor who literally live under the city, telling him, "You care about justice? Look beyond your own pain, Bruce" (*Batman Begins* 2005). Rachel shows Bruce what his new task will be as Batman:

> This city is rotting. They talk about the depression as if it's history. It's not. Things are worse than ever. Falcone floods our streets with crime and drugs . . . preying on the desperate, creating new Joe Chills every day. Falcone may not have killed your parents, Bruce . . . but he's destroying everything that they stood for. You wanna thank him for that? Here you go. We all know where to find him. As long as he keeps the bad people rich . . . and the good people scared, no one'll touch him. Good people like your parents, who'll stand against injustice, they're gone. (*Batman Begins* 2005)

Rachel is as much a teacher to Bruce here as Ducard and the League of Shadows, for Rachel reinforces Bruce Wayne's liberal humanism, which is used to tame the Eastern or "Old World" harshness he learns from the League of Shadows.

Young Bruce's third, frequently unidentified, teacher is Carmine Falcone, whose words in the flashback anticipate Ducard's own. Driven by anger and only briefly tutored by an Ivy League education, Bruce arrogantly tempts the Italian gangster, telling him, "I came to show you that not everyone in Gotham's afraid of you" (*Batman Begins* 2005). Falcone shoots back with "Only those who know me, kid" (*Batman Begins* 2005). Bruce must learn that he is blinded by anger, and these criminals are serious people. Falcone then, like Rachel does and Ducard will do, points out the corruption of Gotham, noting that council men, a union official, and a judge are at his bar, and Falcone wouldn't "have a second's hesitation" of blowing Bruce's "head off in front of them" (*Batman Begins* 2005). The lack of a second's hesitation is a reference to Ducard's later "will to act" (*Batman Begins* 2005). Falcone also notes that Bruce immaturely thinks that because he has lost the will to live, he is immune from harm and thus not afraid of Falcone. However, Falcone tells him: "Because you think you got nothing to lose. But you haven't thought it through. You haven't thought about your lady friend in the DA's office. You haven't thought about your old butler" (*Batman Begins* 2005). Falcone further tells him:

> People from your world . . . have so much to lose. Now, you think because your mommy and your daddy got shot . . . you know about the ugly side of life, but you don't. You've never tasted desperate. You're . . . You're Bruce Wayne, the prince of Gotham. You'd have to go miles to meet someone who didn't know your name. So don't come here with your anger, trying to prove something to yourself. This is a world you'll never understand. And you always fear . . . what you don't understand. All right. Yeah, you got spirit, kid. I'll give you that. More than your old man anyway. In the joint, Chill told me about the night he killed your parents. He said your father begged for mercy. Begged. Like a dog. (*Batman Begins* 2005)

Neither Ducard nor Falcone are entirely wrong. Thomas Wayne was kind but weak. Rachel and Thomas Wayne's humanitarianism must be met by the strength of Falcone and Ducard to form a balanced power. Bruce's exchange with the homeless man right afterward reveals his kindness and desire to help the poor. This scene is repeated in the Narrows by giving the boy a bat device. It is also repeated throughout the trilogy in scenes like that of "escaping the pit" in *The Dark Knight Rises* in which Bruce learns from one of the prisoners that he must learn the fear of death and the will to survive. Echoing Alfred's description of Bane in *The Dark Knight Rises*, the blind prisoners tell Bruce: "How can you move faster than possible? Fight longer than possible? If not from the most powerful impulse of the spirit. The fear of death" (*Batman Begins* 2005). Again, in an Asian, or at least Old World, location, Bruce must learn the wisdom that will be later appropriate for the sake of Gotham (as America).

In yet another flashback, we learn that living as a criminal taught Bruce some beyond good and evil. He explains to Ducard that when he stole to keep from starving, he "lost many assumptions about the simple nature of right and wrong" (*Batman Begins* 2005). Bruce while narrating over a crime he committed in China notes that he learned to experience fear and thrill of crimes, but he "never became one of them" (*Batman Begins* 2005). We also learn that he is stealing from himself. The fact that Wayne Enterprises has a connection with China is interesting as we will see. Shone notes that Wayne's "self-imposed exile" in the Global South is a departure from his wealth and privilege and an opportunity for him to rough "his hands with the criminal fraternity he would one day oppose."[32]

Commenting on Bruce's experience in the criminal underworld, Ducard explains, "But a criminal is not complicated" (*Batman Begins* 2005). As Scarecrow, the Joker, and Bane will prove throughout the trilogy, Ducard is both right and wrong. He tells Bruce: "And what you really fear is inside yourself. You fear your own power. You fear your anger . . . the drive to do great or terrible things" (*Batman Begins* 2005). This same drive is found in

Bane in *The Dark Knight* Rises—as Alfred explains while looking at the footage of Bane's robbery of the Gotham stock market: "Take a good look. At his speed, his ferocity, His training. I see the power of belief. Of the fanatic. I see the League of Shadows resurgent" (*Batman Begins* 2005). Bane, like Ducard (and even like the Joker), has a power drawn from the mysticism and philosophy of the Old World. Batman also has this power, but he learns to temper and control it (for the most part) with liberal humanism. In *Batman Begins*, Ducard gives Bruce the power to overcome his fears and to even become what he feared (a bat), but Bruce cannot accept the ultimate teaching of the League of Shadows and blows up their monastery, a profound symbol of razing the (Orientalized) Old World. Tom Shone sees Wayne's turning against the League of Shadows as being reflective of Nolan's own rebellion against the establishment as well as "that old Etonian James Bond at the end of *You Only Live Twice*."[33]

However, Bruce must change and return to the West to combine his Eastern or Old World wisdom with American technology and put it at the use of Gotham, which serves as a symbol of the Anglo-American world order. The "plane scene" in which Alfred Pennyworth arrives in a private jet and brings Bruce back to Gotham is a liminal point showcasing Bruce's border crossing from East to West. The scene begins with Bruce dressed in his gi set against what appears to be the Himalayan Mountains. The next shot is of a private luxury jet set against the opposite mountains. Commenting on Bruce's gi, Alfred says, "You look very fashionable. Apart from the mud" (*Batman Begins* 2005). The comment is that Bruce does not rightly fit into those clothes. He is not a man of the Old World; he is a twenty-first-century American who owns private jets and mansions and can access the raw material to make the Batsuit. Bruce has changed, for he no longer is fighting for personal reasons, but for the betterment of Gotham as he explains. Alfred asks him, "Are you coming back to Gotham for long, sir?" (*Batman Begins* 2005). Bruce responds, "As long as it takes. I want to show the people . . . their city doesn't belong to the criminals and the corrupt" (*Batman Begins* 2005). Alfred responds by explaining that the death of Thomas and Martha Wayne "shocked the wealthy and the powerful into action" (*Batman Begins* 2005). Bruce grants a different meaning to the symbolism, stating, "People need dramatic examples to shake them out of apathy" (*Batman Begins* 2005). I can't do that as Bruce Wayne. He further notes, "As a man . . . I'm flesh and blood, I can be ignored, destroyed" (*Batman Begins* 2005). However, "as a symbol. As a symbol, I can be incorruptible—I can be everlasting" (*Batman Begins* 2005). One of the key elements that Bruce has learned from the League of Shadows is the ability to transcend narcissism and self-interest. Bruce will create Batman as something superior to himself. However, he will be a kinder, gentler, and more humanistic force. After some discussion of Bruce being declared dead and commenting on protecting Rachel, which Bruce fails to do in *The Dark Knight*, Alfred brings up the fact that as the heir to the Wayne fortune, Alfred cracks, "And you can borrow the Rolls, if you like. Just bring it back with a full tank" (*Batman Begins* 2005). This point is critical; Bruce's wealth makes him powerful and this wealth provided by capitalism is what Bruce is fighting for.

This wealth and its ability to procure items, including military grade weapons and armor, is a key point in the film and strengthens the reading of Batman as a symbol of post-9/11 America. In the Batsuit scene, Alfred and Bruce order parts from Singapore (via a "dummy corporation") as well as China. Like the gun that Sal Maroni's thug with attempts to kill in *The Dark Knight*, the bat mask is made in China and is initially defective. As Alfred says, there is a "problem with the graphite" (*Batman Begins* 2005). The Batsuit itself was designed for "advanced infantry" (*Batman Begins* 2005). *Batman Begins* is thus a deeply Western and European film that positions and frames the East as a source of wisdom that can be appropriated. Bruce never becomes the Oriental "Other"; he comes back as the scion of the Wayne family. He is, as Carmine Falcone calls him, the "Prince of Gotham" (*Batman Begins* 2005). Further noting the parallel between Bruce's suiting up in armor and Renaissance and Medieval armor Gearhart argues that Bruce's armor protects him, but it also symbolizes his "transition from nonwarrior to warrior" and enhances his "masculine silhouette."[34] Bruce does not give up his physical or emotional strength when he appropriates the teachings of the League of Shadows as well as the humanitarianism he learned from his father and Rachel. Gearhart further argues that Bruce, like a "young squire" in Medieval and Renaissance Romance, "enjoys economic resources unavailable to the average citizen"; these resources, Gearhart further argues, allow Bruce to purchase his weaponry and vehicles and affords him the "time for marital training."[35] The suit plays a key role in Bruce Wayne's transformation as well as a "psychological advantage while fighting crime that recalls the advantages medieval and renaissance armor accorded knights."[36] According to Gearhart, the Batsuit is a profound symbol of "Wayne's new identity, drawn from the "ageless traditions" of conceptions of the warrior.[37] This armor is a "symbolic aesthetic image of fierce manliness."[38] Gearhart further argues that the Batsuit "reflects an ingrained sense of moral virtue associated with physical appearance, and bridges the Caped Crusader's status as an outsider with an image the citizens of Gotham fear but ultimately support."[39] The key element here for our discussion is the notion that Bruce Wayne, the icon of American identity is appropriating the medieval European past for his use, just as he utilizes the martial arts, spirituality, and philosophy of the East.

However, Bruce does not simply appropriate the suit for himself; he appropriates the suit for Gotham.

Nonetheless, while Eastern philosophy and Western technology appropriated for American use is enough to stop Carmine Falcone and Scarecrow, it is not enough to prevent the League of Shadows from destroying one of the profound symbols of Batman and America itself: Wayne Manor. The symbolism here is that the Old World values of spirituality and ethics seem superior to capitalism and liberalism; however, in the film's logic, they are not. Like the Joker burning Lau on top of a pile of money in *The Dark Knight*, Ra's Al Gul is frightening to the late capitalist audience because he values something more important than money. The Joker famously tells the Chechen in *The Dark Knight* that he is a man of "simple tastes," enjoying dynamite, gunpowder, and gasoline. Indeed, after burning his own money and before sending the Chechen to his execution, the Joker says, "All you care about is money. This city deserves a better class of criminal, and I'm going to give it to them" (*Batman Begins* 2005). The Joker's values, like Ra's Al Ghul's, are rooted in philosophy and perhaps even (anti-?) theology. The Joker thus, like Ra's Al Ghul, claims the right to rule over Gotham, telling the Chechen, "This is my town now" (*Batman Begins* 2005). The Chechen then realizes that his men are more attracted to Joker's power and strangeness than they are to the money that the Chechen can offer them. This is a terrifying moment for the liberal capitalist audience who encounter something more powerful than money. In a similar manner, in conversation with Bruce before burning down Wayne Manor, Ra's Al Ghul notes that Scarecrow's toxin did not come from himself but from the League of Shadows. Ra's al Ghul further explains that Scarecrow thought that the League was going to "ransom Gotham for money" (*Batman Begins* 2005). However, the plan is the reset or destruction of Gotham by the people "tearing each other apart" (*Batman Begins* 2005).

As a symbol of the Orientalized Old World, Ra's al Ghul's worldview is fundamentally aristocratic, reactionary, and hierarchical. When Bruce tells him that he is "gonna destroy millions of lives," Ra's responds, "Only a cynical man would call what these people have 'lives,' Wayne. Crime. Despair. This is not how man was supposed to live" (*Batman Begins* 2005). There is a lot contained in this passage. Batman's "no-kill" rule is famously humanist in its recognition of the value of every human life from the lowliest villain's henchman to Gotham's leaders. Ra's is not necessarily a nihilist-like Joker, but he views human life as reaching a point of no longer having substantive worth: with the language of both Manicheanism and Nietzschean ranking, Ra's dismisses criminals and sinners as well as the emotionally weak and poor as not being worthy of life or at least worthy of lethal punishment. He sees the premodern or perhaps even futuristic vision of man as being superior to the proletarian and lumpen proletarian masses of Gotham (as well as the rich) who live lives of quiet desperation.

As Ra's further explains, functioning like the "Illuminati" of contemporary conspiracy culture, the League of Shadows has operated as a supranational and superhuman "check" on human behavior. As Ra's explains, the League of Shadows seems to have an omnipotent power and a focus largely on Europe, they "sacked Rome. Loaded trade ships with plague rats. Burned London to the ground" (*Batman Begins* 2005). However, again, rather than being the "yellow peril," the Irish Liam Neeson's Ra's Al Ghul functions like a deity or tyrant-king: a super reactionary force intent on disciplining immorality and chaos among the impure and disobedient. As Ra's says, "Every time a civilization reaches the pinnacle of its decadence . . . we return to restore the balance" (*Batman Begins* 2005). Bruce's response is a deeply (post-)Christian liberal humanist and even echoes Biblical pleas of Abraham and Moses as well as Christ. Dan Hassler-Forest notes, "The League's motivation for this plot sounds remarkably similar to the 'they hate our freedoms' rationale that was repeated so frequently in the wake of the 9/11 attacks, with its emphasis on New York City as the pinnacle of decadence. This resonates once more with Huntington's 'clash of civilization's theory, as the film's dialogue plays up culture values that motivated the villain's plot."[40] Bruce argues, "Gotham isn't beyond saving. Give me more time. There are good people here" (*Batman Begins* 2005). However, instead of being a penitential suppliant, Bruce Wayne is wearing a tuxedo and standing in (the soon to be destroyed) Wayne Manor. He is the beneficent American philanthropist.

When Ra's Al Ghul returns to Bruce's mansion, he begins his attack on Gotham manor, itself a symbol of European aristocracy. The League of Shadows is thus attacking a profound symbol of (Anglo-American) Western capitalism. Bruce's encounter with Ra's is another disenchantment of the supernatural. Ra's asks him, "is Ra's al Ghul immortal? Are his methods supernatural?" (*Batman Begins* 2005). The tuxedo adorned Bruce responds, "Or cheap parlor tricks to conceal your true identity, Ra's?" (*Batman Begins* 2005). Just like the beginning of the film, Bruce is disenchanting the supernatural with the allegedly clear light of Western reason. However, Ra's notes that Bruce is not entirely different from Ra's himself, who taught Bruce how to be Batman: "Surely a man who spends his nights scrambling over the rooftops of Gotham wouldn't begrudge me dual identities" (*Batman Begins* 2005). Ra's and Bruce are very similar in that use theatrics and violence to subdue threats. However, there are two key differences. The first is that Bruce at least thinks that Batman fights for justice with "compassion." As he tells Ra's, "I saved your life," Ra's responds with "I warned you about compassion, Bruce" (*Batman Begins* 2005). Bruce is compassionate. However, he is also fighting to save Gotham or the image of America.

After Bruce confirms that the League of Shadows has attacked Gotham before, Ra's states that he has developed the "more sophisticated" weapon of "Economics" to upset the city. As Ra's further explains, "Create enough hunger and everyone becomes a criminal" (*Batman Begins* 2005). However, Bruce's parents attempted to halt the slide into poverty, and "Their deaths galvanized the city into saving itself" (*Batman Begins* 2005). Ra's al Ghul and the League of Shadows have returned and will not be stopped by Bruce Wayne, whom Ra's identifies as being among the "misguided idealists" like Thomas Wayne who got in the way of the League of Shadow's severity (*Batman Begins* 2005). According to Ra's, Thomas and Bruce's humanism is a demonstration of a lack of "courage to do all that is necessary" (*Batman Begins* 2005). Ra's explains that he and the League of Shadows will provide "true justice," and if someone stands in the way of this harsh justice, "you simply walk up behind them and stab them in the heart" (*Batman Begins* 2005). Wayne Manor is destroyed, but Batman eventually rescues Gotham. The battle in the Narrows and the "monorail" ending of *Batman Begins* has rightly drawn the ire of critics. It seems very much like the dreaded Marvel universe and an unnecessary revisiting of the September 9/11 attacks on the World Trade Center—envisioned, of course, through art in which the American hero can prevent the attacks. Nonetheless, there are several curious moments in the denouement of *Batman Begins*.

The ending scenes are also very redolent of the Orientalism reinvigorated by 9/11. When Bruce meets Rachel at the end of the film in the ruins of Wayne Manor, he is covering the hole to the Batcave. Bruce apologizes to Rachel for not informing her that he is Batman, and Rachel likewise apologizes for scolding him for attempting to kill Joe Chill. Bruce explains that Rachel was right to scorn him, and he has learned true justice: "I was a coward with a gun . . . and justice is about more than revenge, so thank you" (*Batman Begins* 2005). Bruce has reached a higher level of wisdom, but his transformation into Batman has prevented his relationship with Rachel from becoming more intimate. Bruce as Batman is married to Gotham. Rachel then asks what Bruce will do with Wayne Manor; Bruce responds, "Rebuild it. Just the way it was, brick for brick" (*Batman Begins* 2005). Alfred then suggests adding some improvements, which Bruce understands as improving the Batcave. This is a profoundly symbolic scene in as much as Wayne Manor as a profound symbol of the West or, more specifically, a combination of Western aristocracy combined with contemporary American technology. Hassler Forest notes that Wayne Manor has a connection to "the oldest European traditions of the aristocracy and its premodern forms of power."[41] After the tragedy of the Narrows and the attempted destruction of Gotham, a new order will be built.

The ending of *Batman Begins* has likewise been commented on at length by critics. It is a paeon not simply to the eternal reoccurrence of Batman, but, in as much as Batman and Gotham are emblematic of the United States, it represents the need for the American empire to maintain its edge with brute force and military technology. James Gordon has created the Batsignal—again a corporate logo as well as a (myth, political, and cultural) symbol. Batman arrives upon calling like God answering a prayer. After Batman praises the Batsignal as being "nice," the then Lieutenant Gordon tells Batman, "You really started something" (*Batman Begins* 2005). Batman's attempt to restore order and balance to Gotham via an appropriation of Eastern wisdom and Western technology at the service of new world humanism and an attempt at justice. Batman has "Bent cops running scared" (*Batman Begins* 2005). This is a frequent theme in seeming transgressive but, in fact, establishment-affirming films. There are individuals in the police force, military, or intelligence agency that are malevolent, but the system itself is fundamentally sound, and the system will correct itself. Batman's vigilantism working in tangent with the police and getting the job done when the police cannot is a sign of the superpower of the superstructure. As a result of his violent destruction of both petty criminals and homegrown, organized crime, he has brought "Hope on the streets" (*Batman Begins* 2005). Despite his tense relationship with the Gotham PD, Batman is allied with and at the service of the state, utilizing the military technology of Wayne Enterprises to stop the hordes of terrorists at home and abroad.

This is a key point that is especially curious, considering that *Batman Begins*, which premiered in 2005, is a post-9/11 film, the United States was four years into the War on Terror and two years into the Iraq War. Already there was some fatigue with the war, and George W. Bush and the neoconservatives driving the war were attempting to maintain American support through a host of media and other artifacts. James Gordon, in a similar vein, seems to argue that, although Gotham might be temporarily saved, there is still the need to continue the struggle against the threatening criminal Other. However, as Gordon explains, the evil continues out on the streets: "The Narrows is lost . . . And we still haven't picked up Crane or half the inmates of Arkham that he freed" (*Batman Begins* 2005). In language heavily redolent of post-9/11 discourse, Batman assures lieutenant Gordon that they will overcome the criminals and rebuild Gotham, telling Gordon, "We will. We can bring Gotham back" (*Batman Begins* 2005). However, Lt. Gordon, again echoing the phenomenon of the militarization of the police as well as the phenomenon of "blowback" asks, "What about escalation?" (*Batman Begins* 2005). After Batman questions him, Gordon explains, "We start carrying semiautomatics, they buy automatics. We start wearing Kevlar, they buy armor-piercing rounds" (*Batman Begins* 2005). Batman does not seem phased and asks, "And?" (*Batman Begins* 2005). Gordon's response is curious. He reminds Batman that his theatrics will themselves produce strange and new rivals: "And you're wearing a mask . . . and jumping off rooftops. Now, take this guy. Armed robbery, double homicide. Got a taste for the theatrical, like you. Leaves a calling card" (*Batman Begins* 2005). The Joker will be the new wave of terrorism that Batman must fight, as he says, "I'll look into it" (*Batman Begins* 2005). He, is like the soldier or police officer or first responder enshrined after 9/11, a silent protector, keeping the people of America safe from its (largely Orientalized) enemies. This canonization of Batman as the epitome of the "first responder" is echoed in the final lines of the film in which Gordon tells Batman, "I never said thank you" (*Batman Begins* 2005). Batman responds, "And you'll never have to" (*Batman Begins* 2005). The notion here is that Batman is an eternal protector. As such, he, upon first glance represents a Christ figure; however, as we have seen, he is much more a figure of the American state armed with advance military technology; and having appropriated and tamed the wisdom of the (largely Orientalized) Old World, he uses this wisdom, combined with liberal humanism, to protect American from the return of the (again Orientalized) repressed premodern Old World.

Upon first glance, Nolan's most recent film is an embrace of the vanguard Western progressivism. With the release of his 2020 *Tenet*, Christopher Nolan featured, for the first time, an historic black American actor, John David Washington, as his title character. On one level, Nolan's casting is reflective of the wider, post-George Floyd reframing of American culture around people of color as opposed to those of European descent. However, at the same time, such casting, at least for Christopher Nolan, is not necessarily a radical or transgressive act. In *Tenet* John David Washington's character, simply called, "the Protagonist," literally works for the Central Intelligence Agency and labors in collaboration with other Western European powers to stop a Ukrainian arms dealer. The same method of pitting the liberal and capitalist West vis-à-vis the East and continental Europe is continued in the film although the genetic and cosmetic profile of the lead character as changed. Indeed, it might be argued that one of the dominant themes of Nolan's films—or at least his blockbuster films—is the need for the Anglo-American neoliberal world order to be protected at all costs.

To argue that Christopher Nolan's *Batman Begins* (and the bulk of his films) ultimately affirm an Anglo-American capitalist world view as being superior to various totalitarian or reactionary worldviews in Europe and Asia is not to make (herein) a moral judgment on Nolan's oeuvre or his work—for the record, the author of this piece is a huge Nolan fan. Rather, it is an honest assessment of what appears to be one of the intellectual planks of Christopher

Nolan's entire work (especially his post-*Insomnia* blockbusters). In *Batman Begins*, Nolan presents the narrative of Bruce Wayne's transformation into Batman to reform a corruption Gotham, which itself stands for a seemingly corrupt United States. Unsatisfied with early twenty-first century Western liberal education, Bruce must travel to the East or Eurasia to learn martial arts as well as "Old World" psychology and spirituality and even political philosophy. However, this political philosophy must be tamed by a Western humanism and liberalism and be combined with Western technology to be applied in the service of Bruce Wayne, Wayne Enterprises, and, ultimately, Gotham.

NOTES

1. See, for example, Varisco.
2. See, for example, Geary, Schofield, and Sutton as well as Posner and Haynes.
3. See Hassler-Forest, Sisco, McSweeney, Margulies, as well as Laderman Gruenewald.
4. Shone, *The Nolan Variations*, 141–42.
5. McSweeney, *The "War on Terror and American Film*, 215.
6. McSweeney, *The 'War on Terror' and American Film*," 115.
7. Said, *Orientalism*, 19.
8. Said, *Orientalism*, 54.
9. Said, *Orientalism*, 201.
10. Said, *Orientalism*, 204.
11. Ibid.
12. Ibid.
13. Said, *Orientalism*, 263.
14. Brooker, *Hunting the Dark Knight*, 1, 59.
15. Brooker, *Hunting the Dark Knight*, xiii.
16. Brooker, *Hunting the Dark Knight*, 72.
17. Hassler-Forest, *Capitalist Superheroes*, 87.
18. Hassler-Forest, *Capitalist Superheroes*, 88.
19. Shone, *The Nolan Variations*, 135.
20. Shone, *The Nolan Variations*, 133.
21. Hassler-Forest, *Capitalist Superheroes*, 96.
22. Shone, *The Nolan Variations*, 131.
23. Shone, *The Nolan Variations*, 143.
24. Shone, *The Nolan Variations*, 135.
25. Hassler-Forest, *Capitalist Superheroes*, 92.
26. Ibid.
27. Ibid.
28. Ibid.
29. Hassler-Forest, *Capitalist Superheroes*, 96.
30. Hassler-Forest, *Capitalist Superheroes*, 96–97.

31. Gearhart, "Suiting up the Hero," 671.
32. Shone, *The Nolan Variations*, 130.
33. Shone, *The Nolan Variations*, 34–35.
34. Gearhart, "Suiting up the Hero," 666.
35. Gearhart, "Suiting up the Hero," 667.
36. Gearhart, "Suiting up the Hero," 675.
37. Gearhart, "Suiting up the Hero," 680.
38. Ibid.
39. Ibid.
40. Hassler-Forest, *Capitalist Superheroes*, 97.
41. Hassler-Forest, *Capitalist Superheroes*, 174.

Chapter 3

Order and the State in Christopher Nolan's *Dark Knight*

With the release of *The Dark Knight* in 2008, Christopher Nolan established himself as an internationally renowned filmmaker capable of the rare feat of crafting a well-written and intelligent movie while, at the same time, creating a mesmerizing visual feast of stunts and pyrotechnics. Very likely, at least on one level, a reflection on the War on Terror, which was then ramping up at the end of the Bush era and beginning of the Obama era, *The Dark Knight* is exceptionally dark and represents a *realpolitik* assessment of the need for the liberal order to occasionally use the "iron fist" when dealing with especially dangerous enemies, who, in the film, are represented by the Joker and, to a lesser degree, the various mob families. On one level, in *The Dark Knight*, the Joker is a deeply primal and archetypal character who represents the recurrent temptation of evil, to which Batman and the people of Gotham (and the people of the world) are drawn. However, the Joker is also a profound symbol of the anarchy festering among the poor and working class of Gotham, which, in the Batman mythology, often survives as a figure for the archetypal American metropolis, New York, which itself is an image of the United States.

In contrast to the Joker is Batman, his alias Bruce Wayne, and the entire legal and political state apparatus of Gotham. Although imperfect, Gotham is, in the Nolan-verse, worth protecting. It is up to Batman to act in service of the state apparatus in order to rescue Gotham when law enforcement and the legal system fail. Although temporarily needing to use harsh methods with the Joker, Batman eventually returns to a more humane approach at the end of the film, rescuing the Joker after proving to him that the people of Gotham, including the inmates of Gotham Penitentiary, are nobler than the Joker initially assumed. Despite its philosophical, moral, and psychological musings about corruption and the question of human nature, *The Dark Knight* is a deeply political movie that ultimately promotes the American neoliberal world order.

One of the central debates over the film has been the its relationship to the emergent national security state under the Bush administration. In his famous *Wall Street Journal* piece "What Bush and Batman Have in Common," Andrew Klavan argues that *The Dark Knight* is a "a paean of praise to the fortitude and moral courage that has been shown by George W. Bush in this time of terror and war." In a more moderate voice, Patrick Kent Russell places *The Dark Knight* trilogy amid a time in American history in which the United States was pervaded with a "darkness" in which "Americans dealt with multiple traumas, both global and domestic," which included the 9/11 attacks as well as a global financial crisis.[1] Americans thus fled to the world of "archetypal heroes, especially those from comic books—more comics-based films were released between 2001 and 2010, in fact, than in all previous years combined."[2] As a result, Russell writes that similar to the post–World War II fascination with film noir, Americans were interested in a "darker fare."[3] In "Legendary Caesar and the Architect Ariadne: Narrative, Myth and Psychology in Christopher Nolan's *Batman Begins*, *The Dark Knight* and *Inception*," Kresimir Vukovic and Petkovic Rajko note that screenwriter David Goyer has said that the "the main theme of the film is 'escalation.'" Vilja Johnson likewises writes that, rather than being an ethical system, Batman's guiding principles in the films are encapsulated in "a simple desire to thwart the goals of his enemies, forming an "oppositional morality, which "allows Batman the moral flexibility to combat evil in various forms, but it also places his decisions in the hands of his enemies, allowing Nolan to question and test Batman's position as a popular hero."[4] This questioning, Johnson continues, "forces a re-evaluation of traditional, absolute understandings of heroism, allowing for a variety of new distinctions between hero and villain."[5] While it may not necessarily be an endorsement of the Bush administration, The *Dark Knight* is ultimately both a political and moral work that affirms the American world order.

The Dark Knight begins with Nolan's brilliantly choreographed opening, which pays homage to Michael Mann's *Heat* (1995) as well as Stanley Kubrick's *The Killing* (1956). As critics have noted, Joker's appearance on the street corner holding a mask turned away from the camera and entering into a very dated Chevrolet Suburban is representative of Joker as an anonymous force of chaos. However, at the same time, it is a representation of the Joker as a working-class "everyman" waging a war against the system—as a thief, he also fits into the logic of Umberto's 1972 article "The Myth of Superman," in which the Italian semiologist argues that most superhero comics present the hero as a defender of private property. He is dressed at this point in inconspicuous clothes, which sets the tone for the rest of the film: the Joker is a very intelligent and often flamboyant member of the masses, running about in the machinery of the capitalist, neoliberal system and attempting to subvert it. In mimicry of Bruce Wayne, the Joker is also the CEO of the operation and ruthlessly executes his underlines after they finish the job in a parodic form of post-Fordian or "late" capitalism disposing of "temp workers." In *Capitalist Superheroes: Caped Crusaders in the Neoliberal Age*, Dan Hassler-Forest describes the bank robbery scene as being a manifestation of "the kind of logic based on short-term individual gains over long-term benefits that typifies the dangers of neoliberalism and speculative finance capitalism: gang members are dispatched as soon as the application of their particular skill-set has been carried out."[6] Hassler-Forest is correct here, but Joker's enterprise represents a parodic vision of capitalism that rivals the capitalist order of Gotham, which Nolan depicts as being worth preserving. In *The Shock Doctrine*, Naomi Klein identifies neoliberalism with both neoconservativism as well as "Chicago School economics" and defines it as "capitalism stripped of its Keynesian appendages, capitalism in its monopoly phase, a system that has let itself go—that no longer has to work to keep us as customers, that can be as antisocial, antidemocratic and boorish as it wants."[7] Klein's description could apply to the Joker's enterprise, but it also could refer to the authoritarian and transnational corporation known as Wayne Enterprises. In a later scene in which he kills the mobster Gambol, the Joker specifically refers to his operation as being like a company, when attempting to recruit Gambol's men: "Now . . . our operation is small . . . but there is a lot of potential . . . for aggressive expansion. So which of you fine gentlemen would like to join our team? Oh. There's only one spot open right now, so we're gonna have . . . tryouts" (*Dark Knight* 2008). The term "tryouts" is derived from American sports culture, and this mockery or upending of sports culture is something in which Nolan frequently engages throughout his films. Nonetheless, the Joker ironically envisions his criminal enterprise as being like an expanding corporation.

Like Bruce Wayne, the Joker further does not mind getting his hands dirty engaging in the crimes himself. In the opening scene, we are introduced to the Joker's crew, which seems to include high skilled members of the white working class (he will later adopt black teenagers). Overall, there is a primal sense of chaos to the Joker, but he is also a political and economic figure who, like Bane in *The Dark Knight Rises*, represents the fears of the ruling class of subversive element in the 99%. Nolan seems to reinforce this potential reading throughout *The Dark Knight*. Throughout the film, many of the Joker's goons are marginalized figures such as the mentally ill or criminals. Also, his minions appear to be drawn from the working class and operate municipal vehicles and dress like members of the working class. Joker himself dresses as a nurse and a police officer throughout the film, adopting the identity of the working class but also mocking and subverting the established order by infiltrating the apparatus that supports it. The message here is (at least) threefold. The Joker's power is everywhere. His power of chaos is also present among the officials of the government. However, finally, Joker's people are drawn from the working class, including those who work in municipal services. There are thus threats to the established order within the underpinnings of the established order itself. As with Bane in *The Dark Knight Rises*, the Joker has the potential to unleash the power of the poor and working class and upend the social order.

However, the Joker is not a Robinhood figure; he is fundamentally a creature of nihilism. Thinking the Joker is just another "goon," pursuing self-interest and money, during the opening scene, the mob bank manager believes that he can appeal to the street code with this masked character, telling the Joker: "You think you're smart, huh? The guy that hired you he'll just do the same to you" (*Dark Knight* 2008). The mob bank manager further states: "Oh, criminals in this town used to believe in things. Honor . . . respect. Look at you. What do you believe in, huh? What do you believe in?!" (*Dark Knight* 2008). The bank manager seems to think that the Joker represents a decline in the quality of criminal. However, the Joker is not reducible to simply another class of criminal. He is something much more allusive, as he tells the bank manager: "I believe whatever doesn't kill you simply makes you . . . stranger" (*Dark Knight* 2008). The Joker's strangeness is manifested by his ugliness and weirdness, but it is also manifested by his inability to exist in the capitalist system. This exchange presents another key thread that will be developed throughout the film. The Joker does not work for anyone and has no loyalty. He is a primeval and mysterious force of chaos, but he manifests himself as an anti-establishment, anti-liberal, anti-capitalist, and (potentially) anti-American terrorist, who is ultimately drawn from the (white) working class of Gotham. The Joker is an integral part of the system or at least has the ability to hijack the accoutrements of the system, which is symbolized in the opening scene by his driving a school bus into a parade of other buses—as we will see, the Joker frequently commanderies municipal vehicles to use against municipal entities such as the police and Harvey Dent's District Attorney's Office. Although a symbol of chaotic nihilism, the Joker is a deconstructionist and revolutionary who uses the raw material of the political and economic system against the political and economic system itself.

However, there is something bigger than the municipal structure that stands in the way of Joker completely deconstructing and ultimately engulfing Gotham: Batman, who is able to keep the criminals at bay as the next scene in the car garage shows. The criminals are scared on the street, not because of the police or necessarily the reforms Harvey Dent has brought; they are, rather, scared of Batman. There are still villains such as Scarecrow and the mob, but they are easily manhandled by Batman. Moreover, in the parking garage scene in which Batman apprehends Scarecrow and the mobster known as "the Chechen," we are introduced to the copycat Batmen. Like the real Batman, these pretend Batmen are vigilantes; however, unlike the liberal, humanistic Batman, they are quick to apply lethal violence, using guns. Moreover, these pretend Batman are themselves members of the working class and can only afford, "hockey pants" as Batman himself notes (*Dark Knight* 2008). Even Cillian Murphy's Scarecrow recognizes that the real Batman uses both high technology and humanistic methods, commenting "That's more like it" when the real Batman's Tumbler crashes over the wall and blows up some empty vehicles (*Dark Knight* 2008). Batman not only bags the Scarecrow and the Chechen and their goons but also disarms and incapacitates the vigilante Batmen as well. The point here seems to be that the real Batman gains his legitimacy through his wealth and high technology as well as his humanistic methods. As such, Bruce Wayne is representative of the American order that utilizes its high technology and its allegedly liberal credo to fight threats at home and abroad.

The most explicit scene in which Bruce Wayne/Batman is linked with the American intelligence agency is when Bruce and Morgan Freeman's Lucius Fox plan the capture of the Chinese mob accountant Lau. As Lucius Fox explains, "The CIA had a program back in the '60s . . . for getting their people out of hot spots called Sky Hook" (*Dark Knight* 2008). Bruce responds, "We could look into that" (*Dark Knight* 2008). The notion of using military technology is frequent throughout not only *The Dark Knight* trilogy, but also in Nolan films like *Inception*. Nolan is thus not so different from other superhero directors who present elements of their films as being seeming endorsements of at least certain elements of the military industrial complex. As Dan Hassler-Forrest notes in *Capitalist Superheroes*, "since Bruce Wayne must depend wholly on his billionaire status to maintain his alternate crime-fighting persona and pay for his arsenal of technological gadgets, vehicles and costumes, Batman's superpower may be defined as Capital in the most literal sense."[8] Batman is not only simply American military might, but also American capital, which has become increasingly wed to American military power, as Naomi Klein famously demonstrated in *The Shock Doctrine*. *The Dark Knight Rises* is thus very much a post-9/11 film in which the American world order, or, in the words of Hassler-Forest, a "global Empire,"[9] is challenged by subversive enemies who must be converted or eradicated. Rather than being the "end of history," the post-9/11 world has produced, according to Hassler-Forest, "an intensification of the cultures of late capitalism on a global scale."[10] This order of late capitalism, symbolized by the shining postmodern (but ultimately corrupt) Gotham of *The Dark Knight*, is threatened by the Joker but protected by Batman.

Indeed, the conflict between Wayne Enterprises and Mr. Lau is very tense and very much reads as a microcosm of a wider conflict between the United States and the People's Republic of China. In this scene, Morgan Freeman's Lucius performs an intelligence operation, placing a phone that admits sonar into Lau's office. After insulting Lau in a very confrontational manner, Fox meets an incognito Bruce Wayne. He explains the technology he set up in Lau's office to Bruce. Fox explains the sonar device, which Wayne Enterprises (military) "R&D" worked up (*Dark Knight* 2008). It "Sends out a high-frequency pulse . . . records the response time for mapping an environment" (*Dark Knight* 2008). Wayne identifies this as "Sonar," which is like a submarine, as Lucius Fox notes approvingly. In this scene, both Fox and Wayne act as undercover American intelligence agents spying on a Chinese national in Hong Kong. In the actual extradition scene, Batman himself uses extremely sophisticated weapons technology to fly from one Hong Kong skyscraper to the next, breaking through the window of Lau's office and, after evading gunshots and beating up Lau's security, Batman escapes the dumbfounded and incompetent Hong Kong police via a balloon caught by a cargo plane. Batman then finally leaves Lau on the steps of Jim Gordon's office with a humiliating note. The message here is clear: American know-how and technology trumps that of the Chinese, and American intelligence agencies are justified in their extralegal apprehension of America's enemies. In *Living in the End Times*, Slavoj Žižek argues that the "'American century' is over and we are entering into a period characterized by the formation of multiple centers of global capitalism . . . After the failure of the US to impose itself as the sole superpower ('the universal policeman'), there is now a need to establish rules of interaction between these local centers in case of conflicting interests."[11] Batman's kidnapping of Lau is thus a "flex" of American muscle in an era in which such flexing does not draw the respect it once did. As the Joker says during the "group therapy" mob meeting scene: "Batman has no jurisdiction," and neither does the United States (*Dark Knight* 2008). It is quite possible that the puckish Christopher Nolan may be trolling the audience by drawing their sympathy toward this seemingly outrageous extralegal act, but there is little indication of humor or irony in the scene.

If there is criticism of Batman as America's actions in the films it is to be found in the mouth of the Joker. There are numerous passages in which the Joker, echoing American political scientist Chalmers Johnson's notion of blowback, critiques Batman. While torturing the imposter Batman named Brian Douglas in the video given to *Gotham Tonight*, the Joker says, "You see, this is how crazy Batman's made Gotham" (*Dark Knight* 2008). The Joker, echoing Jim Gordon's comments at the end of *Batman Begins*, notes that Batman's pressure on petty criminals and the mob has led to the emergence of the Joker himself. The Joker's political commentary is sustained by the narrative arc of the entire *Dark Knight* trilogy. Batman's ordering power sparks the emergence of a chaotic power to challenge it. In order for there to be peace, Batman has to take off his mask. The state apparatus must come clean as Joker announces: "You want order in Gotham . . . Batman must take off his mask and turn himself in" (*Dark Knight* 2008). The Joker notes that as long as Batman retains his power, people will die: "Oh, and every day he doesn't, people will die. Starting tonight. I'm a man of my word" (*Dark Knight* 2008). The Joker's grainy video, echoing those of Al Qaeda and ISIS and clearly later influencing Paul Dano's Riddler's videos in 2022's *The Batman*, is undoubtedly a "terrorist video." This terrorism is further emphasized by the Joker's demand that Batman as the extrajudicial power of Gotham (America) come out of the shadows and unmask, thus losing his secretive power. Nolan does not necessarily side with the Joker here or with Batman. There is some truth to the idea that Batman has brought this evil upon Gotham. However, as Dan Hassler-Forest argues in *Capitalist Superheroes: Caped Crusaders in The Neoliberal Age*, Gotham itself is a corrupted and "presents the urban landscape as a far more threatening environment [than the Manhattan of the Spider-Man films], constantly plagued by terror, civil unrest, and the systematic failure of its democratic institutions."[12] In this argument then, Gotham as a liberal democracy has failed, and it is necessary for Batman (like the Bush and later Obama administration) to use harsh methods to protect this flawed liberalism.

This quandary is emphasized in a discussion between Bruce Wayne and Alfred. Bruce says, "I knew the Mob wouldn't go down without a fight . . . but this is different. They crossed a line." Alfred responds, "You crossed the line first, Sir. You squeezed them, you hammered them to the point of desperation. And in their desperation, they turned to a man they didn't fully understand" (*Dark Knight* 2008). Quoting Ra's al Ghul, Bruce responds, "Criminals aren't complicated, Alfred" (*Dark Knight* 2008). Alfred reflects on the Joker as a symbol of primal chaos. Bruce tries to use science to understand the Joker, telling Alfred, "We just need to figure out what he's after" (*Dark Knight* 2008). Alfred responds, "With respect, Master Wayne . . . perhaps this is a man you don't fully understand either" (*Dark Knight* 2008). Alfred then gives his famous gem thief story and explains that the Joker is like the gem thief: "Some men aren't looking for anything logical, like money. They can't be bought, bullied, reasoned or negotiated with. Some men just wanna watch the world burn" (*Dark Knight* 2008). The Joker is a force of chaos that, at times, draws the sympathy of the viewer. He does want to watch the world burn, but he destroys the world by taking aim at Gotham, which itself represents America, which thinks of itself as the world's guardian. Gotham's fall would be the world's fall as, in the logic of American imperialism, the fall of America would precipitate the fall of the world into chaos. Dan Hassler-Forest argues that Joker as an agent of chaos affirms a shift from "the Manichean binary of good vs. evil that is so familiar from the standard formula of the popular fantasy film."[13] The Joker threatens the very moral fabric of the film. The Joker does not destroy Batman's legitimacy; however, he, along with the more sympathetic Alfred, challenges it.

However, at the same time, the Joker is someone (or something) that upsets the social order. One of the key scenes in which this anti-social manifestation of the Joker's chaos is present is in the interruption of Bruce Wayne's fundraising party. Interestingly, the Joker enters with his goons behind a police officer (whom we later discover as being owned by the mob) who is upholding a badge. The symbol here is fairly profound. One of Nolan's key interests is doubles. The Joker and Batman function as reciprocal forces of chaos and order and mirror one another. Moreover, the Joker and the mob with whom he is connected are not completely different from the world of the police, Wayne Enterprises, and the municipal government. There is even scene where a much older (and one assumes married) man is caught in what appears to be an act of adultery. This scene, other than serving as comic relief, does not make a great deal of sense and is atypical for Nolan, who generally avoids "love scenes." However, it serves as a slight reminder that Gotham's oligarchy is not pristine but is rather corrupt—if not as corrupt as the mob or as malevolent as the Joker, but they are imperfect. The Joker further ridicules the campiness of the party. His line "good evening ladies and gentleman" is a clearly derisive attack on manners as his own slovenly appearance (*Dark Knight* 2008). Brandishing a shotgun, he further interrogates the party-goers, asking them: "Do you know where I can find Harvey? I need to talk to him about something. Just something little, huh? No" (*Dark Knight* 2008). Through his constant mocking of colloquialisms, Joker is attacking language itself as well as the culture of polite catchphrases. As critics have further noted, Joker is trolling psychology itself. When he tells the elderly man played by Senator Patrick Leahy: You know . . . you remind me of my father. I hated my father" (*Dark Knight* 2008). This is exactly what a traumatized young villain would say, but the Joker may not have actually hated his father. His story, like much of his narrative, is possibly a lie. The Joker is attacking the language, conceptual *apparati* and the manners that support the wealthy of Gotham. In as much as Gotham represents American capitalism, he is, further attacking capitalism itself.

The money pile scene is another a profoundly terrifying image of the Joker's transvaluation of capitalist values. This scene stands in parodic contrast to Batman's high-tech extradition of Lau. The Joker's methods are crude and lethally violence; moreover, they are a bitter and aggressive critique of capitalism. While in the third decade of the twenty-first century, money is increasingly in digital form, the image of an enormous mass of "green backs" being set alight is terrifying but, at the same time, appealing—especially to those who have not benefited from American capitalism. Lao himself is always associated with money in the film and brags of his skill with numbers. Thus, the Joker's incineration of Lao with the money is a profound symbol of the destruction of transnational capitalism—Batman, in contrast, apprehended a criminal for the sake of Gotham. The Joker, however, is attacking capital itself. Hassler-Forest points out that there is a strong parallel between the Joker's view of money and Bruce Wayne's: "The Joker's grasps of the virtualization of money brings him conceptually closer to his nemesis Batman, who consistently adopts the persona of the wasteful billionaire playboy whose financially irresponsible behavior reflects a similar disdain for cash."[14] Hassler-Forest's description here is only partially correct. Bruce Wayne–Batman is reckless at times, but he directs most of his money to the service of Gotham—something that Nolan depicts as positive in his Batman films. At one point, Joker even throws a bundle of bills at Lau, as a way of mocking Lau's attachment to money as well as the money itself. Lao represents the power of money (as to opposed to warcraft or landownership, etc.), which is the basis of power in the twenty-first century. The Chechen, who confronts Joker in the scene, also represents the universal greed for money, expressing his shock when Joker sets the pile of money alight. Disgusted with the Chechen's love of Mammon, the Joker tells him, "all you care about is money. This town deserves a better class of criminal" (*Dark Knight* 2008). The Joker has extra-capitalist values. He thinks of himself as a nihilist philosopher or guru who is teaching the people of Gotham the emptiness of material things. As he comments (to himself?), "It's not about money. It's about sending a message," which he follows with this comment: "Everything burns" (*Dark Knight* 2008). This is true, but this is what Batman, Gordon, and Harvey Dent attempt to hide from the people. Certain elements of Anglo-American liberalism are built upon illusion of the permanence of capital and material prosperity and the illusion that it brings happiness. The Joker seeks to destroy capital and the life it provides, but Batman attempts to defend it.

Batman's humanism that he inherits from Thomas Wayne is also challenged throughout the film. When Batman is interrogating the Italian gangster Salvatori Maroni, Maroni refers to Batman and him as "one professional to another" (*Dark Knight* 2008). Maroni considers Batman to be another criminal or bruiser who works with the police department just as much as Maroni himself works with the police. Maroni further explains that Batman's humanism hinders him, and the criminals of Gotham are not going to adhere to it: "Nobody's gonna tell you nothing. They're wise to your act. You got rules. The Joker, he's got no rules. Nobody's gonna cross him for you. If you want this guy, you got one way. But you already know what that is. Just take off that mask, let him come find you" (*Dark Knight* 2008). Maroni knows that Batman's weakness is his "no kill" rule, which hinders him. Maroni also seconds Alfred and the Joker's request that Batman's secrecy is responsible for the deaths of others. Batman must either come clean or begin to use more brutal methods. However, he instead opts for increased surveillance of Gotham, violating the privacy of the citizens as opposed to brutalizing criminals further.

In fact, in the following scene, Batman affirms his humanism, stopping Harvey Dent from torturing a mentally ill man who has been recruited into the Joker's enterprise. Harvey Dent is the positive image of the administration state as Batman notes when stopping him from torturing one of Joker's goons, telling Harvey: "You're the symbol of hope I could never be. Your stand against organized crime is the first legitimate ray of light in Gotham in decades. If anyone saw this, everything would be undone" (*Dark Knight* 2008). Batman is able to live outside the law engaging in extradition and torture, but Harvey Dent must be the public face of the law, projecting the image of fairness and decency. However, even Batman does not stoop to lethality in the Nolan-verse—if he can help it. Noting that now even Harvey Dent has been tempted by the Joker to engage in torture and possibly murder, Batman decides to come clean, giving Gotham to Dent; as he tells him, "Gotham's in your hands now" (*Dark Knight* 2008). However, Harvey Dent knows Batman is much more powerful than Dent, and thus Dent takes Batman's place as the prisoner as Alfred explains to Rachel: "Perhaps both Bruce and Mr. Dent . . . believe that Batman stands for something more important . . . than the whims of a terrorist, Miss Dawes . . . even if everyone hates him for it. That's the sacrifice he's making. He's not being a hero. He's being something more" (*Dark Knight* 2008). The message here is that the extrajudicial surveillance and extradition and torture in which Batman engages is necessary to keep Gotham safe. Harvey Dent can be replaced, but Batman cannot.

This point is further emphasized in Batman's torture of the Joker at the police station (as well as in the ending scene of Joker's capture on the partially constructed high rise). The Joker taunts Batman for not revealing his identity and allowing people to die, telling Batman, "I wanted to see what you'd do. And you didn't disappoint. You let five people die. Then you let Dent take your place. Even to a guy like me, that's cold" (*Dark Knight* 2008). The Joker, like the terrorists who blame American foreign policy for their actions, is not entirely correct, for it was the Joker who killed the Gothamites. However, there is some sense to his statement in as much as the Batman's system has brought about the Joker. With perhaps a comment on the post-9/11 world of the early twenty-first century, the Joker states, "Those Mob fools want you gone so they can get back to the way things were. But I know the truth. There's no going back. You've changed things. Forever" (*Dark Knight* 2008). It is not just Batman, but the Joker himself who has changed things forever: both the twenty-first-century terrorist, and the twenty-first-century national security state have radically changed the dynamic of the world. In fact, according to the Joker, both terrorism and violence of the state represented by Batman go hand in hand. Joker tells him, "I don't wanna kill you. What would I do without you? Go back to ripping off Mob dealers? No, no. No. No, you. . . . You complete me" (*Dark Knight* 2008). Just as Al Qaeda's predecessor, the Mujahedeen, needed US funding, and the Department of Homeland security needs Al Qaeda to exist, so too do Joker and Batman need each other in order to justify each other's existence.

Batman attempts to reduce the Joker to the level of a petty criminal, but the Joker does not buy it. When Batman tells him, "You're garbage who kills for money," Joker responds: "Don't talk like one of them. You're not. Even if you'd like to be. To them, you're just a freak. Like me" (*Dark Knight* 2008). The Joker is a "freak" who operates outside the law but so is Batman. Moreover, like many of the deserted Vets lying under bridges (perhaps, as we will see, even the Joker himself at one point). Batman, like the US GI, is expendable as the Joker explains, "They need you right now . . . but when they don't . . . they'll cast you out like a leper" (*Dark Knight* 2008). The Joker explains that this utilitarianism is in the selfishness of the people of Gotham: "You see, their morals, their code . . . it's a bad joke. Dropped at the first sign of trouble. They're only as good as the world allows them to be. I'll show you. When the chips are down, these—these civilized people . . . they'll eat each other. See, I'm not a monster. I'm just ahead of the curve" (*Dark Knight* 2008). The Joker ultimately believes that Gotham is so corrupt that it is not worth saving. His response is to torture the city and bring it down to his level, unmasking the alleged lies supporting the system. Batman, however, feels that Gotham is redeemable and worth protecting. The Joker thinks that Batman's humanism is a charade, telling him, "You have all these rules, and you think they'll save you" (*Dark Knight* 2008). Batman says, "I have one rule." The Joker further tempts him: "Oh. Then that's the rule you'll have to break to know the truth." The truth is, as Joker explains, "The only sensible way to live in this world is without rules" (*Dark Knight* 2008). Joker's nihilism is a metaphysical, anti-theological statement, but it is also a political statement. He hopes to bring down the moral order by bringing down the political and legal order of Gotham.

Joker explains this connection between the moral and political orders in his bedside discussion with Harvey Dent, who has turned into Two-Face at Gotham General Hospital. The Joker tells Two-Face that he is not responsible for the death of Rachel or Harvey Dent's mutilation:

"I didn't rig those charges" (*Dark Knight* 2008). However, the angry emergent Two-Face retorts, "Your men, your plan" (*Dark Knight* 2008). Joker ironically attempts to refute this statement with, "Do I really look like a guy with a plan? You know what I am? I'm a dog chasing cars. I wouldn't know what to do with one if I caught it. You know? I just do things" (*Dark Knight* 2008). This is not entirely true, for as the Joker reveals, he has plans to take over Gotham. His plans, however chaotic they are, conflict with Gotham's plans. He derides the others in the movie for their plans: "The Mob has plans. The cops have plans. Gordon's got plans. You know, they're schemers. Schemers trying to control their little worlds" (*Dark Knight* 2008). This cruel statement not only applies to the Joker himself, but to all of Gotham, and is essentially one of the key elements of Nolan's philosophy throughout his films: the desire people have to give meaning to their lives with lies. The Joker further explains, "I'm not a schemer" (*Dark Knight* 2008). The Joker is a deconstructionist: "I try to show the schemers . . . how pathetic their attempts to control things really are" (*Dark Knight* 2008). As he further explains to Two-Face: "It's the schemers that put you where you are. You were a schemer, you had plans and look where that got you" (*Dark Knight* 2008). It is not that Joker is dismissing plans or scheming outright. He is arguing against the idea of unironic seriousness that occupancies the schemers. The Joker views all order as a lie that must be burned down, and that incineration ultimately, in *The Dark Knight*, is a transgressive political act. As Joker tells Two-Face, "I just did what I do best. I took your little plan and I turned it on itself" (*Dark Knight* 2008). This upending of the plan takes the place of a (Rightist? Fascist?) upending of the social order via the intelligence of the deviant and marginalized members of the white working class as the Joker tells Two-Face: "Look what I did to this city with a few drums of gas and a couple of bullets" (*Dark Knight* 2008). The Joker is a violent revolutionary spawned from the working class who uses simple and cheap items to upend the complexity of Gotham's social order. He is thus very much like the terrorist against which the American security state labors at home and abroad.

In his dialogue with Two-Face, Joker specifically notes that there are marginalized groups who are forgotten in the plan for Gotham, which does not take notice of soldiers and criminals: "Hm? You know . . . You know what I noticed? Nobody panics when things go 'according to plan.' Even if the plan is horrifying" (*Dark Knight* 2008). This is an interesting attack on the establishment, whose plans are often "horrifying." Within the establishment's plans, the death of the poor and marginalized are all just "part of the plan" (*Dark Knight* 2008). Joker explains, "If tomorrow I tell the press that, like, a gangbanger will get shot or a truckload of soldiers will be blowing up . . . nobody panics. Because it's all part of the plan" (*Dark Knight* 2008). There are two references here to the war on crime and the War on Terror. In both wars, the poor and marginalized are simply cannon fodder. Their deaths are just part of the plan. However, when Joker speaks truth to power and upsets the established order, things change, as he notes, "But when I say that one little old mayor will die . . . well, then, everyone loses their minds" (*Dark Knight* 2008). The Joker specifically states he is not simply a dog chasing cars or a force of nature; he is a political revolutionary: "Introduce a little anarchy . . . upset the established order . . . and everything becomes chaos" (*Dark Knight* 2008). The Joker says that he is an "agent of chaos." However, he is also a political revolutionary. He is going to bring a true justice and upset the "established order," which he views as being unjust.

The Joker's bullets and gas are symbols of his poverty as well as his intelligence. He represents a terrifying threat not only to the cosmic order, but also to the civil order. As he tells Harvey Dent during the hospital bed scene, "Look what I did to this city with a few drums of gas and a couple of bullets" (*Dark Knight* 2008). Joker here is exaggerating; he obviously uses more than simply gas and bullets, but these gas and bullets, which he describes in the scene in which he sets his pile of money alight, are "cheap" (*Dark Knight* 2008). They are something that are accessible to the poor but are nonetheless a potentially devasting threat to the established order. To stop this chaos and violence, Batman must, once again, use extrajudicial means.

The most poignant and politically relevant scene in which this is revealed is when Batman unveils the sonar grid that, spying on all the citizens of Gotham, he will use to capture the Joker. Upon discovery by Lucius Fox, Batman notes, "Beautiful, isn't it?" (*Dark Knight* 2008). Lucius Fox responds, "Beautiful. Unethical. Dangerous. You've turned every cell phone in Gotham into a microphone" (*Dark Knight* 2008). He continues (explaining to the viewer): "You took my sonar concept and applied it to every phone in the city. With half the city feeding you sonar, you can image all of Gotham. This is wrong." However, both Wayne and Lucius note that, like the Patriot Act, this is a necessary evil and one time affair. Batman states, "I've gotta find this man, Lucius" (*Dark Knight* 2008). Lucius notes, "At what cost?" (*Dark Knight* 2008). Batman continues to deflate Lucius (and the viewer's) concerns, telling him, "The database is null-key encrypted. It can only be accessed by one person" (*Dark Knight* 2008). Lucius protests, "This is too much power for one person" (*Dark Knight* 2008). However, Bruce responds, "That's why I gave it to you. Only you can use it" (*Dark Knight* 2008). Lucius continues to protest: "Spying on 30 million people isn't part of my job description" (*Dark Knight* 2008). Batman explains how useful this surveillance is with an example: "This is an audio sample. If he talks within range of any phone in the city . . . you can triangulate his position" (*Dark Knight* 2008). This is enough to convince Lucius of the efficacy of the project but not necessarily of its morality: "I'll help you this one time. But consider this my resignation. As long as this machine is at Wayne Enterprises, I won't be" (*Dark Knight* 2008). This language could be drawn from any number of CIA dramas in which torture and violation of the Constitutional rights of the American population are just temporary measures to defeat Al-Qaeda, ISIS, domestic terrorists, and so on. Batman echoes this point when he says, "When you're finished . . .type in your name," hinting that the program will be destroyed and no longer be necessary when the Joker is defeated (*Dark Knight* 2008).

In mimicry and parody of the established order of Gotham, the Joker himself attempts exercises control over the population, telling his audience on the ferries near the end of the film, "tonight, you're all gonna . . . be a part of a social experiment. Through the magic of diesel fuel and ammonium nitrate . . . I'm ready right now to blow you all sky-high" (*Dark Knight* 2008). The contrast between the two groups is curiously described by the Joker. There is either "Harvey Dent's most-wanted scumbag collection . . . or the sweet and innocent civilians?" (*Dark Knight* 2008). The choice is theirs: "You choose. Oh, and you might wanna decide quickly . . . because the people on the other boat may not be quite so noble" (*Dark Knight* 2008). It seems as though Nolan is presenting an either/or scenario. Either Batman must use extralegal means to capture the Joker, or the Joker himself will dominate Gotham and torture the people through sadistic experiments. Batman believes that Gotham can be redeemed while the Joker can only see Gotham's wickedness. In the logic of the film, Batman (as an image of the American security state) is thus a (temporary) necessary evil to create a lesser of two evils.

Batman's worldview seems vindicated at the end of the film. After the people of Gotham refuse to kill each other on the ferries, Batman asks, "What were you trying to prove? That deep down, everyone's as ugly as you? You're alone" (*Dark Knight* 2008). The Joker later responds, "You just couldn't let me go, could you? This is what happens when an unstoppable force . . . meets an immovable object" (*Dark Knight* 2008). It is not just Batman who is immovable—at least some of the people on the ferries were not able to be motivated by fear and selfishness. The Joker continues, "You truly are incorruptible, aren't you?" (*Dark Knight* 2008). The Joker does not understand Batman's humanism, telling him "Huh? You won't kill me . . . out of some misplaced sense of self-righteousness" (*Dark Knight* 2008). The Joker in his ludism, however, says, "And I won't kill you . . . because you're just too much fun" (*Dark Knight* 2008). He then presents a deeper Vedic reading: "I think you and I are destined to do this forever" (*Dark Knight* 2008). Batman responds with clinical language, noting that the system will tame him, telling the Joker: "You'll be in a padded cell forever" (*Dark Knight* 2008). The Joker responds by diagnosing Batman as being just as crazy as the Joker is: "Maybe we could share one. You know, they'll be doubling up . . . the rate this city's inhabitants are losing their minds" (*Dark Knight* 2008). Batman reaffirms the people of Gotham's goodness: "This city just showed you that it's full of people ready to believe in good" (*Dark Knight* 2008). However, the Joker has one last trick up his sleeve. The Joker claims to have finally broken the spirit of Gotham, interrupting Batman with "Until their spirit breaks completely. Until they get a good look at the real Harvey Dent and all the heroic things he's done" (*Dark Knight* 2008). The Joker notes that he was fighting for "Gotham's soul" with Batman. Joker explains, "I took Gotham's white knight . . . and I brought him down to our level. It wasn't hard. See, madness, as you know . . . is like gravity. All it takes is a little push" (*Dark Knight* 2008). Joker claims to have destroyed Gotham by destroying Dent, but he was not able to destroy Batman, who is the real hero of Gotham.

Critics have commented at length on the importance of the ending scene of *The Dark Knight*. Nolan reveals (and conceals) the reality that the state relies upon a fictional mythology to support itself. However, it is a fiction that must be preserved because the alternative is the world of chaos initiated by the Joker. Assessing the situation, Jim Gordon notes, "the Joker won" and then lists off everything that will be undone: "Harvey's prosecution, everything he fought for, everything Rachel for. Undone" (*Dark Knight* 2008). The loss of Harvey Dent's sanity and his turn to a life of crime would discredit him as a prosecutor and likely lead to the release of the prisoners he put away. As Gordon further explains, "Whatever chance Gotham had of fixing itself . . . whatever chance you gave us of fixing our city . . . dies with Harvey's reputation. We bet it all on him. The Joker took the best of us and tore him down. People will lose hope" (*Dark Knight* 2008). This brilliant dialogue encapsulates not only Christopher (and Jonathan) Nolan's cinematic *weltanschauung*—present in all of Nolan's films except for *Insomnia*. The world is built upon a series of lies and illusions. Some illusions work better than others. Harvey Dent must remain a hero and become an embodiment of the noble lie. Batman, however, must become a scapegoat and a villain. Batman tells Gordon, "But the Joker cannot win" (*Dark Knight* 2008). Turning Dent to the side to reveal the healthy side of his two faces, Batman says, "Gotham needs its true hero" (*Dark Knight* 2008). The true hero is, in the Deleuzean sense, the *verité du cinema* or the noble lie of Plato. Just as the Joker served as the villainous foil to Batman's redeemer, so now Batman will become a villain to Dent's hero. Reflecting on the anger that emerged when he tortured the Joker as well as when he apparently broke the ankles of Sal Maroni, Batman says, "You either die a hero or live long enough to see yourself become the villain" (*Dark Knight* 2008). Batman has grown aware of the limits of his ability to maintain his moral code and is aware that this moral code or plan could easily be stripped away.

There is also, throughout Nolan's *Dark Knight* trilogy, a profound sense that Batman is a symbol or an ideal. However, he is also the true because, like the American state apparatus, he has both the technology as well as the liberal humanitarian ethos to protect the people. The false Batmen who wear "hockey pants" and use guns are unworthy to become Batman because of their simultaneously sloppiness as well as their recourse to lethal violence (as well as their inability to fight the great evils such as the Joker). The false Batmen also lack the money and resources to fight terrorism. As a symbol, Batman is ultimately the servant of the common good of Gotham; as Batman tells Gordon, "I can do those things because I'm not a hero, like Dent. I killed those people. That's what I can be" (*Dark Knight* 2008). Batman can take the guilt for Harvey Dent, and Dent can, even after the murders, still be a hero. Within Batman is the dual nature of being both a hero and villain—and the two "torture scenes" reveal, just as within Harvey Dent were the two faces. Moreover, in as much Harvey Dent is the symbol of the white knight, he must be the symbol of goodness and remain a hero, while the vigilante Batman must be a dark knight. As Batman tells Gordon, "I'm whatever Gotham needs me to be" (*Dark Knight* 2008). Batman as a symbol is at the service of Gotham, willing to serve the city's interest. The torture scenes (like the torture of Abu Ghraib) were momentary aberrations in which Batman's love of Rachel (and the wider city of Gotham) gets the best of him.

The montage of the aftermath of Batman's acceptance of the blame for Harvey Dent's crimes is deeply revealing of the need for a lie to maintain the order of the state. As Gordon announces with an enlarged picture of Harvey Dent in the background, Dent is "a hero. Not the hero we deserved—the hero we needed. Nothing less than a knight. Shining. . . ." (*Dark Knight* 2008). This language is very revealing, for the knight is the archetypal symbol of Western masculinity (later appearing as the American cowboy—this scene in *The Dark Knight* famously represents elements of the classic 1953 Western *Shane*). As the audience knows, Harvey Dent is not a white knight, and so Nolan directly challenges the notion of the knight in shining armor on which so much of Western mythology rests. During these back-and-forths and cuts, Gordon destroys the Bat Symbol, which is the (albeit temporary) dethroning of the symbol of Batman, for the sake of Gotham. During this mashup, Batman comments that "sometimes the truth isn't good enough . . . sometimes, people deserve more" (*Dark Knight* 2008). What is more than the truth is the noble lie that achieves its verity and power from its practical service of the political common good. Gordon further explains that Batman is "the hero Gotham deserves . . . but not the one it needs right now" (*Dark Knight* 2008). Batman's life and work is at the service of Gotham. Batman is "not our hero . . . he's a silent guardian, a watchful protector . . . a dark knight"

(*Dark Knight* 2008). Batman, the dark knight, who used irregular methods to capture the Joker (as well as Lau), is the real hero who, having lost Rachel, sacrifices himself for Gotham. Batman, like the National Security State, is watching and protecting Gotham (America) from the shadows. Even though there was rising animosity toward the Bush administration and the alphabet agency because of their prosecution of the War on Terror at home and abroad, such anger is ok because like Batman, the superstructure "can take it." This does not mean that, contrary to the view of Andrew Klavan, that Nolan is supportive of the Bush administration; rather Nolan is supportive of the wider Anglo-American system that the Bush administration temporarily claims to serve.

During this montage, Lucius Fox destroys the sonar machine. For viewers living late in the War on Terror, this scene is ironic, for the National Security State and monitoring of the civilian population has only increased over time. However, the American public is told to forget about the Snowden and other revelations of intrusive spying to maintain the noble lie that the surveillance of the civilian population had disappeared or at least was only targeting Muslims. At the end of the film, the audience knows that Dent had become a villain, and that, despite his temptations, Batman did not succumb to the villainy present within himself. However, a lie must be constructed to support the political and economic order of Gotham, which itself is a figure for the United States.

From the advent of the New Left to the Bush administration, much of American critical discourse has been focused on attacking and deconstructing the superstructure of the newly emergent National Security State. However, with the election of Barrack Obama, the National Security State became chic and cool, and much of radical discourse was stymied.[15] During the Trump administration, the rapprochement between the mainstream left and capital as well as the federal government became more solidified as Donald Trump established his identity as an outsider fighting against the "swamp." The left, for the most part, has largely abandoned critique of capital. Indeed, the last major populist uprisings prior to the Trump era, Occupy Wall Street and the Tea Party were either themselves integrated into the establishment system or were, in the case of Occupy Wall Street, violently suppressed by the police.

Although being known as a transgressive and avant-garde filmmaker, or at least a filmmaker who introduces transgressive and avant-garde techniques and ideas to popular audiences, Christopher Nolan nonetheless affirms the dominate Anglo-American social order in *The Dark Knight*. The Joker does represent a primal chaos or evil, which Nolan seems to believe will be endemic in the universe in perpetuity. However, the Joker also represents the threat of the poor and working class upsetting the social order either through a left- or right-wing insurrection. Like Krishna in the Vedic stories, Batman is tasked with not only affirming the order of the universe, but more so the order of Gotham, which is a city emblematic of America and wider Western civilization. At the end of *The Dark Knight*, Batman must even sacrifice himself for the sake of Gotham, becoming a hunted villain and outlaw. However, in *The Dark Knight Rises*, Batman must face down Bane, an even more explicit threat to the social order of Gotham, and the Batman must come back.

NOTES

1. Russell, "Christopher Nolan's The Dark Knight Trilogy as a Noir View of American Social Tensions," 171.
2. Ibid.
3. Russell, "Christopher Nolan's The Dark Knight Trilogy as a Noir View of American Social Tensions," 172.
4. Johnson, "'It's What You Do that Defines You': Christopher Nolan's Batman as Moral Philosopher," 952.
5. Ibid.
6. Hassler-Forest, *Capitalist Superheroes*, 149–50.
7. Klein, *The Shock Doctrine*, 349.
8. Hassler-Forest, *Capitalist Superheroes*, 147–48.
9. Hassler-Forest, *Capitalist Superheroes*, 2.
10. Hassler-Forest, *Capitalist Superheroes*, 4.
11. Žižek, *Living in the End Times*, 166.
12. Hassler-Forest, *Capitalist Superheroes*, 143.
13. Hassler-Forest, *Capitalist Superheroes*, 145.
14. Ibid.
15. Exceptions include Hastings and Sanger.

Chapter 4

Defending the Status Quo in *The Dark Knight Rises*

Christopher Nolan's 2012 *The Dark Knight Rises* is frequently overshadowed by its much more popular and critically acclaimed 2008 predecessor, *The Dark Knight. The Dark Knight Rises*, which is battered by criticism of the plot as well as complaints that the dialogue of Tom Hardy is unintelligible, is often presented as the "worst" of Christopher Nolan's trilogy, which began with the 2005 *Batman Begins*. There are, however, critics who find *The Dark Knight Rises* to be a film very similar to the other two films, and, indeed, the most fertile film for political analysis—script writer Jonah Nolan himself has referred to the film as being "underrated."[1] As Shone has remarked, *The Dark Knight Rises* is modeled after Charles Dickens's *A Tale of Two Cities*.[2] Bane's revolution is a (perhaps parodic) reframing of the French Revolution, which, at least in some of its forms, sought to retool the French and the wider global social order into a radically egalitarian society. Director Christopher Nolan himself has remarked that the film is a "historical epic" and "disaster film."[3] Both Heath Ledger's Joker in *The Dark Knight* and Tom Hardy's Bane's rhetoric are very attractive to a host of individuals living in the postmodern and now postmillennial world, in which many feel a profound sense of alienation vis a vis the state apparatus. Nonetheless, as in *The Dark Knight*, in *The Dark Knight Rises*, Christopher Nolan ultimately seems to support the dominant Anglo-American order represented by Gotham.

From his first appearance in the film, Bane presents himself as an adversary of the established order of Gotham as well as the United States. Bane and his mercenary crew, described as "Eastern Europeans" in the shooting script, are able to hijack a US military plane and to foil the plans of the CIA. When greeting the Russian nuclear physicist who will play a pronounced role in the plot, the character referred to as the "CIA Man" says, "Dr. Pavel, I'm CIA" (*The Dark Knight Rises* 2012). The CIA Man is standing confidently in front of the plane, certain that he and the American intelligence agencies have the power to nab terrorists. However, as in *Batman Begins* and *The Dark Knight*, the American (Gothamite) state apparatus does not have the power alone to stop Bane—ultimately, Batman must intervene. In this odd scene, the CIA Man mimics Batman's fatal flaw in that he does not kill his prisoners but merely threatens to do so. Martin Fradley writes that *The Dark Knight* as well as the wider trilogy "systematically fails to condemn torture per se as a moral, ethical, and political obscenity . . . "[4] Regardless, Bane sees through his deception. When the CIA Man expresses his confusion why a hired gun will not talk, he says, "Lot of loyalty for a hired gun!" (*The Dark Knight Rises* 2012). Bane responds with, "Or perhaps he's wondering why someone would shoot a man before throwing him out of plane" (*The Dark Knight Rises* 2012). As in the other scenes in the film, the scrawny but big mouthed CIA agent cannot stand up to Bane's intelligence or brutality. Bane is both a reactionary and revolutionary force from the old world like the League of Shadows itself in *Batman Begins*. These people are dedicated to a cause greater than themselves, and their "plan" is more important than their individual worth. These figures, like Ra's al Ghul, are dedicated to a plan higher than themselves. They represent an alternative but not necessarily better philosophical order than American liberalism, which Bane and his "mercenaries" challenge throughout the film.

The stadium scene in which Bane exercises his control over Gotham is also a profound attack on an important American symbol. As the boy is singing "the star-spangled banner," the football stadium in which the Gotham Rogues are playing collapses. Just as the Joker mocks American sports culture in *The Dark Knight*, Bane says, "let the games begin" (*The Dark Knight Rises* 2012). Bane attempts to destroy the entertainment complex of Gotham as America. Bane thinks that by destroying it, he is liberating America. He tells them, "Gotham, take control of your city . . . ," and the nuclear bomb is the "instrument of your liberation" (*The Dark Knight Rises* 2012). These scenes are interspersed with a pentagon war room filled with military personal and intelligence analysts. Bane is challenging the establishment of America and presenting himself and the League of Shadows as the new statement. He, like the Joker, envisions himself as a purveyor of rival entertainment. He tells the people of the new game he has crafted. The bomb is "mobile," and there is an anonymous "triggerman." Bane further uses a deceptive revolutionary message, telling the people, "we come not as conquerors, but as liberators to return control of this city to the people" (*The Dark Knight Rises* 2012). The "triggerman" will be prompted to set off the bomb if there is "interference from the outside world or of people attempting to flee," and, as Bane tells them, the people of Gotham should return to their homes, for "Tomorrow you claim what is rightfully yours" (*The Dark Knight Rises* 2012). His language is like the Joker's in *The Dark Knight*, and he utilizes the mockery of the image of the hero. In addition to physical attacks on American symbols, Bane's attack on Gotham as America is also rhetorical.

Much of the film's controversy deals with the appeal of Bane. The neoconservative commentator John Podhoretz, writing in *The Weekly* Standard, argues that Nolan put "the rhetoric of the Occupy Wall Street movement in the mouth of" Bane. Slavoj Žižek countered in *The New Statesman* that the fact that Bane's rhetoric and (temporary) revolutionary success was a radical gesture by Nolan, for in the age of "capitalist realism" even the mention of socialist ideas is a dangerous violation of a taboo. Taking note of Donald Trump's use of Bane's rhetoric in his campaign, Tom Shone argues in *The Nolan Variations* that "[j]ust as Burke predicted the rise of Napoleon Bonaparte, so *The Dark Knight Rises* could take some credit for intuiting the seismic shifts that would lead to the election of Donald Trump."[5]

Christopher Nolan, however, made it clear that the film is about "a demagogue," and Bane is the "bad guy" of the film, further arguing that he was trying to capture the psychological or emotional zeitgeist of the period immediately following the 2008 financial crash. Nolan further told Tom Shone, "The film was not supposed to be political. It's not intended to be; it's about primal fears. At the time we were writing there was this sense of false calm; everything things okay, we got through the financial crisis, but there are underlying things brewing that could lead to difficult places."[6] In the above quoted interview with Tom Shone, Nolan both recognizes and denies the political implications of the film, stating that although "The Occupy Wall Street movement was right there," the films in the *Dark Knight* series are not "political acts"; *The Dark Knight Rises* in particular is about "the upending of society."[7] Nolan, in an earlier 2008 interview with *IndieLondon*, had stated that he and his cowriters "try and be pretty rigidly not aware and no conscious of real world parallels in things we're doing." Nonetheless, Shone argues, "Written as the 2008 financial collapse began to rumble and shot as Occupy Wall Street movement gathered strength, *The Dark Knight Rises* shrewdly intuits the press points of the postindustrial economy with its vision of a modern American city torn apart by internecine class warfare."[8] Nolan, who has made a tremendous amount of money from the *Dark Knight* movies, solidifying himself as a "blockbuster" director, may simply being trying to deflect a political reading of the film that would alienated some moviegoers. Despite such apparent deflections, *The Dark Knight Rises* is a deeply political film.

Benjamin Winterhalter, however, argues that Nolan's film is more about psychology than it is about politics, and the film's "political message . . . is decidedly psychological; it is the politics of the inner: We can only resolve the thorny political questions in which we inevitably become entangled by first tending to our inner lives."[9] Perhaps the most controversial suggestion is that all of these readings have some truth to them. Bane's rhetoric is seductive and compelling, and much of the film is about psychological growth—although Winterhalter may be incorrect in seeing Batman's transition into a more "moderate" conservative. *The Dark Knight Rises*, like *The Dark Knight* and *Batman Begins*, however, ultimately affirms the dominant order that Gotham represents and Batman protects.

In contrast, Martin Fradley argues that Bane is whatever the viewer wants him to be: "rather than having any legible political viewpoint, *The Dark Knight Rises* deliberately concedes to the individual viewer the authority to decide what it means. One might find in Bane a psychotic radical leftist whose muffled, incoherent proclamations and violent agenda provide a pro-hegemonic caricature of oppositional politics. Equally, the film deliberately grants Bane more than enough ingenuity, intelligence, and pathos, to allow a less conservative viewer to interpret him as a heroic martyr."[10] Nonetheless, Fradley concludes that *The Dark Knight Rises* quashes "the insurrectionary flames in the interests of an unconvincing and untenable status quo."[11] Nolan himself seems to affirm this view of Batman as a champion of the established order, writing in his forward to Jody Duncan Jesser and Janine Pourroy's *The Art and Making of the Dark Knight Trilogy*, "Gotham was rotting away at its foundations. A new evil bubbling up from beneath. Bruce had thought Batman was not needed any more, but Bruce was wrong . . . The Batman had to come back." There is a clear statement here of Bane's revolutionary ethos as being ultimately evil—despite its allure. Nolan's *The Dark Knight Rises* might be "polyphonic" and not easily categorized as political propaganda, but it is, nonetheless, a work that affirms the established order.

Although overshadowed by Heath Ledger's Joker, Tom Hardy's Bane and his rebranded "League of Shadows" present a powerful argument for its own case. Bane's recruits are among the poor and marginalized of Gotham as well as the Orientalized European, Asian, and African mercenaries. Bane and his crew live in the sewers of Gotham and are frequently shown preparing denotations throughout the city of Gotham. As Shone notes, "[t]he idea of self-detonating buildings is purest Nolan: both constructivist and deconstructivist urges combined. . . . *The Dark Knight Rises* is a thunderous paean to *un*building, detonation, demolition."[12] Bane, however, is not simply a destroyer and builder; he is a master of political rhetoric. He can move the people (including the audience) with his words and manipulate them with promises of a utopia.

Perhaps the most famous piece of rhetoric is Bane's Blackgate prison speech. After seizing Gotham, Bane comes to Gotham's prison and announces to its people: "Behind you stands a symbol of oppression. Blackgate Prison . . . " (*The Dark Knight Rises* 2012). This statement has been voiced by left-wing as well as various black nationalist groups for generations. The prison system in America (Gotham) is ultimately corrupt and built on lies. Bane goes on to explain that Blackgate is a place where "a thousand men have languished for years. Under the Dent Act" (*The Dark Knight Rises* 2012). The prisoners are in fact victims of an unjust system. Bane emphasizes that the prisoners have been held under the name of Harvey Dent, who was held up "as a shining example of justice . . . " (*The Dark Knight Rises* 2012). However, in the key of Nietzsche and a host of deconstructionists who followed in his wake, Bane announces, "You have been supplied with a false idol," ripping up the picture of Dent and exclaiming, "to stop you from tearing down this corrupt city" (*The Dark Knight Rises* 2012). Bane's rhetoric is deceiving. It is true that elements of Gotham are corrupt, but police commissioner Jim Gordon, who hid helped Batman to hide Harvey Dent's crimes, has sacrificed him as well as Bruce Wayne for the sake of the city. Also, Bane does not simply want just Blackgate prison torn down, but also the whole system.

Bane does reveal the truth of what happened. Bane unveils an inconvenient truth that Gordon himself had hoped to reveal. The Dent Act is thus simultaneously good and bad in as much as it did imprison genuine criminals, but it also harshly imprisoned potentially good men like the prisoners who prevented the ferry explosion in *The Dark Knight*. Reading from Jim Gordon's letter, Bane says, "The Batman didn't murder Harvey Dent—he saved my boy. Then took the blame for Harvey's appalling crimes, so that I could, to my shame, build a lie around this fallen idol" (*The Dark Knight Rises* 2012). The idol of Dent here represents various institutional powers that keep peace and order in society. Bane's revelation of the corruption of the system is an unveiling or disclosing of truth, but it is a painful truth that may have been better hidden. Bane further quotes Jim Gordon, "I praised the madman who tried to murder my own child" (*The Dark Knight Rises* 2012). This line is very curious considering the revelation that Barbara, Commissioner Gordon's wife, left him and moved to Cleveland; she was perhaps all too aware of Gordon's lie and hypocrisy and Jim Gordon's willingness to sacrifice the truth for Gotham. He further argues, reading Jim Gordon's words, that he can no longer live with his lie and must resign. Jim Gordon did not resign for a variety of reasons. Perhaps he wanted to retain power. Perhaps he genuinely wanted to help Gotham. We know that Gordon's kindness was appreciated by Batman, who, in *The Dark Knight Rises*, thanks Gordon for comforting a young Bruce Wayne after his parents had died. Perhaps he, like many of Nolan's characters, was addicted to the thrill of the chase: in much of the films Gordon is helping Batman chase down villains and even fakes his own death in *The Dark Knight* to help catch the Joker. The ambiguity here is the film's overall point as it is for all his characters in his films: the truth of the matter is ultimately complicated.

Bane, despite some sympathetic depictions of him later when Miranda reveals herself as Talia al Ghul, has corrupt intentions in seizing Gotham—however strong his criticisms of Gotham might be. Once unearthing the corruption of Gotham, Bane hopes to exploit the situation for his benefit, like Ra's Al Ghul, Scarecrow, and the Joker, and to topple the entire system. "Do you accept this man's resignation? Do you accept the resignation of all the liars?! All the corrupt?!" (*The Dark Knight Rises* 2012). Bane is not entirely wrong here. The Dent Act and much of Gotham's functioning is built on a lie. Batman is built on a lie. All these figures are corrupt and are "liars." However, perhaps the central theme of all of Nolan's film is that everyone is a liar. Everyone—from *Memento*'s Leonard Shelby to *Insomnia*'s Will Dormer to *Inception*'s Dominic Cobb—grasps hold of a lie that they desire in order to give meaning to their happiness. What Bane is doing is simply focusing on one of the many lies that structure much of social reality. This is not to suggest that all ideas are lies or that Nolan does not believe in truth. Rather, it is to suggest that Nolan, throughout his films, points to the tenuousness of truth.

The rookie orphan cop Blake points out the terrible nature of the Dent Act and the consequences it had on the men who were sent to prison: "These men, locked up in Blackgate for eight years, denied parole under the Dent Act. Based on a lie" (*The Dark Knight Rises* 2012). This passage is important because Gotham is, in effect, acting like the League of Shadows in as much as it is exercised brutal (legal) force to keep order. As in Nolan's earlier *Insomnia*, a lie cannot last forever. Jim Gordon attempts to defend his actions, saying, "Gotham needed a hero" (*The Dark Knight Rises* 2012). The manufacturing of the hero, which cost Gordon his family, now is revealed to be a lie. Blake tells Gordon, "It needs it now more than ever. You betrayed everything you stood for" (*The Dark Knight Rises* 2012). Gordon explains, "There's a point. Far out there. When the structures fail you. When the rules aren't weapons anymore, they're shackles, letting the bad get ahead. Maybe one day you'll have such a moment of crisis. And in that moment, I hope you have a friend like I did. To plunge their hands into the filth so you can keep yours clean" (*The Dark Knight Rises* 2012). This is the noble lie with which Jim Gordon has lived. The rule of law is effective only to a point; eventually, one must cross over the law to affect a greater good. However, this crossing of the law has consequences which Gordon and the city of Gotham must reap. Moreover, as Blake tells Gordon: "Your hands look pretty filthy to me, Commissioner" (*The Dark Knight Rises* 2012). There are few "innocents" in the Nolan-verse. Some are perhaps nobler than others.

Bane, however, sees things, like Ra's al Ghul before him, in purer terms. There are corrupt and noble people. There are those who must be destroyed and purified. This does not mean that Bane considers himself to be among the pure, but his "plan" is pure. In his Blackgate speech, Bane tells the people of Gotham that he will take Gotham and give it to the people, allowing them a Saturnalia: "We take Gotham from the corrupt. The rich. The oppressors of generations who've kept you down with the myth of opportunity. And we give it to you, the people. Gotham is yours none shall interfere. Do as you please" (*The Dark Knight Rises* 2012). Bane's critique, repeated by various left- and right-wing revolutionaries, is that Gotham has oppressed the people and given them false idols to adore and empty promises. This is not entirely false; Selena Kyle, the Joker, and a host of other figures have echoed this point. The very existence of the "narrows" in contrast to the opulence of Wayne Manor in *Batman Begins* echoes this point. However, Bane himself is a false idol or at least the creator of false idols, and the Anglo-American order, reflected in Gotham, is something worth fighting for. Bane provides a whole series of lies and half-truths to seduce the people of Gotham into overthrowing the established order. He commands them: "But start by storming Blackgate and freeing the oppressed . . . Step forward, those who would serve. The powerful will be ripped from their decadent nests and cast into the cold world that we know and endure. Courts will be convened. Spoils will be enjoyed. Blood will be shed. The police will survive, as they learn to serve true justice. This great city . . . it will endure. Gotham will survive" (*The Dark Knight Rises* 2012). This is all an elaborate lie, for Bane plans on destroying the whole city.

On the one hand, the shots of poor and working-class people storming the homes of the urban rich are disturbing and depict the common people of Gotham stealing from the rich as being the acts of vicious animals. Bane's mercenaries give military-grade weapons to the Blackgate prisoners. An elderly wealthy man is dragged out from under his dresser by marauding citizens, and a woman in a fur coat is dragged away by what looks like her doorman. However, the film's depiction of the working class is complicated. Selina Kyle herself is a figure for the revolutionary working class as well. She kidnaps a congressman, outfoxes the mob, and penetrates Wayne Manor, stealing Martha Wayne's pearl neckless. She also outfoxes the police, feigning a damsel-in-distress pose. She and her friend Jen rob a "yuppie" of his watch and $60. Bruce Wayne and Selena argue during the ball, and her class consciousness and insecurity come to the surface. Noticing her cat ears, Wayne says, "Brazen costume for a cat burglar" (*The Dark Knight Rises* 2012). Selina responds, "Yeah? Who are you pretending to be?" (*The Dark Knight Rises* 2012). Wayne states, "Bruce Wayne, eccentric billionaire" (*The Dark Knight Rises* 2012). This line is ironic, for the "real" Bruce Wayne is something and somebody else. It may be Batman, or it may be the scared boy who never grew up after his parents' death, but the eccentric billionaire is a role that Bruce plays.

He then asks Selina who her date is. She responds, "His wife's in Ibiza. She left her diamonds behind, though. Worried they'd get stolen" (*The Dark Knight Rises* 2012). Throughout the film, Selina has advanced through her wit and ability to subvert the system. However, Bruce unmasks her and humiliates her noting, "It's pronounced 'Ibeetha.' You wouldn't want these folks realizing you're a crook, not a social climber" (*The Dark Knight Rises* 2012). The shooting script refers to Selina as being overcome with a "flash of anger." To defend herself, Selina questions, "You think I care what anyone in this room thinks about me?" (*The Dark Knight Rises* 2012). Bruce responds with some sarcasm, "I doubt you care what anyone in any room thinks of you" (*The Dark Knight Rises* 2012). Selina defends herself: "Don't condescend, Mr. Wayne. You don't know a thing about me" (*The Dark Knight Rises* 2012). Most of the villains in the *Dark Knight* trilogy have mysterious pasts that enable them to slip away from being easily categorized. Like the other villains, Selina thinks this protects her. This scene echoes the dance between Michael Keaton's Bruce Wayne and Michelle Pfeiffer's Selina Kyle, although Pfeiffer's Kyle is more bluntly aggressive, pulling out a gun to kill the robber baron Max Shreck.

In *The Dark Knight Rises*, Bruce, however, has used his surveillance technology to gather information about Selina, which he presents in an insulting manner: "Well, Selina Kyle, I know you came here from your walk-up in Old Town—modest place for a master jewel thief. Which means either you're saving for your retirement—or you're in deep with the wrong people" (*The Dark Knight Rises* 2012). Bruce Wayne is uncharacteristically snobbish toward her, but he pushes the right buttons with Selina. Moreover, we here clearly see the social divide of Gotham, which has been present throughout all three. Ra's al Ghul, the Joker, and Bane have some validity to their claims of the corruption within Gotham's class divide. Selina gives a typical response that Bruce was simply born into power: "You don't get to judge me because you were born in the master bedroom of Wayne Manor" (*The Dark Knight Rises* 2012). Bruce responds with even further condescension: "Actually, I was born in the Regency Room" (*The Dark Knight Rises* 2012). Selina then, à la Fredrich Engels and Alain Badiou, shows Bruce the reality of the poor, which the rich often cannot see, explaining, "I started off doing what I had to. Once you've done what you had to, they'll never let you do what you want to" (*The Dark Knight Rises* 2012).

They then discuss the problem of being a criminal in a digital world with Selina saying, "There's no fresh start in today's world. Any twelve-year-old with a cell phone could find out what you did. Everything we do is collated and quantified. Everything sticks" (*The Dark Knight Rises* 2012). Selina curiously is describing what the audience knows what Bruce and Lucius did in *The Dark Knight*; she is one of the people who are victims of the surveillance grid that the establishment (of which Bruce is a part) laid over the people of Gotham. Wayne calls her actions "stealing," while Selina explains, "I take what I need to from those who have more than enough. I don't stand on the shoulders of people with less" (*The Dark Knight Rises* 2012). Wayne mockingly asks, "Robin Hood?" Selina, however, responds, "I think I do more to help someone than most of the people in this room. Thank you" (*The Dark Knight Rises* 2012). Rob White, in an interview in *Film Quarterly*, states, "in terms of outright political content, it's surely Selina Kyle . . . who gives Robin Hood–style voice to Occupy's ideas about economic equality." On one level, the audience knows this is false: Bruce Wayne has given nearly literally everything for Gotham. Wayne himself states, "you think you're assuming maybe a little too much" (*The Dark Knight Rises* 2012). Neither Selina nor Bane is entirely accurate in their understanding of Gotham or Bruce Wayne. He, along with Jim Gordon and others, sacrifice themselves for the city.

Selina attacks the rich as being just rich, but she is assuming. Thus, the film appears to be defending the wealthy establishment. Whatever the criticism the villains have of the establishment, the establishment itself must remain in power. Selina even explicitly threatens to overthrow the establishment: "You think all this can last? There's a storm coming, Mr. Wayne. You and your friends better batten down the hatches, because when it hits, you're all gonna wonder how you ever thought you could live so large and leave so little to the rest of us" (*The Dark Knight Rises* 2012). This is a threat to the established (Anglo-)American order, just like the one Bane provides. This threat is, in fact, realized in all three of the *Dark Knight* films. In each film, the villain presents a convincing case that the corruption in Gotham must be upended, but, in the end, the audience is drawn back to supporting Batman's re-establishment of the status quo. In *The Dark Knight Rises*, Wayne comments, "Sounds like you're looking forward to it" (*The Dark Knight Rises* 2012). Selina responds, "I'm adaptable" (*The Dark Knight Rises* 2012). What Selina does not realize is that Bruce Wayne is Batman and is adaptable. In a profoundly symbolic gesture, the wealthy Bruce Wayne reasserts his rule over the poor Selina, telling her "These pearls do look better on you then they did in my safe . . . " (*The Dark Knight Rises* 2012). He says, "But I still can't let you keep them," taking them from her (*The Dark Knight Rises* 2012). Selena then upends Wayne by stealing his Lamborghini.

Later, after Bane seizes power over Gotham, Selina's comments are revisited as she realizes that the rich of Gotham are more complex than she initially thought. Foraging through the apartment of a wealthy family, Selina and her friend Jen comment on a destroyed framed picture of a family. Selina states, "This was someone's home" (*The Dark Knight Rises* 2012). Using communitarian language, Jen responds, "Now it's everyone's home" (*The Dark Knight Rises* 2012). She further refers to Selina's own words: "'Storm's coming,' remember? This is what you wanted" (*The Dark Knight Rises* 2012). The message here is that she did not get what she wanted. Revolutions do not usually grant what they promise and the new situation, in Nolan's view, is worse than the previous. However, this does not mean that Gotham and the America that it represents are not beyond reproach in *The Dark Knight Rises*.

The Dark Knight Rises begins with a partial lie. Commissioner Gordon says that he knew Harvey Dent and was his friend, "And it will be a very long time before someone inspires us the way he did" (*The Dark Knight Rises* 2012). Gordon's statement here is not a total lie. He did, indeed, know Harvey Dent, whose actions were initially well intentioned in trying to clean up Gotham—although we do see that the inmates that Dent locked up prove themselves to have noble qualities in the boat scene. Gordon further states, "I believed in Harvey Dent" (*The Dark Knight Rises* 2012). This is clearly a connection with the "silent protector" scene at the end of *The Dark Knight*. The audience knows that, upon becoming Two-Face, Harvey Dent became a murderer and even threatened Jim Gordon's family. However, Dent's noble lie was necessary to reward the faith of the people of Gotham. On the other hand, this noble lie is constantly under threat and must be countered by the Gotham PD, the military and intelligence agencies, and especially the Central Intelligence Agency, as demonstrated in the next scene, which has Bane and his minions destroy a CIA plane and upend the CIA's "plan," a popular and important word in the *Dark Knight* trilogy. Within the Blackgate prison speech, we also see the unraveling of the lie of Harvey Dent. The people of Gotham (and the people of the world) learn that Harvey Dent was in fact a murderer and that Jim Gordon lied to them. While it would be foolish to commit the cardinal sin of criticism and look for real-world parallels between post-9/11 American *The Dark Knight Rises* (although many have done so), there is nonetheless a parallel between the sense of anger and frustration at both the Bush and Obama administrations' seeming deceptions and failures in the prosecution of the War on Terror.

Despite this disenchantment, Nolan crafts in his film a vision of the importance of the political and social order of Gotham. While celebrating "Harvey Dent Day," the mayor says, "Harvey Dent's uncompromising stand against organized crime and, yes, ultimately, his sacrifice, have made Gotham a safer place than it was at the time of his death, eight years ago" (*The Dark Knight Rises* 2012). This is a paradox, for, like Batman, the "uncompromising stand" of Harvey Dent ultimately led to his downfall and threatened Batman's own. The major enumerates several positive outcomes of the Dent Act: "This city has seen a historic turnaround. No city is without crime. But this city is without organized crime because the Dent Act gave law enforcement teeth in its fight against the mob. Now people are talking about repealing the Dent Act.

And to them I say . . . not on my watch" (*The Dark Knight Rises* 2012). In this case, the teeth are not only simply strict laws, but also the violence of the state and its adjutant, Batman.

As the mayor notes, Bruce Wayne is paying for the event: "I want to thank the Wayne Foundation for hosting this event. I'm told Mr. Wayne couldn't be here tonight, but I'm sure he's with us in spirit" (*The Dark Knight Rises* 2012). Wayne's money has paid for the event, but the money of the establishment of Gotham (America) is not enough to protect the people of Gotham from figures like Bane. It is Batman who is needed, a person the mayor ironically calls a murderous thug in a mask and a cape. A thug who showed his true nature when he betrayed the trust of this great man. . . . And murdered him in cold blood" (*The Dark Knight Rises* 2012). The irony is here, as the audience knows that it was Batman who was able to protect Gotham and defeat the mob and then the Joker. However, the noble lie is necessary to prop up the state.

Interestingly, the film shows that the description of the "enemy" can also be a lie as well since Batman is somewhat innocent of the accusations the mayor levies against him. There is an ironic and tense scene in which the mayor says, "Jim Gordon can tell you the truth about Harvey Dent . . . But I'll let him tell you himself—Commissioner Gordon?" (*The Dark Knight Rises* 2012). Gordon explains, "I have written a speech telling the truth about Harvey Dent" (*The Dark Knight Rises* 2012). However, he states, "Maybe the time isn't right . . . " (*The Dark Knight Rises* 2012). These comments in the film are interspersed with images of the wild Two-Face threatening Gordon's son. The repressed does return, but it can only be hidden for a brief while. Gordon continues, "Maybe right now all you need to know is that there are a thousand inmates in Blackgate Prison as a direct result of the Dent Act. These are violent criminals, essential cogs in the organized crime machine . . . Maybe, for now, all I should say about Harvey Dent's death is this . . . it has not been for nothing" (*The Dark Knight Rises* 2012). The truth will eventually come out, but there is a time for the lie to stabilize the social order.

The importance of the Batman myth and the broader myth of the hero in the work of Christopher Nolan is emphasized in the scene in which John Blake meets Bruce Wayne and reveals that he knows that Wayne is Batman. Like Wayne, Blake is an orphan, and he understands the pain of losing one's family as he tells Bruce Wayne, "See, my mom died when I was small. Car accident, I don't really remember it. But a couple of years later my dad was shot over a gambling debt. I remember that just fine. Not a lot of people who what it feels like, do they? To be angry. In your bones. People understand, foster parents understand. For a while. Then they expect the angry kid to do what he knows he can never do. To move on. To forget" (*The Dark Knight Rises* 2012). He has been traumatized, but he turned to a life of service of the state and others as opposed to a life of crime like Scarecrow, the Joker, Ra's al Ghul, and so on. He further explains that he understands the importance of masks and lies. Blake tells Wayne, "We made up stories about you. Legends. The other boys' stories were just that. But when I saw you, I knew who you really were . . . I'd seen that look on your face. Same one I taught myself. I don't know why you took the fall for Dent's murder, but I'm still a believer in the Batman. Even if you're not" (*The Dark Knight Rises* 2012). Batman is something bigger than Bruce Wayne. In *The Dark Knight*, there is a famous scene in which the police discuss the investigation into who Batman is, and the camera pans to a board with images of Elvis, Bigfoot, and Abraham Lincoln. Although perhaps simply humorous, this scene also refers to Batman's status as a mythic figure like Bigfoot, an American celebrity like Elvis, and an enforcer of the law through "extralegal" means like Abraham Lincoln. In *The Dark Knight Rises*, Bruce Wayne's money is necessary to help the orphans of Gotham, and the image of Batman as the defender of Gotham is essential for the city's functioning.

However, it is hard for Bruce to return. He very much represents the post-9/11 European and American male who is wounded by desires to keep fighting. As Alfred tells Bruce, "That was then. And you can strap up your leg and put the mask back on. But it won't make you what you were" (*The Dark Knight Rises* 2012). Nevertheless, Wayne tells Alfred that he wants to keep fighting to protect Gotham from Bane: "If this man is all the things you say he is, then this city needs me" (*The Dark Knight Rises* 2012). Alfred, on the other hand, envisions Bruce Wayne as a philanthropist as opposed to the brutal Batman, as he tells Bruce: "This city needs Bruce Wayne. Your resources, your knowledge. It doesn't need your body or your life. That time has passed" (*The Dark Knight Rises* 2012). Wayne, nonetheless, sees the social order of Gotham as being flawed and in need of help.

The police are not entirely trustworthy and there is a need for Batman to support the system. When Wayne returns as Batman, Alfred questions him on it being the police should be gathering the evidence. However, Bruce responds, "They don't have the tools to analyze it" (*The Dark Knight Rises* 2012). Alfred retorts, "They would if you gave them to them" (*The Dark Knight Rises* 2012). Bruce Wayne, however, does not trust the police, stating, "One man's tool is another man's weapon." After some banter, Wayne further states, "The police weren't getting it done . . . " (*The Dark Knight Rises* 2012). Alfred notes that Bruce must become something more powerful than the Batman he is to beat Bane. Showing Bruce a surveillance video of Bane, Alfred says, "Take a good look. At his speed, his ferocity, His training. I see the power of belief. Of the fanatic. I see the League of Shadows resurgent" (*The Dark Knight Rises* 2012). This scene precipitates the revelation that Rachel left Bruce for Harvey Dent and the split with Alfred. Bruce must once again hit a low point to come back stronger. He must confront the truth. As Alfred says, "I'm using the truth, Master Wayne. Maybe it's time we all stopped trying to outsmart the truth and just let it have its day" (*The Dark Knight Rises* 2012). The truth must be kept away from the people at times, but it is something the hero must confront. Bane is a new devil who resembles the earlier fears of bats that Bruce thought he could overcome. He must become a better version of Bane like he became a better version of the bat to fight Bane. However, Bane is something new and more powerful.

Throughout *Batman Begins*, Scarecrow was able to play upon the fears of his victims. For Bruce, there was a connection between bats, the death of his parents, and the devils in the *Mefistofele* opera that the Wayne family was watching the night of the parents' death. There is thus a sense in which Bruce's maturation includes overcoming the fear of the devil. In *The Dark Knight Rises*, Bane is this devil. This reality is emphasized in the scene in which he murders Daggett. When Daggett expresses his frustration at Miranda Tate's rise to power, asking where Bane is, Bane announces, "Speak of the devil, and he shall appear" (*The Dark Knight Rises* 2012). Like the mobsters in *The Dark Knight*, Daggett must learn that there is a "plan" bigger than his own greed (*The Dark Knight Rises* 2012). As Bane, says, "The plan is proceeding as expected" (*The Dark Knight Rises* 2012). Bane shows his tremendous strength, asking Dagget, "Do you feel in charge?" (*The Dark Knight Rises* 2012). Daggett attempts to reason with Bane over money, telling him, "I've paid you a small fortune" (*The Dark Knight Rises* 2012). Bane however, responds, "And that gives you power over me?" (*The Dark Knight Rises* 2012). The plan is bigger than Daggett's financial scheming. Also, brute force is more powerful than money. Bane explains, "Your money and infrastructure have been important. Till now" (*The Dark Knight Rises* 2012). When Daggett asks, "What are you?" (*The Dark Knight Rises* 2012). Bane explains, "I'm Gotham's reckoning. Come to end the borrowed time you've all been living on . . . " (*The Dark Knight Rises* 2012). Unable to understand this evil force, Daggett calls Bane "pure evil," while Bane responds, "I am necessary evil" (*The Dark Knight Rises* 2012). This scene shows that there are forces more powerful than money and, as we will see, even more powerful than the military and police. Rob White describes Bane as "a Shock Doctrine fundamentalist, who wants to use Gotham as a lab to see what happens when people are no longer shackled by regulation." Mark Fisher, however, refers to the Bane's plan as "fascist project."[13] Whether a devil or a fascist, Bane is something, like Joker, outside of capitalism. This scene immediately contrasted with Bruce Wayne and Blake talking about the mask. Like Joker, Bane is outside the capitalist system. So, however, is Batman, who protects the system. Ultimately, he tells Blake, "The idea was to be a symbol. Batman could be anybody, that was the point" (*The Dark Knight Rises* 2012). Batman tries to protect while Bane hurts; Batman uses compassion; Bane uses violence and pain. Nonetheless Batman must get stronger.

Wayne, like the "Last Man" living at the "end of history," has gotten weak and frail after the victory of the Cold War. As Bane tells him: "Peace has cost you strength. Victory has defeated you" (*The Dark Knight Rises* 2012). When Batman attempts to use the tricks he learned in the League of Shadows, they do not work on Bane as the brute explains, "Theatricality and deception are powerful agents . . . to the uninitiated. But we are initiated, aren't we, Bruce?" (*The Dark Knight Rises* 2012). Moreover, Batman's fighting is immature as well: "You fight like a younger man with nothing held back. Admirable. But mistaken" (*The Dark Knight Rises* 2012). Finally, Batman attempts to utilize the darkness he befriended, but, again, Bane has a response, taunting him: "You think darkness is your ally. But you merely adopted the dark. I was born in it. Molded by it. I didn't see the light until I was already a man. And by then it was nothing to me but blinding" (*The Dark Knight Rises* 2012). Bane is smarter than Bruce. Bruce's methods that were used to defeat Scarecrow and the Joker no longer work. Something else is needed. Bruce needs a greater spiritual and physical strength, and he must thus go back to the Old World to find it, Bane tells Bruce: "I will show you where I've made my home while preparing to bring justice. Then . . . I will break you" (*The Dark Knight Rises* 2012). During this scene, Bane also steals American technology, stating, "Your precious armory. Gratefully accepted. We will need it" (*The Dark Knight Rises* 2012). Bane pulls off Batman's mask. He is the deconstructionist who unveils and destroys; but returning to the East is what makes Batman strong.

When he brings Bruce to the East, Bane further explains how the pit transformed him and how he will use it to destroy Bruce; he tells Bruce that is where he "learned the truth about despair" (*The Dark Knight Rises* 2012). He will give Bruce the illusion of hope with the light coming down from the well and with the people of Gotham as well. He will make them "believe they can survive so that you can watch them clamber over each other to stay in the sun. You will watch as I torture an entire city to cause you pain you thought you could never feel again. Then, when you have truly understood the depths of your failure, we will fulfill Ra's al Ghul's destiny. We will destroy Gotham. And when it is done . . . when Gotham is ashes . . . then you have my permission to die" (*The Dark Knight Rises* 2012). Bane here reveals that he does not believe in the goodness of the people but has a fundamentally reactionary worldview. The people are in fact animals, but it is Bane who has reduced them to this state, not Gotham or Wayne, or Anglo-American capitalism.

The fact that Bane wants to destroy Gotham as well makes him a villain. Batman thinks he can reform Gotham. Bruce Wayne is stripped of wealth. There must be more to Batman, Bruce Wayne, Gotham, and America than its wealth and technology, which can be appropriated and taken away. Wayne must re-orient himself and relearn the teaching of the east. This is demonstrated in his ability to make the climb. The prisoner in the pit contrasts Wayne with the child who escaped who is "No ordinary child. A child born in hell. A child forged by suffering, hardened by pain. Not a man from privilege" (*The Dark Knight Rises* 2012). Wayne was born into privilege, but his suffering strengthened him; he proves he is just as strong as the reactionary Old World by climbing out of the pit.

While he is gone, the American military apparatus tries to protect Gotham. In *The Dark Knight Rises*, the military comes in on bridges with conventional weapons. However, as Bane's lead mercenary tells them: "Tanks and planes cannot stop us detonating our device" (*The Dark Knight Rises* 2012). The police and military can help, but Gotham needs something more. The film reinforces the idea that Gotham is representative of the United States when the president of the United States (William Davane) refers to Gotham as America's "greatest city" and using language redolent of that used for New York after 9/11: "The people of our greatest city are resilient. They have proven this before, they will prove this again" (*The Dark Knight Rises* 2012). He further states in very post-9/11 terms: "We do not negotiate with terrorists, but we do recognize realities" (*The Dark Knight Rises* 2012). Like the terrorists who attacked the Twin Towers and the Pentagon, Bane's mercenaries are trying to topple a powerful symbol of America. However, like Occupy Wall Street and other revolutionaries, they are trying to establish a new order. Interesting, as Martin Fradley notes, there is a further connection between *The Dark Knight Rises* and terrorism, for, during a screening of the film in Aurora, Colorado, a young man named James Holmes killed twelve people, "resulting in a tragedy that doubled as something of a grim metaphor for the fate of a generation doomed to be lost in the long-term socio-economic aftermath of the global economic meltdown."[14] *The Dark Knight* thus became an important culture touchstone in the rise in domestic terrorism in the United States as lethal violence committed either for political or personal motives increased in frequency. Fradley further comments that "the massacre of a predominately youthful audience became synergistically incorporated into the promotional machine of *The Dark Knight Rises* when widely disseminated footage of millionaire actor Christian Bale, visiting survivors in the hospital, uncannily mirrored images' of Bale's character, philanthropic capitalist Bruce Wayne, in Nolan's trilogy."[15] The key point here is that regardless of Nolan's intent, the *Dark Knight* trilogy is charged with a political messaging that was in (occasionally violent) dialogue with day to day "current events" in America.

One of the most pronounced and explicitly political scenes in the film is when one of Bane's mercenaries arrests Jim Gordon. After the mercenary places him under arrest, Gordon asks, "On whose authority?" (*The Dark Knight Rises* 2012). The mercenary responds, "The people of Gotham" (*The Dark Knight Rises* 2012). This scenario has been repeated throughout various revolutionary events in which the power that was previously in authority is overturned, and a new government is established in the name of the "people." Bane's mercenaries here represent a direct challenge to Gotham's system, which itself is an image of America. When he is standing before Jonathan Crane's court, Gordon asks, "No lawyer, no witnesses. What sort of due process is this?" (*The Dark Knight Rises* 2012). Here the film is pointing out that the allegedly egalitarian regime of Bane is in fact a draconian and illiberal state far worse than the corrupt Gotham—in *The Dark Knight*, there was a lot of talk of "lawyers," which were even provided to the mob. Crane's response, in the shooting script, packs a much bigger punch than the lines that made it to the big screen. In the shooting script, the initial script used for production prior to changes, Crane says, "More than you give Harvey's prisoners, Commissioner" (*The Dark Knight Rises* 2012). This is a direct and perhaps even legitimate critique of Gotham's harsh criminal justice system. In the film, Crane responds, "Your guilt is determined, this is merely a sentencing hearing. What's it to be, death or exile?" (*The Dark Knight Rises* 2012). The only option in Bane's system, which is far worse than the admittedly harsh system of Gotham is death. Crane frames his court as a revolutionary tribunal seeking justice for the poor and accuses Philip Stryver of having "lived like a prince off the blood and sweat of people less powerful . . . " (*The Dark Knight Rises* 2012). The sentence meted out to Stryver is unfair, but it resonates better with the viewers, Philip Stryver had himself helped to bring about Bane's reign, and, like the other mobsters in the Nolan-verse, he serves as a symbol of capitalism without a conscience or the shadow side of Anglo-American liberalism. This dual nature of capitalism or perhaps the wider reality of political power is further represented by the nuclear fusion reactor in the film, which can either be a bomb or a source of clean energy depending in whose hands it ends up. The rule of Bane is, as Blake himself says to the special forces soldiers who attempt to liberate Gotham, the rule of a "warlord" under a "failed state."

Nonetheless, once again, the film emphasizes the fact even though Gotham itself is corrupt and harsh and built on lies, it is far better than the alternatives. As Peter Foley says when charging Bane's mercenaries: "There's only one police in this city" (*The Dark Knight Rises* 2012). Foley makes the ultimate sacrifice for Gotham, giving his life, and there is some irony in this, for as Catwoman states, she and Batman may be "suckers" for sacrificing themselves for Gotham. A likely hallucination of Ra's al Ghul tempts Bruce while he is hanging from a rope in the pit attempting to fix his back: "You yourself fought the decadence of Gotham for years. With all your strength and resources, all your moral authority. And the only victory you could achieve was a lie. Finally, you understand . . . Gotham is beyond saving. And must be allowed to die" (*The Dark Knight Rises* 2012). This belief has been disproven frequently throughout *The Dark Knight*. There are wicked elements in Gotham, but there is good as well, and the American system, of which Gotham is a part and which the city symbolizes, best enables these good elements to flourish. As Talia notes, like her father before her, Gotham is not "innocent," but contrary to the belief of the Joker in *The Dark Knight*, it is redeemable.

The ending sequence of *The Dark Knight Rises* seeks to recapture the pathos of *The Dark Knight*'s own powerful closing, which helped shape the understanding of the image of the hero in the film. However, the ending of *The Dark Knight* is more about the city of Gotham than it is about the legend of Batman. While the shots of the poor and working-class districts of Gotham pan on screen, Commissioner Gordon reads from Charles Dicken's *A Tale of Two Cities*: "I see a beautiful city and a brilliant people rising from this abyss" (*The Dark Knight Rises* 2012). As the Gotham PD patrol around the defeated and apprehended mercenaries of Bane's rebranded League of Shadows, Gordon continues with the extract from Dickens: "I see the lives for which I lay down my life, peaceful, useful, prosperous and happy" (*The Dark Knight Rises* 2012). While Gordon further reads, we eventually see he is reading in the family cemetery at Wayne Manor: "I see that I hold a sanctuary in their hearts, and in the hearts of their descendants, generations hence. It is a far, far better thing that I do, than I have ever done" (*The Dark Knight Rises* 2012). Both Gordon and Bruce Wayne have sacrificed themselves and their families for the sake of Gotham. Just as the rescue of Gotham would not have been possible without Batman, so too were Gordon and Lucius Fox and a host of other unsung heroes necessary for Gotham's continuation. The scene is thus connected to Batman's earlier statement to Gordon: "A hero can be anyone. Even a man doing something as simple and reassuring as putting a coat around a little boy's shoulders to let him know that the world hadn't ended" (*The Dark Knight Rises* 2012). Who Batman is does not matter. Nolan is inviting the audience to be a hero as well—Nolan had played with this idea in *Inception* and would revisit it in *Tenet*. In Nolan's view, the hero must serve the system while occasionally clashing with and transgressing it.

This point is reiterated in the initiation of Blake, aka Robin, into the world of Batman. After quitting, Blake tells Gordon that he cannot work within the system of the Gotham PD due to its corruption: "What you said about structures. About shackles. I can't take it. The injustice" (*The Dark Knight Rises* 2012). He further explains his frustration at how noble lies are necessary for the functioning of Gotham, telling Gordon, "I mean . . . no one's ever going to know who saved an entire city" (*The Dark Knight Rises* 2012). Gordon responds with "They know. It was Batman" (*The Dark Knight Rises* 2012). However, it is important to note that Commissioner Gordon is not clapping when the Batman statue is unveiled at the end of the film. Perhaps Gordon himself realizes the ultimate hollowness of many political symbols. Nonetheless, there is another sense in which Batman is a symbol that must be maintained for Gotham to function. The image of the hero must be upheld and then filled by heroes who come every generation to do good—this point is emphasized by Nolan's ending shots of the orphans in the school bus, who, like Blake and Bruce Wayne, could possibly become the next generation of heroes. The final shots of Gordon patting a new Batsignal as well as Blake entering the Batcave further emphasize this idea. There is also a curious link with the historic black American football player who affects a similar pose as Robin after the Bane blows up Gotham Stadium. This is an interestingly link between the continuation of Batman and a revolutionary ethos—especially in the wake of the Colin Kaepernick protests. Like Batman those who kneeled in protest of the National Anthem found themselves simultaneously part of the American system and in an act of rebellion against it.

Finally, however, the scene of Bruce and Selina in Florence is itself another noble lie. Some critics have even suggested that this scene is merely Alfred's imagination. In *The Traumatic Screen*, Stuart Joy argues that this scene, since it is shot from Alfred's point of view, "undermines its own structure as an object reality, especially when considered in relation to Alfred's own experience of trauma regarding Wayne's apparent death.[16] Moreover, the film introduces the notion of a hallucination with Bruce's vision of Ra's al Ghul in the pit. Nonetheless, as with *Inception*, for Nolan the answer does not matter. Certainly, Bruce and Selina are two very wounded individuals, who have likely lost all their money and will have a rough go of it together. However, the happy ending of them together in Florence validates the notion that everyone can be a hero and change—and is capable of good. And all of this is made possible by the American liberal capitalist order that the heroes of Gotham defend.

To argue that Christopher Nolan ultimately supports a frail and deeply corrupt (Anglo-)American world order in *The Dark Knight Rises* (and his other films) is not to claim that the Anglo-American director is a propagandist. Rather, it is to contend that Nolan's films depict American late capitalism as the best of a series of bad systems. *The Dark Knight Rises*, in a certain sense, is a validation of Mark Fischer's notion of "capitalist realism" or zombie capitalism. As Fisher notes, "Since 2008, neoliberalism might have been deprived of the feverish forward momentum it once possessed, but it is nowhere near collapsing. Neoliberalism now shambles on a zombie."[17] Many across the world have realized the limits of capitalism and neoliberalism, but they are unable to see an alternative. As Fisher state writes, "It is by no means clear that the public has ever embraced neoliberal doctrines with much enthusiasm—but what people have been persuaded of is the idea that there is no alternative to neoliberalism."[18] The *Dark Knight* trilogy, although entertaining various revolutionary ideas, ultimately shows the viewer there is no alternative to the capitalist world order that Gotham represents.

In *The Dark Knight Rises*, although built on a series of (noble) lies, Gotham as a symbol of America is a place that allows anyone to be a hero, and its leadership, although corrupt, contains several unsung heroes. This system is challenged from without and within by various reactionary and revolutionary forces, represented in various forms by Talia al Ghul, Bane, Selina Kyle, as well as the various members of the marginalized poor and working class who are drawn into their orbit. It is not as though these villains are entirely incorrect in critiquing Gotham. However, the alternatives that they provide are ultimately far more brutal and worse than the America that Gotham represents, which despite its flaws, is still, in the film's view, a city shining on a hill.

NOTES

1. Shone, *The Nolan Variations*, 236.
2. Shone, *The Nolan Variations*, 235.
3. Ibid.
4. Fradley, "What Do You Believe In?," 18.
5. Shone, *The Nolan Variations*, 251.
6. Shone, *The Nolan Variations*, 252.
7. Shone, *The Nolan Variations*, 246.
8. Ibid.
9. Winterhalter, "The Politics of the Inner," 1046.
10. Fradley, "What Do You Believe In?," 18–19.
11. Fradley, "What Do You Believe In?," 27.
12. Shone, *The Nolan Variations*, 249.
13. Fisher, "The Politics of 'The Dark Knight Rises': A Discussion."
14. Fradley, "What Do You Believe In?," 15.
15. Ibid.
16. Joy, *The Traumatic Screen*, 66.
17. Fisher, "How to kill a zombie."

18. Ibid.

Chapter 5

Dreaming of Capitalism in Christopher Nolan's *Inception*

Since its release in 2010, Christopher Nolan's *Inception* has proved itself to be a fertile ground for philosophical, theological, and aesthetic analysis. Indeed, there are two essay collections—Thorstein Botz-Bornstein's *Inception and Philosophy: Ideas to Die For* and David Kyle Johnson's *Inception and Philosophy: Because Its Never Just a Dream*—dedicated to exploring philosophical themes in the film. The bulk of the discussion of *Inception* focuses upon existential, psychological, and metaphysical-phenomenological issues—the primary question has been who is truly dreaming in the film and when/if the dreams stop. However, with a few exceptions, critics have largely avoided a political and/or economic analysis of the film. Upon first glance, with its depictions of global corporations attempting to "hack" (to use an antiquated term) the minds of human beings, the film appears to be critiquing late capitalism and the penetration of capitalism into the minds of twenty-first-century humans. Yet, throughout *Inception*, contrary to the claims of many critics, Christopher Nolan does not depict "corporations" as such as being evil. In fact, the rapacious and crafty Proclus Corporation, headed by the ruthless but ultimately charming and sympathetic Saito (played by Ken Wanatabe) is a key component in the engine of the film's plot, enabling, via a legal power play and chicanery, Leonardo DiCaprio's Cobb to return home to his children. Rather than being a critique of transnational global capitalism, Christopher Nolan's *Inception* is at the very least an acceptance of, if not a potential endorsement of, what the late philosopher Mark Fisher called "capitalist realism," or the twenty-first-century global triumph of capital.

There are many of Christopher Nolan's films that have ignited political discussion—most notably the *Dark Knight* trilogy (2005–2012) as well as, to a lesser extent, *Dunkirk* (2017). In *The Fictional Christopher Nolan*, Todd McGowan argues that Nolan engages in "a politically engaged film making."[1] However, upon first glance, *Inception* seems to be an apolitical film. Some critics nonetheless have identified political themes in the film. Drew Winchur rightly notes that outright propaganda films in the West are rare; however, even though Nolan's *Inception* "completely omits any explicit reference to politics," by hiding the film's political message in "the uncontroversial circumstance of Cobb's emotional struggle, *Inception* covertly legitimizes the routine and far-reaching violence used to sustain corporate empires"; as a result, "in practice, if not by design, the film proves to be a highly sophisticated vehicle for capitalist propaganda."[2] Nolan's treatment of corporations has been the dominant theme of political discussion of the film.

Much of *Inception* (and perhaps all of it—if we are simply watching Cobb's dream) is merely projections of someone else's fantasy and dreams. That is also one of Christopher Nolan's main points: that film itself is like a dream and we are all watching the dreamscape of Christopher Nolan and his creative crew. Tyler Shores adds that *Inception* is not only about the ability to create other characters with our minds; it is also about the mind's ability to create things, "ranging from fantastic, physics-bending displays of cityscapes folding on top of themselves to Cobb's guilt-driven projections of Mal."[3] Joseph Garvin refers to these projections as "near-perfect simulations of people"; however, they are "not exactly like the real person they are a projection of."[4] The film itself is an image, but those elements of *Inception* that are constructed from CGI are images of images. It is a world of illusion showcasing the power of American Cinema and the capitalism that funds it. Fredric Jameson describes this world of illusion in his *Postmodernism, or, The Cultural Logic of Late Capitalism* as "a delirious vision" of electronic objects, which are themselves "mesmerizing properly aesthetic postmodern structures in which the identity of the media and the market is perceptually reenacted, something like a high-tech special effects dramatization of the ontological proof."[5] Although Jameson uses the examples of early 1990s technology, the phenomenon he describes here is even more intense in the digital era of the 2010s and 2020s. Most—if not all—films are themselves stunning advertisements for America and American capitalism. What makes *Inception* unique is that Nolan is drawing attention to the illusory nature of late postmodern existence, but, at the same time, if not endorsing, at least accepting this reality. Moreover, the world of illusion in which the characters live, again, is enabled and, in the film, funded by large corporations that control the world, manipulating humans like chess pieces. As a treat, we humans are given the ability to have bold and exciting dreams, which the technology powered by capitalism provides.

Released in 2010, *Inception* came at a precarious time in both world media and world political culture. Although not a superhero movie per se, *Inception* was released amid the initial cresting of twenty-first-century superhero movies—Nolan's own *Dark Knight* was released two years earlier in 2008, and the first *Avengers* movie would appear in 2012. As Dan Hassler-Forest writes in *Capitalist Superheroes: Caped Crusaders in the Neoliberal Age*, many of these films were not as overtly nationalistic as their twentieth-century predecessors, but they nonetheless affirmed the global dominance of an "American" militarized capitalist order.[6] Hassler-Forest explains that superhero films should be read "in the light of globalization and the forms of 'flexible accumulation' that typify neoliberalism and cultures of postmodernity." The twenty-first-century superhero, he further argues, is presented as "a benevolent peacekeeper who stand for supposedly universal interests."[7] Rather than history ending, the fallout from 9/11 has produced "an intensification of the cultures of late capitalism on a global scale."[8] Ultimately, the post-9/11 world contains a "neoliberal shift from nation state to market state is not so much that the neoliberal agenda of late capitalism has subverted the established order, but that it has come to supersede it, taking the place of the establishment while forcefully eradicating its former institutions."[9]

Critical theorists were already diagnosing this phenomenon in the twentieth century. The global dominance of capitalism and a postmodern culture is the domination of an American culture, which itself is, in the words of Frederic Jameson, "the internal superstructural expression of a whole new wave of American military and economic domination throughout the world: in this sense, as throughout class history, the underside of culture is blood, torture, death, and terror."[10] This global culture is furthermore an "the imaginary museum" in which all the artefacts of world culture are stockpiled.[11] However, this imaginary museum is more a memory of images and simulacra than memory of the Real.[12] Late capitalism is also forward-looking in as much as its technological products seem "to offer some privileged representational shorthand for grasping a network of power and control even more difficult for our minds and imaginations to grasp: the whole new decentered global network of the third stage of capital itself."[13] *Inception* is, at heart, a film about many things. It is, however, a film about human life in the era of postmodernism, late capitalism, or neoliberalism, and, at its heart, *Inception* affirms this order.

On its surface, the plot of *Inception* revolves around (software?) architect Dominick Cobb's attempt to find his children. The family that Cobb has is always present with him via memory and fantasy but is, simultaneously (and seemingly), always out of reach. If the audience accepts the film as being about a commentary on the tenuousness of reality and its relationship to the human experience, then it does not matter which reality Cobb is in, because all these realities are simultaneously fake and real. As Thomas Kapper notes, in *Inception*, the "question is not so much what's real but rather how we know what's real."[14] Like his wife, Mal, whom we assume has committed suicide,

Cobb finds it exceptionally difficult to keep track of which reality is, in fact, real. As a result, when he is awake, he thinks he is dreaming, and sometimes when he is dreaming, he thinks of himself as awake. If Mal could have convinced herself that she was dreaming when she was awake, then the audience can assume (and intuit via the experience of other characters in the film), that a character can convince him or herself that he or she is dream.

Some critics have even suggested that Cobb is dreaming and could go home to his kids and his wife anytime he wants by simply waking up; however, he prefers to stay in the dream. Even if he is not dreaming, there is the possibility that Cobb could use some of his technical savvy to find a way back home. However, it is quite possible that, if Cobb could wake up and go home to his children, he doesn't necessarily want to. Like the bulk of Nolan's characters in his films, Cobb is driven by the fantasy of the chase or heist. There is a sense in which Cobb wants to live in the world of fantasy, working away on elaborate technical feats for large amounts of money. This does not mean that Cobb does not experience any sort of existential dread or anxiety; in fact, he is perhaps the most tormented figure in the film outside of Mal. The scene of Cobb in a Tokyo apartment alone with his top and his gun is a deeply "existential" scene in the key of Hamlet's "To be or not to be" speech." Cobb spins the top and raises the gun to his head and then talks with his children on the phone. His children want him to come home, but he can't because he is "working." This is a loaded statement, for like many parents separated from their children by work in the global neoliberal economy, Cobb is working away from home. In the movie's context, he is legally prevented from seeing his children; however, in as much as the dreamworld is something he willed into living, he is apart from his children because he chooses the fantasy world of corporate espionage and incepting the dreams of billionaires. The temptation is to escape into the fantasy world provided by technocratic neoliberal American cinema. *Inception* is, in fact, more postmodern than the 1980s and 1990s world of fax machines and MTV that Frederic Jameson describes. The contents of postmodernism "are just more images, which are themselves the result of the eradication of nature through the process of modernization when it is "complete and nature is gone for good."[15] Drawing from Walter Benjamin, Jameson notes that postmodernism accelerates the process of the "aestheticization of reality."[16] Drawing from Baudrillard, Lyotard, and Žižek, Hassler-Forest likewise notes that postmodern life is "a form of simulation" and punctuated by "the unreal quality of the contemporary Western existence."[17] This is precisely what *Inception* is about. As Thorstein Botz-Bornstein notes, "the atomized dreams of *Inception*" contain "pictures of the real world"; however, the real world consists simply of "impressions" and "streaming media images that can be switched off at any moment."[18]

Cobb lives in a dreamworld constructed from simulacra and guided and shaped by corporate powers but so too does the viewer.

Capitalism and the corporations who marshal it control the world of *Inception*, swallowing the lives the films of character. Nolan illustrates this phenomenon when in Tokyo, Cobb's ruminations following his conversation with his children is interrupted by Arthur. Arthur questions Cobb about the appearance of Mal, and her frequent interruptions into Cobb's subconscious. However, this personal discussion is swallowed up by work that the team must do. In *Inception*, the personal and the professional and mutually intertwined, capital has colonized our dreams and every waking hour in the neoliberal order. Corporations also control the lives of the characters in *Inception*. Cobb notes to Arthur that they are in trouble with Cobol corporation, telling him, "We were supposed to deliver Saito's expansion plans to Cobol Engineering two hours ago. By now they know we failed. Time to disappear" (*Inception* 2010). The postmillennial global system is on 24 hours a day using various forms of media and communication to track and trace the global citizen throughout the world at all times. Cobb is afraid the judicial system in the United States, but he seems as more afraid of the corporate entities that have the ability to manipulate and even control the justice systems of various countries.

Indeed, the scene in which Cobb's physical safety is most prominently found in Mombasa when he chased by the goons from Cobol Engineering. Cobol seems to control Mombasa as Tom Hardy's Eames says to Cobb: "Word is, you're not welcome in these parts" (*Inception* 2010). Eames explains, "There is a price on your head from Cobol Engineering. Pretty big one, actually" (*Inception* 2010). Arthur also describes Mombasa is "Cobol's backyard" (*Inception* 2010). In the shooting script, Eames further explains that the people of Cobol Engineering "pretty much own Mombasa" (*Inception* 2010). The corporations have a God-like role in the film and can traverse the world. At the same time, *Inception* is not necessarily condemnatory of global capitalism. Cobb himself has a global company—albeit a criminal enterprise of which he is the CEO. Moreover, in as much as Cobb is an image of a movie director, he is a globe-trotting international movie director. The world is, in effect, a playground for the Anglo-American (and, in the case of Ken Watanabe's Saito, Japanese) subject.

The twenty-first-century viewer delighting in the sublime panoply of CGI-enhanced battles across the globe creates an experience, which, in the words of Greg Tuck, "seems to mimic aspects of the religious spectacle, at a distance, which engenders a sense of sublime community and shared being."[19] This shared being is likewise called "postmodern group consciousness" by Frederic Jameson.[20] The characters are exciting props who talk wildly and excitedly or who duck out of the way of expensive vehicles. In the end, however, this is precisely Nolan's point. The movie offers a fantasy to not only the Western but also the wider global subject of traveling around the world dressed to kill and shooting at enemies while various onlookers—whether French or Kenya—look on in admiration. In Nolan's *Inception*, the Anglo-American filmmaker provides just such an endorsement of Anglo-American capitalism and the global films that promote this worldview. Auxier argues that Nolan is attempting to manipulate the mind of the viewer, telling his reader, "If you want to protect yourself from being deceived by Christopher Nolan's movies, stay away from the movies altogether. To place yourself in the theater is to place yourself at his mercy to invite him into your dreams. He knows that you go to the movies to be able to dream, with others. And after all, Nolan is Cobb."[21] Critical theorists have noted the tremendous power of corporations, who, in late capitalism, have become integrally wedded to the state. From other Frankfurt School thinkers such as Theodor Adorno and Max Horkheimer, as well as Michel Foucault, Jameson argues that late capitalism involves an "administered society," which includes "a tendential web of bureaucratic control" and the "the interpenetration of government and big business . . . ,"[22] which has created the "inauguration of a whole new type of society, most famously baptized 'postindustrial society' (Daniel Bell) but often also designated consumer society, media society, information society, electronic society, or high tech, and the like."[23] This high-tech society is the world of *Inception*. It is a world dominated by corporations that can hack and control the human mind—something they have been doing for a long time in the "real" world via art and film.

We further see the lethality and aggression of this global capitalism when Saito offers Cobb the opportunity to kill Nash, who has betrayed him and the team. Cobb refuses and asks as Nash is drugged and taken away, "What will you do to him?" (*Inception* 2010). Saito responds with the menacing, "Nothing. But I can't speak for your friends from Cobol Engineering" (*Inception* 2010). Upon first glance, this brutality seems to a profound condemnation of the ruthlessness of global capitalism. Just as Saito can resolve Cobb's charges with a phone call, so too do corporations appear to be able to harm and likely kill others with impunity. However, immediately after this seeming warning of the dangers of corporate power, we see the fantastic potential of transnational capitalism. Saito offers Cobb one of his planes, which can take him wherever he wants to go, as Saito tells Cobb, "Tell the crew where you want to go" (*Inception* 2010). Cobb then tells him that he has the potential to get him home, asking Cobb, "How would you like to go home? To America. To your children" (*Inception* 2010). Cobb warns that such an act is impossible, telling Saito, "You can't fix that. Nobody could" (*Inception* 2010). However, Saito responds, "Just like inception" (*Inception* 2010). Saito as a representative of transnational capitalism, enabling Cobb to travel the world and make a great deal of money. He also has the power to manipulate the American criminal justice system. Here, Nolan appears to be depicting transnational capitalism as a potential force for good. Saito then recruits him as part of his ambition to break up Fischer-Morrow Energy, telling Cobb: "My main competitor is an old man in poor health. His son will soon inherit control of the corporation. I need him to decide to break up his father's empire" (*Inception* 2010). Saito's goal is to destroy his competitor by tampering with the mind of his son. Cobb is recruited to serve this task. As critics have noted, Nolan does not seem to depict this task as immoral. Cobb and Saito discuss the power of Saito's Proclus Global in almost religious terms. When Cobb asks Saito how Cobb can know that Saito will "deliver" and erase his criminal charges, Saito responds, "You don't. But I can. So do you want to take a leap of faith, or become an old man, filled with regret, waiting to die alone?" (*Inception* 2010). Happiness is provided by Proclus Global and the capitalist system, which has the power to manipulate the law and give Cobb what he wants. As critics such as Winchur argue, this gives Cobb the role as a key participant in the capitalist system that infiltrates the minds and, as Mark Fisher notes, the sub- or unconsciousness of Cobb. Daniel P. Molloy argues that the "major players" in inception are not people; rather, "[t]hey are corporations."[24] For Molloy it is corporations who move the characters and who dominate and control their lives: "Cobol Engineering sends Cobb after Saito. Saito, acting as head of Proclus Global, sends Cobb after Robert Fischer. Fisher becomes a target not because of anything he's done or even knows, but because of his impending ascension to the chairmanship of Fischer-Morrow."[25] In *Inception,* the world is dominated by corporations. The age of the nation-state is over—the fact that Saito can simply make a phone call to clear Cobb's charges show that corporate billionaires control the legal system. While both Eastern and Western religions inform the film's structure and themes, there are no religious organizations in the film. Everything is ruled and dominated by capitalism. Molloy further explains that, in the film, people "are just pieces, moved about at the will of the company."[26] The age of "Late Capitalism" or "Capitalist Realism" is an anti-human or anti-humanist age in which the emergent subject or transcendental ego of the Enlightenment has been replaced by the new model servant of capital and corporations.

Inception also contains the postmodern, late capitalist contrast between First World and the Third World. The First and Third worlds are integrally linked but at the same time mediated to each other via simulacra. Botz-Bornstein further that in *Inception* the "political turmoil that takes place in the chaotic Third World country in which the team is operating" is itself simply a "dream" and "isn't supposed to be real."[27] He further notes that the dreaming machine in Yusuf's basement likewise points to the possible reality that this scene may argue that the depiction of "ramshackle Mobasa" is not "supposed to be real," although Mombasa is a reality for the people living in it even if it is not for those watching the film.[28] At the same time, this worldview reinforces Western capitalism as the epoch of world civilization. Maybe the dreamers in Mombasa are dreaming of Western capitalism. This world of mass culture has colonized and connected with the deepest elements of the global subject.

This phenomenon is revealed in the Mombasa bar scene in which Cobb and Tom Hardy's Eames discuss the phenomenon of *Inception*. Eames explains, "If you're going to perform inception, you need imagination" (*Inception* 2010). Eames explains that this imagination must figure out how to truly penetrate the mind of the subject. Cobb asks Eames if he didn't plant the idea "deep enough" (*Inception* 2010). Eames responds, "It's not just about depth. You need the simplest version of the idea the one that will grow naturally in the subject's mind" (*Inception* 2010). Cobb explains that they want "the heir to a major corporation to break up his father's empire." Understandingly, Eames responds, "See, right there you've got various political motivations, anti-monopolistic sentiment and so forth. But all that stuff's at the mercy of the subject's prejudice you have to go to the basic" (*Inception* 2010). For Eames this most basic element is "The relationship with the father" (*Inception* 2010). This phrase is critical because we see that the deepest core of Fischer's mind and heart will be penetrated by an artist working on behalf of a global corporation. Winchur argues that this brutality is hidden behind Cobb's personal struggles in the film, and "*Inception* renders the violence motivated by corporate profit unremarkable and incidental to a 'real' personal story such as Cobb's True happiness, we learn, requires only the talent to successfully alienate oneself from moral and civic responsibilities."[29] However, Nolan provides a number of clues that allow the viewer to see how he carefully criticizes but nonetheless ultimately endorses global capital. Postmodernism further has a profound effect on the human body; according to Jameson, "postmodern bodies are bereft of spatial coordinates and practically (let alone theoretically) incapable of instantiation."[30] There is thus an attack on the body itself while "multinational capital ends up penetrating and colonizing those very precapitalist enclaves (Nature and the Unconscious) which offered extraterritorial and Archimedean footholds for critical effectivity."[31] Capitalism swallows and invades everything. The subconscious is colonized by capital as has been nature. Postmodernism is the "third great original expansion of capitalism around the globe."[32] This is precisely what happens to Fischer in *Inception*: his mind is colonized on behalf of a rival capitalist corporation.

The scene in Yusuf's basement is another critical one in which shared dreaming is marked as a positive product of global capitalism. This is Mombasa, an African city; however, it is dominated by two factors: corporate capitalism, represented by the Cobol Engineering, and American media, represented by the "shared dreaming" that Yusuf puts the men in. As an Indian running a dream room in Africa, Yusuf is representative of the global reach of shared dreaming or film or mass culture. Yusuf announces to Cobb and his team, "They come every day. To share the dream" (*Inception* 2010). Cinema is a global phenomenon. As the old man slaps the occupant, Yusuf says, "See? Very stable" (*Inception* 2010). Cobb asks, "How long do they dream" (*Inception* 2010). Yusuf responds, "Three, four hours. Every day" (*Inception* 2010). Cobb then asks, "How long in dream time?" Yusuf responds, "With this compound . . . about forty hours. Each and every day" (*Inception* 2010). The billionaire head of Proclus Global, Saito, is disgusted by this and asks, "Why do they do it?" (*Inception* 2010). Yusuf has Cobb tell him; Cobb responds to Saito, "After a while . . . It becomes the only way you can dream" (*Inception* 2010). When Eames asks, "They come here every day to sleep?" The elderly bald man responds, "No. They come to be woken up . . . the dream has become their reality . . . And who are you to say otherwise?" (*Inception* 2010). Even prior to the twenty-first century, Jean Baudrillard developed the concept of "hyperreality" for those living in the electronic age and experiencing the world through television and film. In the twenty-first century, this phenomenon has only been increased as billions of humans access the Internet and immerse themselves in digital worlds. This shared dreaming has allowed the dissemination of ideas in rapid form throughout the world. Randall E. Auxier argues that the group dreaming scene in *Inception* "connects the idea of group dreaming to mythic consciousness" because it is commonly understood that "modern life has made group dreaming impossible"; nonetheless, some desire to escape to a premodern life that "existed before civilization became so much controlled by greed and technology."[33] This shared dreaming, in Auxier's view, is "the power to find the way out of the labyrinth of modern consciousness and into genuine, shared, collective consciousness," making Yusuf a "Medicine Man."[34] However, the dreams that the dreamers dream are facilitated by the technology. Nolan's point is not that we should lament the loss of group dreaming so much as we can relive it while watching movies, and it is precisely the process of capitalist globalism that has enabled Christopher Nolan to share his dreams of with the world and allow a form of "packaged" group dreaming.

Moreover, this Third World of dreamers exists as an ancillary part of the First World of globetrotting inceptors. As Frederic Jameson notes, postmodernism is the combination of the "slum" with "the postmodern United States of extraordinary technological and scientific achievement; the most 'advanced' country in the world, in all the science fictional senses and connotations of that figure, accompanied by an inconceivable financial system and a combination of abstract wealth and real power in which all of us also believe, without many of us ever really know what that might be or look like."[35] Jameson further argues that "the totalizing account of the postmodern always included a space for various forms of oppositional culture . . . "; however, this marginal culture is the result the "uneven development of late capitalism, whose First World produces a Third World within itself by its own inner dynamic."[36] There is thus a tension between the two worlds that Nolan does not address, merely making Mombasa a playground for his characters.

This notion of the world (and the mind) as a playground is essential to the meaning of *Inception* as a showcase of postmodernism. There is much evidence that Cobb further does not want to return home to his family just yet. When encountering Professor Miles, who is either his father or father-in-law, Cobb reinforces the narrative that there is a legal apparatus preventing him from seeing his children. Professor Miles asks him, "Is it safe for you to be here?" (*Inception* 2010). Cobb responds, "Extradition between France and the U.S. is a bureaucratic nightmare" (*Inception* 2010). Miles returns with "I think they'd find a way to make it work in your case" (*Inception* 2010). We don't know exactly who to trust in this situation. Certainly, some effort could be made to extradite Cobb from France to the United States—if he, in fact, killed his wife. One might wonder how a criminal mastermind such as Dominic Cobb could be able to travel the entire world on private airplanes—including one that Saito tells him will take him whenever he wants to go and not devise a way to get back home. The image of a talented individual who is consumed by his or her work and ultimately ends up destroying their family is ca common theme in Nolan's filmography—*The Prestige* has it has its central theme. Cobb curiously has stuffed animals to send back to his kids and he calls them. It seems that whatever law and enforcement agency that is investigating Cobb's case might intercept or at least investigate these gifts and communications. Professor Miles makes the interesting comment, "It'll take more than the occasional stuffed animal to convince those children they still have a father" (*Inception* 2010). Gifts are not enough nor is calling; what is needed is the real presence of the children's father. Throughout the film, Cobb either sees the world through fantasy or through commercial exchange. In an essay on *Inception* reprinted in his *Ghosts of My Life*, Mark Fisher refers to Cobb's grief as ultimately "hollow," which is a "stand in for something else, another sadness—a loss that the film points to but can't name."[37] Fisher argues that the loss here includes the loss of the unconsciousness itself, writing, "*Inception's* arcades and hotel corridors are indeed those of globalized capital, whose reach easily extends into the former depths of what was once the unconscious. There is nothing alien, no *other place* here, only a 'subconscious' recirculating deeply familiar images mined form an ersatz psychoanalysis."[38] Fisher holds that Cobb's subconscious has been colonized and destroyed by late capitalism. There is much to Fisher's argument, and most of Nolan's characters in his films are not comfortable living in the twentieth or twenty-first century and often turn to realms of fantasy for escape. Indeed, there is much in *Inception* that suggest the world of global capitalism is one of terror and menace.

When Professor Miles expresses his disapproval with Cobb, Cobb responds to Miles, "This is what you taught me" (*Inception* 2010). Professor Miles returns, "I never taught you to be a thief." Cobb states, "No, you taught me to navigate other people's minds. But after what happened with Mal there weren't a whole lot of legitimate ways for me to use that skill" (*Inception* 2010). This is a deceptive statement, for Cobb is assuming that invading another's mind is a legitimate act, while doing so for a corporation is not. Cobb here represents the combination of art and capital or, perhaps more specifically, the big-budget films—including those produced by Christopher Nolan himself that combine Nolan's genius with the marketing desires of a major studio. This major studio enables Nolan to make his films and market his films to an enormous global audience, thus allowing Nolan to "incept" his audience with thoughts. David Carter writes, "Fundamental to the whole process of inception is the assumption that the human mind can be controlled and its motivations modified."[39] Carter additionally explains that within Nolan's films, the normal world with which humans surround themselves "is essentially an illusion"; everyone is trapped within him or herself, and "Nolan believes that the creative person can enable this trapped individual to understand how others view the world."[40] This solipsistic world is a world of dreaming and games, which can be facilitated by the postmodern structure that undergirds the film.

Instead of sneaking back into the United States or contesting his charges in court, Cobb has an elaborate scheme to get back into the United States as he explains to Professor Miles why he came to see him: "I found a way home. A job. For powerful people. If I pull it off, I can get back to my family. But I need help" (*Inception* 2010). This line should be read considering Teddy's comments in Christopher Nolan's earlier film *Memento* about Lenny making a puzzle that he can never solve for himself. It is certainly possible that Cobb, like Leonard Shelby, is creating puzzles for himself that he never will be able to solve. It is curious that he frames his offer for who we will discover is Ariadne in both financial and imaginative terms. Cobb's words then combine the two means through which Cobb functions in the world: money and art. When asking for a new architect, Cobb says to Professor Miles, "You know what I'm offering" (*Inception* 2010). Miles responds, "Money?" (*Inception* 2010). Cobb says, "No, not just money: the chance to build cathedrals, entire cities things that have never existed, things that couldn't exist in the real world" (*Inception* 2010). This language sounds very much like the forging of a contract between an ambitious and creative director and a studio. The director is given money to produce their art. The studio, moreover, demands that certain elements of the film be palatable to a global audience. This is perhaps the key to understanding the core of *Inception*, which is a film about not just about filmmaking and the power it has on the audience; it is also a film about the culture and finance of filmmaking, and, as Mark Fisher noted, the entire state apparatus that accompanies American filmmaking.

Professor Miles's response is, however, curious. He tells Cobb, "Come back to reality, Dom. Please" (*Inception* 2010). This phrase has drawn the interest of a host of critics, but it seems to mean, in essence, that Cobb is in some way not in reality—either that he is literally dreaming, or he is simply delusional. Commenting on this scene, critic Todd McGowan writes, "Paternal identification is simultaneously a physic investment in the real world and a rejection of the dream. To help bring his son back to reality Miles sends him to Ariadne."[41] McGowan further notes that "Though *Inception* stresses Cobb's decision to cede his desire for the sake of paternity, the film also makes it clear that our desire is never simply our own," and our ideas often, unacknowledged, come from others.[42] McGowan writes of this scene: "Cobb must identify with the paternal position, which necessarily involves placing oneself in the social reality rather than into the fantasmatic world of the dream. Paternal identification is simultaneously a psychic investment in the real world and a rejection of the dream. To help bring his son back to reality, Miles sends him Ariadne."[43] It is possible that Cobb is dreaming and needs to come out of it to return to his children. Regardless, the real in the film is posited as Cobb's relationship with his children, to which he ultimately is being steered in the film. However, before returning to the real and to home, Cobb desires some more adventure in the fantasy world.

This world in which Cobb chooses to live has a distinctly labyrinthian character as the training scenes with Ariadne indicate. Interestingly, the icon for Christopher Nolan's own legendary productions is a maze. It is thus curious that Cobb asks Ariadne to draw mazes as part of what he is doing, which is, as he tells her, "not, strictly speaking, legal" (*Inception* 2010). Cobb then gives her the first lesson in "shared dreaming," which critics recognize as being a symbol for movie watching. What they do in this movie is interesting; they blow up a street in Paris and bend a neighborhood in half. The (Anglo-)American creators of the shared dreaming world can shape Paris into their own image and likeness. Fisher writes that, in the Paris scenes, Ariadne "is behaving more like the CGI engineer who is creating the scene than any dreamer. This is a display of technical prowess, devoid of any charge of the uncanny."[44] The dreaming allows the subject to bend the world to his or her will, and this act is not that of a great artist but of what Fisher sees as an uncreative act of software engineering.

As Cobb further tutors Ariadne, the viewer learns that the world of the dream is centered around the individual ego. The characters in the dream are projections of one's subconscious. This is curious because the characters are a diverse cast of figures across the globe. This is a strong symbol if we see Cobb as the Western subject par excellence: the director as a corporate spy incepting the minds of the audience. Daniel Molloy notes the moral quandary of Cobb as a corporate spy: "Aside from breaking and entering, we could draw a parallel between Cobb's activities and stalking."[45] Cobb's actions are further "an invasion of privacy, and a worse one that any other conceivable. This is not going through someone's garbage—its rummaging around inside someone's mind."[46] Thus, if Cobb is Nolan, then the director is a thief as well incepting the minds of the audience. Inasmuch as the director represents a major studio's interest, then that person is a corporate thief committing corporate espionage.

This is to say that the people of the world are shaped and molded by his subconsciousness. For Cobb as an image of Nolan or at least an image of the American film director, this connection is even more pronounced, for the people of the world are shaped by the director's mind. Cobb tells Ariadne: "Sure—you are the dreamer, I am the subject. My subconscious populates your world. That's one way we get at a subject's thoughts-his mind creates the people, so we can literally talk to his subconscious" (*Inception* 2010). This is a profound image of the power of film to infiltrate the mind of the audience. But the world of the film is not multipolar. It is the mind of a specifically Anglo-American director who affects the minds of those around him. Commenting on the dream, Ariadne says, "I thought a dream space would be all about the visual, but it's the feel of things. Question is, what happens as you start to mess with physics" (*Inception* 2010). Ariadne then bends a Parisian neighborhood on top of itself in one of *Inception*'s most famous scenes. Here again Nolan is making a poignant comment on the nature of the imagination as well as film.

There is a notable scene in which Cobb realizes that Ariadne is making a part of Paris Cobb calls out, "I know this bridge. This place is real. You didn't imagine it, you remembered it" (*Inception* 2010). Ariadne responds, "I cross it every day on my way to the college. Never recreate places from your memory. Always imagine new places" (*Inception* 2010). There is an interesting and perhaps many layered readings here. Cobb explicitly fears that Mal will appear if he enters a memory. But there is a commentary on the confusion of fantasy and reality. Ariadne responds, "You have to draw from what you know" (*Inception* 2010). If we follow Mark Fisher's logic here, the mind of the director has been colonized by capital as well as militarized. He or she projects that mind on to the world via the shared dreaming of movies (or another mass produced, globalized) and filling the minds and dreams by of the world's population through the process of inception.

Cobb again warns Ariadne again about building dreams out of her memories because, as he tells her, it is "the surest way to lose your grip on what's real and what's a dream" (*Inception* 2010). Ariadne is eventually killed in the dream by Mal after rearranging the area around a Parisian bridge. Mal represents the menacing return of the family or the repressed real from which Cobb is trying to escape. As Ariadne tells Arthur, "Maybe you can't see what's going on, maybe you don't want to. But Cobb's got problems he's tried to bury down there" (*Inception* 2010). Mal is representative of Cobb's repressed guilt, but she is also a figure for the family from which he cannot escape. After Ariadne leaves, Cobb notes, "She'll be back" (*Inception* 2010). Despite the destructive trauma and the empty plasticity of the shared dream world of liberal capitalism and its cultural artefacts, it is nonetheless addictive. Postmodernism is according to Jameson, a continuation of modernist anxiety perpetuated by "the messiness of a dispersed existence, existential messiness, the perpetual temporal distraction of a post-sixties life."[47] The post-sixties life is marked by "psychic fragmentation," which "is raised to a qualitative new power, the structural distraction of the decentered subject now morphed to the very motor and existential logic of late capitalism itself."[48] Even Cobb's state of confusion, mediated to the viewer, is a product of postmodernism. According to critical theorists, mental illness is the de facto mental state of not only modernism, but postmodernism as well. Drawing from Marxist thinker Christian Marazzi as well as Deleuze and Guattari, Mark Fisher writes, that, if schizophrenia is the "condition that marks the outer edges of capitalism," then "bi-polar disorder is the mental illness proper to the 'interior' of capitalism."[49] However, Mark Fischer notes that film and other "screening narratives," which cover the "unbearable" "Real."[50] Indeed, Fisher argues that the "idea that the world we experience is a solipsistic delusion projected from the interior of our mind consoles rather than disturbs us, since it conforms with our infantile fantasies of omnipotence; but the thought that our so-called interiority owe its existence to a fictionalized consensus will always carry an uncanny charge."[51] This is the layout of *Inception*. The entire world is fantasy covering over the trauma of Mal's death (if she did, in fact, really die) or it is a fantasy, like Leonard Shelby's *Memento*, covering the reality of his life with a fiction. At the same time, we ourselves as viewers are watching *Inception* and at least potentially escaping from the monotony of late postmodern existence. *Inception* is a film about trauma and the desire to escape trauma through imagination, technology, and narrative. However, it is also a film endorsing the capitalism that makes this escape possible.

Saito later explains that scenario of Robert Fischer, describing Fischer in financial terms. At this point, Winchur is correct to note that the personal qualities of Robert Fischer are completely ignored. Saito describes him as "Robert Fischer. Heir to the Fischer-Morrow Energy conglomerate. He's spent his whole life being groomed as successor-breaking up his father's empire will take a radical shift in his thinking" (*Inception* 2010). When Cobb asks Saito, "What's your problem with Fischer?" (*Inception* 2010). Saito responds, "That's not your concern" (*Inception* 2010). However, Cobb explains the critical nature of inception and how it can radically affect someone's life: "This isn't the usual corporate espionage, Mr. Saito. This is inception. The seed of the idea we plant will grow in this man's mind. It'll change him. It might even come to define him" (*Inception* 2010). Saito gives a moral excuse for his actions, telling Cobb: "Fischer-Morrow has the regulators in their pockets. We're the last company standing between them and total energy dominance and we can no longer compete. Soon they'll control the energy supply of half the world. They'll be able to blackmail governments, dictate policy. In effect, they become a new superpower. The world needs Robert Fischer to change his mind" (*Inception* 2010). This rationale seems convincing, but, from one of Fischer-Morrow's competitors, it is less convincing. Moreover, it does not necessarily justify the hacking of another human being's mind. We further see how much emotional manipulation is going on when it is revealed that they are going to exploit Fischer's, in the words of Saito, "complicated" relationship with his father (*Inception* 2010). As critic Mark Fisher notes, this is the notion that capitalism has colonized our dreams. Here media is an adjunct of capitalism. Some critics have treated the film as a "dystopia" in which corporations such as Fischer-Morrow, Proclus, and Cobol battle each other across the globe for control of resources and human capital.

In "Honor and Redemption in Corporate Espionage," from *Inception and Philosophy*, Albert J. Chan argues that the audience roots for Cobb in his battle against the corporations because in the "economic climate" of the twenty-first century, "a thief captures more sympathy from the public than the corporate CEO."[52] Chan further notes that Cobb's highest values are not money making or capitalism, but rather to get home to his family.[53] Cobb nonetheless functions within the capitalist system that the film endorses. The most important thing to Cobb is his family, or at least the idea of his family. However, this family, to enjoy the lavish life that they enjoyed before, during, and even after Mal's apparent death. Cobb is fundamentally the capitalist dream and consumer. His desire to risk the lives of his teammates in *Inception*, moreover, is indicative of a selfish impulse to sacrifice the lives of others to fully his capitalist dream.[54] Kimberly Blessing likewise notes this selfishness in Cobb. For Blessing, "Cobb is not a heartless monster"; nonetheless, his regret in incepting Mal is fueled by what happened to his once very happy family as a result of the inception," and "Cobb what he did because it didn't bring about his desired outcome."[55] Blessing may be too harsh on Cobb here, but she is right to note that Cobb sees things in terms of how they benefit him. His family is always an image or fantasy in his mind. It is a postmodern pastiche that is enabled and supported by capitalism. David Carter writes (regarding deal with Cobb), "Saito's own motivation clearly arises from his need to protect his business interests."[56] Business and the capitalist model dominates the world—a phenomenon that Mark Fisher has called "capitalist realism."

Mark Fisher's most famous work is his 2009 *Capitalist Realism: Is There No Alternative?*. Written in the wake of the 2008 stock market crash and housing crisis, *Capitalist Realism* bemoans the full spectrum dominance of capital in the twenty first century while, at the same time, arguing that the 2008 crisis provides a crack in edifice of capitalism, which Marxist critics can exploit. Fisher sees capitalist realism as being a new stage after postmodern in which there are no political alternatives to capitalism and in which there dominates a "pervasive sense of exhaustion, of cultural and political sterility."[57] Capitalist realism, Fisher argues further, "successfully installed a 'business ontology' in which it is *simply obvious* that everything in society, including healthcare and education, should be run as a business."[58] This commentary also explains Capitalism, according to Fisher, demands the acceptance of the "incommensurable without question"; this incommensurable include the "dreaming up and junking of social fictions is nearly as rapid as its production and disposal of commodities."[59] In the world of *Inception*, Capitalism mediated through cinema completely dominates the world, and, while Nolan criticizes certain elements of capital and global blockbuster cinema that acts as its adjutant, Nolan ultimately presents the world of capital as being a positive good in which the view is invited to indulge and pursue happiness.

The big issues of the nature of reality and consciousness in *Inception* have been mined by critics for over a decade. The principal debate is when and where and if Cobb begins and stops dreaming. Some critics argue that the whole film is a dream in which Cobb is trapped. They take Mal's doubting words to him seriously. When Cobb and Ariadne attempt to recover Fischer from Mal in Limbo, Cobb tells her, "I know what's real," Mal responds: "No creeping doubts? Not feeling persecuted, Dom? Chased around the globe by anonymous corporations and police forces? The way the projections persecute the dreamer?" (*Inception* 2010). There is no question, as the various interruptions of the memories of his children as well Mal indicate, that Cobb is no longer living in a real world. However, critics have failed to ask the question: what is the fantasy world in which he lives? Mal states, "Admit it, Dom. You don't believe in one reality anymore. So choose. Choose your reality like I did. Choose to be here. Choose me" (*Inception* 2010). These words reveal that Mal is wrong because she at least appears to be talking about Limbo as opposed to the "real world" or "up there" (*Inception* 2010). Mark Fisher argues that the Limbo scenes and the cities that Cobb and Mal have created a world that is "like a PowerPoint presentation of a love affair rendered as some walk-through simulation: faintly haunting in its very lack of allure, quietly horrifying in its solipsistic emptiness."[60] Rather than being a "meta-meditation on the power of cinema," *Inception* is, Fisher argues, "a reflection of the way in which cinematic techniques have become imbricated into banal spectacle which—fusing business machismo, entertainment protocols and breathless hype—enjoy an unprecedented dominion over our working lives and our dreaming minds."[61] Even though Mal and Cobb thought they could escape the humdrum of postmodern existence, they, according to Fisher, cannot. However, Nolan does not seem to think it is a bad thing. *Inception* also presents the tremendous ability to create realities. However, these realities are artificial in the film and in the reader's experience of the film. Thorsten Botz-Bornstein writes that in their stay in Limbo, Cobb and Mal create a "space reminiscent of computer games."[62] The still standing "New World" that remain is "absolutely modern, sterile, and impersonal, in which the nostalgic and melancholic childhood home and the old apartment look like architectural projections."[63] It is a "deserted and "uncanny" space "apparently meant to represent the wasteland of a failed utopia," which resembles the "contemporary neoliberal 'paradises' such as Dubai."[64] The modernist and postmodernist architecture of Cobb and Mal's dream world is very much in key with the architecture Nolan celebrates throughout his films. If the world of Limbo in *Inception* is a PowerPoint presentation, it is one that Christopher Nolan seems to enjoy.

In addition to the connection between capital and film, the audience learns in *Inception* that there is a specific connection, as with the technology showcased in the *Dark Knight* trilogy, between the dream-sharing technology and what former president Dwight Eisenhower called the "military industrial complex." Critics have taken note of *Inception*'s exploration of the militarization of the mind. Mark Fisher writes that in *Inception* is reflective of the world of neoliberalism: "*Inception's* dreamsharing technology is—like the internet—a military invention turned into a commercial application" in which the mind has become a "militarized zone."[65] The most pronounced scene in which the militarization of the mind is show cased is when the extraction theme assaults Robert Fisher's fortified subconscious, which is in a snow-covered mountain range. There is an army defending the mind from intruders. However, Randall E. Auxier notes that this militarization is "not driven by ideals of honorable combat, and even if it is about mind-control, in some sense, this militarization isn't brain-washing."[66] Rather, within Robert Fischer's mind is some "kind of control over the way the subconscious energies enter the conscious mind" which enables Fischer to undertake a "total, violent elimination of foreign presences" in his dreams.[67] However, what is important about militarization of the mind is that such militarization, in the logic of late capitalism, is part of the process of postmodernization which involves a colonization of the mind itself.

While in the Parisian warehouse, Arthur states, "That's why the military developed dream sharing-a training program where soldiers could strangle, stab and shoot each other, then wake up" (*Inception* 2010). It is hinted that Cobb himself formerly worked for the military. Ariadne asks, "How did architects get involved?" (*Inception* 2010). Cobb responds, "Someone had to design the dreams" (*Inception* 2010). Mal and Cobb however utilized this military branded technology, and it took them too deep down the rabbit hole of their minds. The almost parodic action sequences in *Inception* play a crucial role in the film's endorsement of the capitalist world order. The crew of the film battle a host of enemies throughout a variety of dream levels and topography. This is one of the standard tropes of (Anglo-)American action films: the ability for the American hero to defeat their enemies in a variety of fields. While the gruff Tom Hardy plays the part of a tough guy well, both Joseph Gordon Levitt and Leonardo DiCaprio do not fare as well. The action sequences, although modeled, in the case of the hotel fight on the films of Jean Cocteau, are, nonetheless, more based, as many critics have noted, on video game logic. This is not necessarily a criticism. Perhaps Tom Hardy best puts it when wielding a rocket launcher like an upgrade in *Call of Duty*, telling Joseph Gordon Levitt's, "You mustn't be afraid to dream a little bigger, darling" (*Inception* 2010). This comment is a key to understanding the action sequences that feature hard-bodied action in a soft-body, digital world. It is important to further note that many characters in the film are what Susan Jeffords would call "soft bodies."[68] In the digital age, the "hard bodies" of the Cold War, Reagan Era action hero are no longer needed. *Inception* is, like much of lived human experience in the realm of Web 2.0, a digital playland—the celebration of weapons here conveys some of the edge of hard science fiction in which there is a "love of hardware for its own sake, especially military hardware."[69] Matthew Brophy further explains, "Cobb's life captivates us. Its's full of action, thrills, adventure, struggle, failure, and triumph, colored by car chases, gunfire, fist-fights, daring escapes, forbidden romance, tragic temptations. It seems epic and meaningful. Real life is not like that."[70] It is not a real world; it is an illusion provided in the film by Cobb and the corporations for which he works and for the viewer of *Inception* by Christopher Nolan and the corporations for which he works. Hassler-Forest writes that after 9/11, we saw "the privatization of the military as well as "the militarization of the public space."[71] In *Inception*, the mind has been militarized and commodified as well, but, for Christopher Nolan, it does not matter, for all of it is (at least potentially) an exciting dream made possible by the wealth, technology, and alleged freedom of postmodernity.

In July 2021, *Screen Rant* released a controversial article titled "10 Unpopular Opinions About Christopher Nolan Movies (According to Reddit)," noting several criticisms of Christopher Nolan's movies.[72] The article ultimately touched on a key point among the Nolan fandom as well as among Nolan critics: is Christopher Nolan an overrated movie director? Such a question has been asked of other directors such as Quentin Tarantino whose works display technical mastery, intellectual depth, as well as a thoughtful attunement to the cultural zeitgeist, but which are at the same time paradoxically criticized for their shallowness and their derivative nature. Nonetheless, Christopher Nolan's *Inception* is unquestionably a multilayered film that deals with the craft of filmmaking, human consciousness as well as the very nature of reality. However, at the same time, it is a film that, although presenting a mild criticism of the world of corporate espionage and competition, nonetheless, in a similar manner to the James Bond film series or other action thriller celebrates the world of capitalism. If *Inception* is about movie making, it is also about big budget transnational twenty-first-century moviemaking—something that has catapulted Nolan to the heights of fame and wealth with *The Dark Knight*. This, however, is not to criticize Nolan herein from a moral standpoint, nor is it to label Nolan as an advertiser for capitalism. Rather it is to argue that, like most of his films, Nolan depicts the twenty-first-century Anglo-American world order as something positive. Capitalism and the world created in the American Century is so good that Nolan's characters even dream about it.

NOTES

1. McGowan, *The Fictional Christopher Nolan*, 10.
2. Winchur, ""Ideology in Christopher Nolan's Inception," 44.
3. Shores. "Paradox, Dreams and Strange Loops in *Inception*," 337.
4. Garvin, "Right and Wrong in Dreams," 113.
5. Jameson, *Postmodernism*, 353.
6. Hassler-Forest, *Capitalist Superheroes*, 11–12.
7. Ibid.
8. Hassler-Forest, *Capitalist Superheroes*, 4–5.
9. Hassler-Forest, *Capitalist Superheroes*, 193.
10. Jameson, *Postmodernism*, 5.
11. Jameson, *Postmodernism*, 19.
12. Jameson, *Postmodernism*, 38.
13. Jameson, *Postmodernism*, 124.
14. Kapper, "Ariadne's Clue to Life, the Universe, and Everything, 119.
15. Jameson, *Postmodernism*, ix.
16. Jameson, *Postmodernism*, x.

17. Hassler-Forest, *Capitalist Superheroes*, 39.
18. Botz-Bornstein, "The Movie as a Thinking Machine," 211.
19. Tuck, "When more is less: CGI, spectacle and the capitalist sublime," 271.
20. Jameson, *Postmodernism,* 347.
21. Auxier, "Once Upon A Time," 147.
22. Jameson, *Postmodernism,* xviii.
23. Jameson, *Postmodernism*, 3.
24. Molloy, "The Business of *Inception*," 81.
25. Ibid.
26. Ibid.
27. Botz-Bernstein, "The Movie as Thinking Machine," 211.
28. Botz-Bernstein, "The Movie as Thinking Machine," 211–12.
29. Winchur, "Ideology in Christopher Nolan Inception," 47.
30. Jameson, *Capitalism*, 49.
31. Ibid.
32. Ibid.
33. Auxier, "Once Upon a Time," 134.
34. Auxier, "Once Upon a Time," 134–35.
35. Jameson, *Postmodernism*, 128.
36. Jameson, *Postmodernism,* 159.
37. Fisher, *Ghosts of My Life*, 218.
38. Ibid.
39. Carter, *Constellations: Inception*, 42.
40. Carter, *Constellations: Inception*, 52.
41. McGowan, *The Fictional Christopher Nolan,* 157.
42. McGowan, *The Fictional Christopher Nolan*, 160.
43. McGowan, *The Fictional Christopher Nolan,* 157.
44. Fisher, *Ghosts of My Life*, 214–15.
45. Molloy, "The Business of *Inception*," 83.
46. Ibid.
47. Jameson, *Postmodernism*, 117.
48. Ibid.
49. Fisher, *Capitalist Realism*, 35.
50. Fisher, *Capitalist Realism*, 55.
51. Fisher, *Capitalist Realism*, 55–56.
52. Chan, "Honor and Redemption Corporate Espionage," 167.
53. Chan, "Honor and Redemption Corporate Espionage," 171.
54. Chan, "Honor and Redemption Corporate Espionage," 172.
55. Blessing, "Mal-Placed Regret," 303.
56. Carter, "*Constellations: Inception*," 82.
57. Fisher, *Capitalist Realism*, 7.
58. Fisher, *Capitalist Realism*, 17.
59. Fisher, *Capitalist Realism*, 56.
60. Fisher, *Ghosts of My Life*, 214–15.
61. Fisher, *Ghosts of My Life*, 215.

62. Fisher, *Ghosts of My Life*, 214.
63. Ibid.
64. Fisher, *Ghosts of My Life*, 214.
65. Fisher, *Ghosts of My Life*, 212.
66. Auxier, "Once Upon A Time," 133.
67. *Ghosts of My Life*, 133.
68. Jeffords, *Hard Bodies*, 33.
69. Cramer, "Hard Science Fiction," 189.
70. Brophy, "Shared Dreams in Virtual Worlds," 193.
71. Hassler-Forest, *Capitalist Realism*, 73.
72. McGinley, "10 Unpopular Opinions About Christopher Nolan Movies (According to Reddit)."

Chapter 6

Discovering America in Space

Christopher Nolan's Interstellar

In the third decade of the twenty-first century, Frederic Jameson's 1991 *Postmodernism or The Cultural Logic of Late Capitalism* sits uneasily in critical discourse. On one hand, the work has been completely vindicated as American-style capitalism has come to dominate world culture, continuing the process of postmodernization in a manner similar to how postmodernism continued the process of modernization. On the other, history has not ended and various forms of premodern thought have returned, and American capitalist hegemony has been challenged by various forms of reactionary and authoritarian regimes such as Russia, Syria, Iran, China, and others. Throughout much of twenty-first-century film, these regimes have provided the foil to America as the home of liberal tolerance—the plot of the recent *Top Gun: Maverick* is a perfect of example of this. However, other films provide a more nuanced and critical vision of America in a multipolar world. Christopher Nolan's 2014 film *Interstellar* sits at the crux of the Obama era in which a kindler gentler version of President Bill Clinton's Pax America was rolled out before the turbulence of the Trump and now post-Trump eras. While not as aggressively patriotic as post-9/11 superhero films, the film nonetheless presents a future in which America continues to dominate space.

The original "Spielberg" script for *Interstellar* was, in fact, much more focused on an aggressive space with China that America ultimately "wins."[1] Prior to its release in 2014, *Interstellar* had been a work in progress for some time. The narrative arch of the space mission initially began in 2006 as a collaborative effort at Paramount Pictures among gravitational physicist Kip Thorne, director Steven Spielberg, screenwriter Jonathan (Jonah) Nolan, who was hired by Spielberg in 2007, and producer Lynda Obst. Spielberg eventually abandoned the picture after Spielberg's DreamWorks was purchased from Paramount by Disney.

The original script places much more emphasis on a future space race with China and has a number of plot differences, but the basic narrative arc of Cooper's journey through a wormhole remains. Upon the recommendation of Jonah Nolan, his brother Chris was brought on as director. It is curious that Nolan would drop the notion of space race from the work of Spielberg who often has set his works in a good-versus-evil struggle between America and its enemies such as National Socialist Germany and Russia. In *Interstellar*, Nolan did not only erase the space race element of Spielberg's proposed version of the film but added a touching story of the love between a father and his daughter. These two stories in Nolan's film are integrally linked and form a political message. The story of the father daughter relationship has an interesting back story as Nolan scholar Tom Shone writes in his book, *The Nolan Variations*. The story of Murph's relationship with her father Cooper was developed by Christopher Nolan and Hans Zimmer over a winter evening dinner. As Shone narrates, while dining at the Wolseley restaurant in Piccadilly Square, Hans Zimmer said to the Nolans, "Once your children are born, you can never look at yourself through your own eyes anymore; you always look at yourself through *their* eyes."[2] While, as some critics have complained, these two threads are in so great of tension that they form one (mediocre) film as opposed to a potentially very good Christopher Nolan flick, the stories nonetheless are very much independent upon one another. Coop, like innumerable other characters in the Nolan-verse as well as other science fiction film's like Kubrick's masterpiece *2001: A Space Odyssey* (1968) and the neglected Brad Pitt film *Ad Astra* (2019), the obsession of the father is a price the entire family has to play. However, due to the father's absence in the film, the entire world is saved, and American flags are firmly planted on new worlds.

However, while *Interstellar* does not have the motif of a space race against America's rivals and is undergirded by a story of familial love, it is nonetheless a film that celebrates American space travel. It is also a film very much in the tradition of sci-fi flicks. As Tom Shone notes, *Interstellar* is Nolan's "conscious effort yet to bridge the gap between the optimism of his early childhood, spent glued to Carl Sagan's *Cosmos* and Spielberg's *Close Encounters of the Third Kind* with Jonah, and the darker, more cerebral fiction of Kubrick and Roeg he had explored in his teens."[3] More optimistically, Mark Cotta Vaz writes in *Interstellar: Beyond Time and Space*, "Recapturing the early space program's spirit of adventure is one of the driving themes of behind director Christopher Nolan's *Interstellar*."[4] *Interstellar* is a film about the vastness and seeming cruelty of space as well as the cruelty human beings have toward one another, but its message is also a message of hope and endurance and the ability for America to overcome its twenty-first decline and ultimately overcome space and time.

Interstellar is also a deeply "patriotic" film that celebrates America's achievements in space and seeks to encourage further space exploration by the United States. Vaz notes that the pre-production research involved a visit to the last space *Interstellar's* pre-production research included a visit to the space shuttle *Endeavour*, the last shuttle to be put out of service as well as several visits with Elon Musk.[5] Christopher Nolan himself further emphasizes the connection of the film with early patriotic depictions of American space travel: "We had screened a print of *The Right Stuff*, a film embodying a lot of the spirit of what we were trying to get across about the character of Cooper and the drive to get off of earth."[6] Vaz further comments on the historical placement of *Interstellar* during the Obama era in which America seemed to be bowing out from space travel: "*Interstellar* seemed to come together at a propitious time, with America cutting ack its space program—even as new breed of space explorer was emerging in the private sector—and China, India, and other countries embarking upon their own ambitious space programs. Many in the *Interstellar* production team saw the film as a call for America to return to greatness."[7] Producer Lynda Obst as well emphasized the importance of the film as a way to show the more tolerant side of America, telling Vaz, "A lot of what America used to be, what we stood for, was wrapped up in our space program,'. . . . 'We showed our best selves to the world through the space program and our ability to use technology for all mankind, as the saying goes, not for drones or bunker bombs."[8] This quote is key to understanding the *Interstellar*. It is not simply a film that celebrates and encourages American space exploration or simply a film about family ties. It is a film calling America to a kinder and gentler version of itself.

Although not a superhero film, per se, in as much as the film is a late post-9/11 film about American greatness, *Interstellar* reflections many of the themes that Dan Hassler-Forest develops in his critical 2012 work *Capitalist Superheroes: Caped Crusaders in the Neoliberal Age*. In this work, Hassler-Forrest notes a twenty-first-century "conflation of politics with entertainment and celebrity culture."[9] Echoing Frederic Jameson, Hassler-Forest further implies that American neoliberalism has become the exclusive political system although, in the twenty-first century, much of culture masks American interest.[10] However, Hassler-Forest further notes, "This does not mean, however, that the films no longer represent American geopolitical interests. Instead, one should see this re-engineering of superhero characters in the light of globalization and the forms of 'flexible accumulation' that typify neoliberalism and cultures of postmodernity. Instead of representing American neoliberal policies in terms of the iconography of the nation state, the twenty-first-century superhero is instead presented as a benevolent peacekeeper who stands for supposedly universal interests."[11] This is exactly what

Interstellar accomplishes. Without the aggressive patriotism of earlier films, the Nolan sci-fi flick presents a future in which a tolerant and humanistic America continues to rule both time and space. Some scholars have argued that "hard" science fiction is fundamentally apolitical, and "when politicians appear at all, they are usually ignorant fools or outright villains, reflecting the experiences of actual working scientists."[12]

Although shot at an Alberta farmhouse, the first portion of *Interstellar* takes place in middle America. Coop is introduced as a farmer. As an elderly Murph says, "my dad was a farmer—like everybody else back then" (*Interstellar* 2014). However, she then says, "Of course, he didn't start that way" (*Interstellar* 2014). We then cut to a scene in which Matthew McConaughey's Cooper is flying a prototype spaceship through the earth's atmosphere. He is directed away from flying as someone tells him he is "shutting it down" (*Interstellar* 2014). It appears as if Cooper was attempting to do something dangerous and was "reeled in" by NASA in a very similar manner to Jack Yaeger in *The Right Stuff*. We then cut to a seen of Murph waking her dad up. Murph tells her dad that she thought he was the ghost, which, as we will see by the end of the film, he is the "ghost" communicating to her through the tesseract. He is also the metaphorical "ghost" who inspires Murph's career and helps her to progress as a scientist in imitation of her father. He looks out at the field of corn as Murph explains, "The wheat had died" (*Interstellar* 2014). We learn about the blight and that Coop's family, America, and the world have declined and, in a certain sense, have died. The rest of the film is about Cooper's relationship with his family, but it is also about the family and America saving the world. The blight in the film is reflective of the malaise that had set in during the Obama era (and which would eventually explode in the Trump era). America seemed to be floundering in the War on Terror and the great hopes of the End of History were gone. Nonetheless, in the film, America saves the world. The blight in the film is both a physical catastrophe as well as a spiritual or emotional one. Commenting on the 2008 Pixar film, *Wall-E*, Mark Fisher notes in *Capitalist Realism*, a work that is, in many ways, an update of Jameson's *Posmodernism*, that "environmental catastrophe features in late capitalist culture only as a kind of simulacra, its real implication for capitalism too traumatic to be assimilated into the system."[13] *Interstellar* is not a film about economics; it is a film about America, and a worldwide blight is not severe enough to destroy Americans who triumph over it and, in fact, make their way into colonization of space by the end of the film. Interestingly, Slavoj Žižek notes in his 2002 tome reflecting on the post-9/11 world, *Welcome to the Desert of the Real!*, "it is easy to account for the fact that poor people around the world dream about becoming Americans—so what do the well-to-do Americans, immobilized in their well-being, dream about? About a global catastrophe that would shatter their lives."[14] *Interstellar* is a catastrophe film sent during a period of (relative) quiet in American history, but it is also a film about the triumph of a new America tutored by a reinforced message of love.

As the film progresses, Cooper is drawn toward space flight and engineering in both his dreams and waking life. After their truck gets a flat tire while driving down a dirt road, Cooper stops to fix the tire but his imagination is captured by a drown that he chases down in his truck. They capture what Coop calls an "India surveillance drone" and plan on harvesting its solar cells (*Interstellar* 2014). It is clear that Cooper has talents and desires that are hindered by his life as a farmer. When Murph complains about Cooper's cannibalization of the Indian surveillance drone, Cooper responds, "This thing needs to learn how to adapt, Murph—like the rest of us" (*Interstellar* 2014). The viewer is set up for a space exploration journey in which Cooper will end up saving America and the world, but this is not quite what happens in the film. Cooper is very much a sci-fi hero in the tradition of Robert Heinlein who helped to create what has been called the "*Astounding* hero" or the "tough, taciturn engineer who uses reason and practical know-how to solve seemingly insurmountable problems."[15] Cooper and Murph do end up saving the world, but they do so through ingenuity as well as the power of a personal love that extends to the whole human race.

The film adds a further political dimension when Cooper and his son and daughter arrive at school. During a parent teacher conference at Murph and the boy's school, Ms. Hanley, Murph's teacher, comments that Murph brought an "old federal textbook" with a "section on the lunar landings" (*Interstellar* 2014). This is not acceptable according to Ms. Hanley because these books have been "corrected" to explain "how the Apollo missions were faked to bankrupt the Soviet Union" (*Interstellar* 2014). This statement prompts Cooper to ask, "You don't believe we went to the moon?" Ms. Hanley explains, "I believe it was a brilliant piece of propaganda. The Soviets bankrupted themselves pouring resources into rockets and other useless machines" (*Interstellar* 2014). The comment "useless machines" "triggers" Cooper (*Interstellar* 2014). This scene is very Nolan-esque. We (along with Nolan) clearly sympathize with Cooper, although because of his rough impulsivity, Cooper is not necessarily to be trusted. However, Ms. Hanley is not necessarily a touchstone herself. She explains to Cooper, "Yes, Mr. Cooper. And if we don't want a repeat of the wastefulness and excess of the twentieth century, our children need to learn about *this* planet, not tales of leaving it" (*Interstellar* 2014). However, Cooper strongly retorts, "One of those useless machines they used to make was called an MRI. And if we had any of them left, the doctors might have been able to find the cyst in my wife's brain before she died, rather than afterwards. Then she could be setting here listening to this" (*Interstellar* 2014). This gives more of a strong argument in favor of Cooper. Although notoriously adverse (but not completely opposed to) CGI, Christopher Nolan's films generally celebrate technology as an advantage. Ms. Hanley here represents a small-minded luddite attitude; she lacks the ambition and imagination of Cooper (and, we will see, the treacherous Dr. Mann). However, Cooper's ambition and patriotic drive will have to be later tempered and educated in the tesseract scene.

When Cooper returns and speaks with his father-in-law Donald, this notion of America being in a temporary malaise that will eventually be overcome by technology and a moderated and liberalized will to power is further emphasized. Donald ask Coop, "Sounds like your meeting at school didn't go so well" (*Interstellar* 2014). Cooper responds, "We've forgotten who we are, Donald. Explores, pioneers. Not caretakers" (*Interstellar* 2014). Donald responds, "When I was a kid it felt like they made something new every day. Some gadget or idea. Like every day was Christmas. But six billion people . . . just try to imagine that. And every last one of them trying to have it all" (*Interstellar* 2014). The problems of the old world seem to include not only militarism, but consumerism as well. However, the American spirit of adventure is something that must continue into the future, as Cooper states, "We used to look up and wonder at our place in the stars. Now we just look down and worry about our place in the dirt" (*Interstellar* 2014). America is in a malaise and needs to get out, but this getting out, but this transformation will have to be achieved through love as well as will to power.

Throughout the film, Murph encounters further phenomena in her room, and she eventually is given a message of coordinates, which Cooper decides to follow. Coop and Murph head out to an abandoned military facility that turns out to host NASA while it previously held NORAD. The notion that American agencies are continuing in the future is key to the film. Murph and Cooper encounter a robot that threatens them but turns out to be benign. The theme of "toning it down" from the "hardbodies" of 1980s action films is present in *Interstellar* as well. *Interstellar* further harkens back to the "passivism" of sci-fi writers like Isaac Asimov and Arthur C. Clarke who protested the Reagan SDI initiative.[16] This reality is humorously reflected in Cooper's comment to the robot: "You might think you're still in the Marines, but the Marines don't exist anymore, pal. I've got grunts like you mowing my grass" (*Interstellar* 2014). Cooper further tells Amelia Brand in the shooting script, "You're taking a risk using ex-military for security. They're old, their control units are unpredictable" (*Interstellar* 2014). The old militaristic America still haunts the future with its ghosts, but they have been re-tooled. Like Cooper himself they are undergone a domestication. On one level, *Interstellar* is about this change and then retooling of a new, kinder, gentler America. When Cooper first encounters Professor Brand, the younger Anne Hathaway's Brand makes it clear that they are NASA, pointing around the table: "Williams, Doyle, Jenkins, Smith, you already know my father, Professor Brand. We're NASA" (*Interstellar* 2014). Cooper asks, "NASA?" Professor Brand Responds, "NASA. Same NASA you flew for" (*Interstellar* 2014). This is in response to Professor Brand's question, "Don't you know who we are, Coop?" (*Interstellar* 2014). To which Cooper responds, "No. No, I don't." The point here is that the old NASA has been reborn; it continues. Cooper rhetorically states, "I heard you got shut down for refusing to drop bombs from the stratosphere onto starving people" (*Interstellar* 2014). This is the old mentality of the military industrial complex or the (New) Right as well as the neoconservatives: using military violence to suppress America's enemies. This however, is (at least upon first glance) the methods of NASA. Professor Brand instructs Cooper: "When they realized killing other people wasn't a long-term solution they needed us back. Set up in the old NORAD facility. In secret" (*Interstellar* 2014). The point here is that the age of the military industrial complex is over. There is no need for NORAD, but there is a need for NASA. The mission of the United States will be one of peace making through scientific discovery and exploration. This peaceful mission is at the heart of the space program. However, even this space program must be kept secret, as Professor Brand explains, "Public opinion won't allow spending on space exploration. Not when we're struggling to put food on the table" (*Interstellar* 2014). This point of a "secret space" program has been popular with conspiracy theorists. However, it is not the only conspiracy in the film.

Brand and Cooper's conversation further emphasizes this notion of some sort of change from the old America to the new. They discuss the retooling of American spacecraft and talk about the "Lazarus missions" (*Interstellar* 2014). Cooper does not like the term, but Brand emphasizes, "Lazarus came back from the dead—" (*Interstellar* 2014). Cooper comments, "He had to die in the first place. You sent people out there looking for a new home . . . There's no planet in our solar system that can support life . . . and it'd take them a thousand years to reach the nearest star—that doesn't even qualify as *futile* . . . Where did you send them, Professor?" (*Interstellar* 2014). This is the first point in which we note the key divide between Brand and Cooper or between the residual old America and the new. The old America was willing to sacrifice individuals lives for the greater good—especially in the American space program as chronicled in films like *The Right Stuff* and *First Man*. However, the new America, represented by Cooper, will be more humanistic and liberal. As we later learn, Professor Brand lies to Cooper when he tells him to "Get out there" and "save" his kids (*Interstellar* 2014). Doyle later explains how the Lazaraus mission sent out several astronauts to twelve planets. These astronauts would, however, possibly not return if the planet was inhabitable. Once again, we see the utilitarian approach to human life. Brand further tells Cooper about a "Plan B" in which there will be a "population bomb" of humans from fertilized embryos (*Interstellar* 2014). This Plan B, however, requires giving up on the people on earth as Cooper asks, "We just give up on the people here?" (*Interstellar* 2014). Cooper here is compassionate toward those who are left on Earth, but this compassion must be watered and developed in space. Cooper agrees to the mission, thinking he will save humanity and return to his family. He is impelled to go back out into space by his sense of adventure as well as his love for his family. However, along the way he must encounter both the evil and selfishness within himself, mirrored in Dr. Mann, and learn from Amelia Brand what true love is and how this true love will save America and the world.

Dr. Hugh Mann, the leader of the Lazarus missions, who is stranded on a beautiful frozen planet and is awakened, Lazarus-like from his sleep chamber by Cooper, is strongly representative of the old America of the Apollo program, the Cold War and the tough as nails Jarhead of the War on Terror before the Lazarus-like re-tooling that Cooper will go through. Dr. Mann, played by Matt Damon, represents the older, more ruthless, and less liberal idea of American identity. He is fundamentally selfish and is concerned with survival. He is willing to kill Cooper as well as Romilly, although Romilly's death seems to have been potentially an accident. There is no question that Dr. Mann is brave and heroic; Amelia Brand describes him as being "Remarkable. The best of us. My father's protégé. He inspired eleven people to follow him on the loneliest journey in human history" (*Interstellar* 2014). However, at the same time, Dr. Mann's bravado and aggression lead to his death. He, like Cooper, undergoes a transformation, yet his transformation is into a more primitive and violent state of survival. As he tells Cooper: "Pray you never learn just how good it can be to see another face. I hadn't much hope to begin with. After so much time, I had none. My supplies were exhausted. The last time I sent to sleep, I set no waking date. You have literally raised me from the dead" (*Interstellar* 2014). Mann's explanation is clearly a reference to Lazarus, and like Cooper, he has undergone a metamorphosis, but his metamorphosis leads him to a selfish and more regressive state. He has become a reptilian deceiver as opposed to a more generous explorer like Cooper will become. Like Professor Brand, Dr. Mann lies to Cooper, telling him that close to the surface of the planet, life is more habitable, and this is a viable planet.

Dr. Mann further reveals that he knew that Plan A was all an illusion after Murph sends a transmission to the planet saying that Dr. Brand died revealing that there was supposedly no hope of saving Earth. Dr. Mann further emphasizes the evolutionary logic behind Dr. Brand's decision: "He knew how much harder it would be for people to come together and save the species, instead of themselves. Or their children" (*Interstellar* 2014). This is the old notion of nationalism or ethnocentrism that powered America's initially ascendency. According to this logic, humans a fundamentally tribal and selfish. The notion of universal brother is, in this view, an (albeit noble) lie presented by Christianity and then various forms of liberalism and Marxism. Dr. Mann further explains this (semi-)social Darwinist view: "Evolution has yet to transcend that simple barrier—we can care deeply, selflessly for people we know, but our empathy rarely extends beyond our line of sight" (*Interstellar* 2014). Dr. Mann looks out for himself and is dedicated to the mission; he manifests this belief in his deeds.

Interestingly, he also embraces the "noble lie" concept so present in so many of Nolan's films. When Amelia Brand calls her father's deception a "lie. A monstrous lie," Dr. Mann interestingly agrees, telling Amelia and Cooper: "Unforgivable. And he knew it. Your father was prepared to destroy his own humanity to save the species. He made the ultimate sacrifice" (*Interstellar* 2014). Dr. Mann sees self-sacrifice as part of a logic of sacrifice of others as well. Cooper, who is learning to view love and self-sacrifice as being intertwined with a "big picture" view of universal love, responds with "No. That's being made by the people of Earth who'll die because, in his arrogance, he declared their case hopeless" (*Interstellar* 2014). Dr. Mann retorts, "I'm sorry, Cooper. Their case is hopeless. We are the future" (*Interstellar* 2014). There is a cruel and bravado message to Mann here. He views individual life as worth sacrificing for the greater good.

As he and Cooper walk toward the supposedly more temperate surface, he further explains to him his cold evolutionary logic, "You have attachments. I'm not supposed to, but even without family, I can promise you that the yearning to be with other people is massively powerful. Our instincts, our emotions, are at the foundations of what makes us human. They're not to be taken lightly" (*Interstellar* 2014). This explanation is fundamentally self-centered, but it is not entirely different from the message of love that Cooper finally learns. Dr. Mann further notes, "A trip into the unknown requires improvisation. Machines can't improvise well because you can't program a fear of death. The survival instinct is our single greatest source of inspiration. Take you—a father. With a survival instinct that extends to your kids" (*Interstellar* 2014). Here Mann reveals more of the logic of his thinking. In his view, a human's relationship with his or her offspring is defined by instinct as opposed to love. As Dr. Mann reveals to Cooper that he lied about the habitability of the planet, he explains his rational for deceiving, "I tried to do my duty, Cooper, but the day I arrived I could see this place had nothing. I resisted the temptation for years . . . but I knew there was a way to get rescued" (*Interstellar* 2014). Dr. Mann operates according to a quasi-Stoic logic; he views life in terms of instinct and will; the missing ingredient is the love of which Amelia Brand speaks and which Cooper learns in the tesseract. As Cooper struggles after Dr. Mann smashes Cooper's Helmet, Dr. Mann also states, "Please don't judge me, Cooper—you were never tested like I was. Few men have been" (*Interstellar* 2014). Dr. Mann further notes, "You're feeling it, aren't you? That survival instinct—that's what drove me. It's always driven the human race, and it's going to save it now. I'm going to save it. For all mankind. For you, Cooper" (*Interstellar* 2014). Both Cooper and Dr. Mann are selfish and altruistic at the same time. Or, better yet, they their selfishness is tied to their altruism. However, Dr. Mann is willing to sacrifice billions of lives while Cooper is hoping to save them. Moreover, Cooper learns that it is love, not instinct that should be the driving force of human life, and it is this love that, in *Interstellar*, ultimately saves humanity.

The film is not just about survival or American achievement or a eugenic and utilitarian approach to preserving the future as represented by the older Dr. Brand and Dr. Mann (as well as a host of James Bond villains). It is ultimately love that impels Cooper and drives him to find Murph on the other side of the tesseract. Before leaving to go on the mission, Cooper tells Murph, "I love you, Murph. Forever. And I'm coming back" (*Interstellar* 2014). This statement is very bold and strong, but it strangely is fulfilled in the film. The love of Cooper for Murph impels him, with the help of the mysterious beings called "they" in the film (very likely humans from the future, a theme Nolan will repeat in *Tenet*), to transcend space and time and to find the child Murph and encounter the older dying Murph at the end of the film. However, this communicative love between father and daughter has a political meaning in as much as it is love—not the sleight of hand and aggressive machinations of Dr. Brand and Dr. Mann. It is Amelia Brand who gives (a perhaps too on the nose) explanation of the power and logic of love. Brand gives a lesson about how she explains her feelings for Wolf Edmunds: "So listen to me when I tell you that love isn't something we invented—its observable, powerful. Why shouldn't it mean something?" (*Interstellar* 2014). Cooper responds, "It means social utility—child rearing, social bonding—" (*Interstellar* 2014). Brand retorts with an explanation worth quoting in full:

> We love people who've died . . . where's the social utility in that? Maybe it means more—something we can't understand, yet. Maybe it's some evidence, some artifacts of higher dimensions that we can't consciously perceive. I'm drawn across the universe to someone I haven't seen for a decade, who I know is probably dead. Love is the one thing we're capable of perceiving that transcends the dimensions of time and space. Maybe we should trust that, even if we can't yet understand it. (*Interstellar* 2014)

One of the dominant themes of *Interstellar* is the possibility for humans—both as individuals—and as a species to undergo a death and resurrection and to "evolve" into a better state of being. Amelia Brand, at this point in the journey, believes in the power of love to transcend space and time and to form a bound between people. Cooper is the hardheaded engineer and pilot who loves his daughter. However, as the film progresses, Cooper discovers that his love for Murph will be a powerful engine that will enable him and Murph to save the world. Cooper undergoes and education and an evolution in love as he progresses through Gargantua and the tesseract. Amelia Brand has some awareness of the bound between personal love and its connection to a wider love that could save humanity, explaining to Cooper, "yes—the tiniest possibility of seeing Wolf again excites me. But that doesn't mean I'm wrong" (*Interstellar* 2014). This is the core of the film: selfishness is tied to altruism.

When Cooper goes through the black hole, he ends up in the tesseract a four-dimensional region in which he can access time periods of Murph's bedroom. This tesseract has been designed by "them" or the future humans or aliens to enable Coop to communicate with Murph and help her to solve the crisis on Earth. This scene is, once again, a reinforcement of the idea that the love between Cooper and his daughter is strong enough to transcend time and space as well as powerful enough to serve as an impetus to deeper love that saves the whole human race. There is also a political message: Cooper is an American everyman—more of a product of the twentieth century than the first. Cooper travels across the solar system, through a wormhole, through a black hole, and ends up back in an American Midwestern home. Thus, Cooper's journey back home ultimately leads him back to America.

The journey is not simply a voyage back to America. Rather, it is an interior journey in which Cooper relinquishes the selfish part of himself that wanted to keep exploring for the sake of exploring or regain his identity as an engineer/fighter pilot. In the tesseract scene, Cooper sees himself leaving Murph. The older astronaut Cooper in the screams, "Don't go!" (*Interstellar* 2014). This scene is crucial not becaue Cooper renounces his pride and ambition, but because his journey through Gargantua and the tesseract was necessary—indeed, it was literally orchestrated by what is quite likely the people of the future saved by the act—Cooper had no choice to go. He was fated to go, but now he performs the mission for the sake of humanity as opposed to satisfy his own ego. Murph and Coop's love save the world, but the world they save, as we will see, is on dominated by America. TARS (in perhaps overkill or too much telling as opposed to showing for Nolan) tells Cooper via radio, explaining, "They saved us . . . " (*Interstellar* 2014). Confused, Cooper asks, "Who's 'They'? And why would they help us?" (*Interstellar* 2014). TARS responds, "I don't know, but they constructed this three-dimensional space inside their five-dimensional reality to allow you to understand it"

(*Interstellar* 2014). We get a better understanding of who "they" likely are in the film when after Cooper exclaims that he doesn't understand what is going on, and "It isn't working" (*Interstellar* 2014). Tars states, "Yes, it is. You've seen that time is represented here as a physical dimension—you even worked out that you can exert a force across spacetime" (*Interstellar* 2014). They can use gravity (but also Amelia brand's "love") to transmit messages across space and time. Cooper later explains that he "can find Murph and find a way to tell her" (*Interstellar* 2014). When Tars ask how, Cooper responds, "Love, Tars. Love—just like Brand said—that's how we find things here" (*Interstellar* 2014). Love and science propel Cooper and Murph to saving the world.

The tesseract scene further emphasizes the fact that the "they" are likely (American) humans from the future. TARS explains to Cooper, implicitly, that he was not supposed to change the past or prevent himself from leaving: "They didn't bring us here to change the past" (*Interstellar* 2014). Cooper realizes that it was (likely) humans in the future, as he says, "We brought ourselves here" (*Interstellar* 2014). As Cooper deduces, they choose Murph to "save the world." Americans in the future choose Americans in the past to save the world. It is the job of an American Midwestern woman, played by Jessica Chastain—who in *Zero Dark Thirty* (2013) helped save the world from Osama bin Laden—to save the world. Murph has the help of her father as she announces to her confused brother Tom, "Dad. It was him. All this time . . . it was him. He's going to save us" (*Interstellar* 2014). As the tesseract closes, Coop further explains to TARS, "'They' aren't 'beings' . . . they're *us* . . . What I've been doing for Murph, they're doing for me . . . for all of us" (*Interstellar* 2014). When TARS states that "People couldn't build this," Cooper responds with "Not yet . . . but one day. Not you and me but a *people*, a civilization that's evolved beyond the four dimensions we know" (*Interstellar* 2014). Due to Nolan's frequent use of deception—especially self-deception—in his films, we cannot tell if Cooper's assessment is accurate. However, if we do, then very likely this evolved civilization is an American one that chooses earlier Americans to save the world and then subsequently colonize space. As the tesseract dissolves, Cooper then reaches out to touch Amelia Brand's hand in mimicry of God touching Adam's hand in the Sistine Chapel. There is clearly, like Stephen Spielberg's similar scene in *E.T.*, a theological message (that the real "gods" are allegedly humans), but there is also implicitly a political message as well. In *Interstellar*, the gods are Americans helping each other to save the world.

Even when Cooper gets back to the solar system surrounding Earth, he returns to America. After the doctor explains to him his age, the first thing a resuscitated Cooper hears is the crack of a baseball bat. He opens the window curtain to see young (American) boys playing baseball in a replica of what appears to be small, Midwestern American town, complete with a cornfield. The doctor tells him that he was rescued by the "Rangers" (a very American-sounding term). This sound takes Cooper, and the viewer, back to *Interstellar* ends with American dominance of space. There is a humorous scene that followers in which Cooper thinks the space station they are on, named "Cooper Station," is named after him, when, in fact, it is named after Murph. This scene is curious—especially when we look at it through the very Nolan-esque lens of self-deception and illusion. It is a supreme fantasy to have monuments named after oneself. Discovering that the station is named after Murph helps to deflate Cooper, but even then, it still draws attention to the fact that the film is a film; it is a fantasy of (especially American) ego to conquer space and name the things in it. This drawing of attention does not mean that Nolan is mocking this dream, however; he is, in fact, endorsing it throughout the whole film.

At the end of the film, after the saving the world, Coop reconciles with his daughter. He as the American man of resolve can conquer time and space. He can see Murph before she dies. Interestingly, all Murph's family, who are also Cooper's family, leave the room so he can be alone with her. The first thing Cooper says to her is, "You told them I like farming" (*Interstellar* 2014). This, of course, is a joke, but is also a reflection on one of Nolan's perennial themes, the use of the noble lie. Todd McGowan argues in *The Fictional Christopher Nolan* that the characters in Nolan's movies "constantly find themselves deceived by others and caught up in a vast web of deceit that transcends individual lies."[17] McGowan further explains:

> In the filmic universe of Christopher Nolan, truth is neither relative nor non-existent. There is truth, but one arrives at it only by passing through the lie. Lies establish the path through which one discovers the truth, and one can make this discovery only by accepting and investing oneself in the lie. A lie establishes a fictional version of events that don't correspond to what is actually happening or what has happened. The problem with our usual conception of truth is that it separates truth from this fiction and views truth as an original state that fiction or deceit corrupts. But for Nolan's cinema, the link between truth and fiction always remains clear: if one wants to discover the truth, one must first succumb to the fiction that seems to obscure it.[18]

Nolan, according to Todd McGowan, tries "to develop a politically engaged filmmaking that takes up and makes explicit use of cinema's tendency toward the lie."[19] McGowan writes, "We cannot leave the fiction and enter reality. We live our lives within the fiction, and when we encounter truth, we necessarily do so from with the terrain of some controlling fiction."[20] Cooper then reveals that he was her "ghost," and she confirms that she knew it was him all along (*Interstellar* 2014). The "they" in the film are very likely Americans in the future who are using time travel to communicate with and ultimately save their "ancestors" (*Interstellar* 2014). This scene further emphasizes a parody of Michelangelo's Sistine Chapel creation painting by showing a hand-to-hand connection between Cooper in the tesseract and Amelia in the ship earlier in time. Murph further emphasizes her faith in Cooper's return: "People didn't believe me, they thought I'd done it all myself . . . But I knew who it was" (*Interstellar* 2014). The will of the American pilot is able, with the help of aliens or his descendants, to conquer space and time and return to his daughter. At the same time, Murph tells Coop to leave to join Brand. Brand is at station in which there is a torn American flag and a robot. It is an American colony on another planet. She buries Edmunds and adorns his tomb with his Nasa identification tag. Over shoots of Amelia, Murch narrates that "She's out there . . . Setting up camp . . . Alone in a strange galaxy . . . Maybe, right now, she's settling in for the long nap . . . By the light of our new sun . . . In our new home" (*Interstellar* 2014). Brand is an American colonist who has a new American flag above a base. Although not a film about a space race between China and the United States, Nolan's *Interstellar* ends with the triumph of America—implicitly above India and other rivals.

Christopher Nolan is one of the most important film directors of the twenty-first century. To argue that his films endorse "late capitalism" or "American hegemony" is not to argue that Nolan is reducible to merely being a propagandist. It is not further an attempt to belittle the achievements of the American space program, American astronauts, or even American patriotism. Rather, it is to argue that *Interstellar* is very much a political film. Like a host of other films of the Obama era, *Interstellar* opts for a softer vision of American global (or in the case, universal) hegemony. While films like *The Hurt Locker* and *Zero Dark Thirty* seemed to present violence and even torture as a potentially necessary evil, *Interstellar* omits celebration or war or even competition among nations. The older more aggressive and ruthless vison of American dominance reflecting the spirit of *The Right Stuff* and the Cold War as well as the Bush-era prosecution of the War on Terror is represented by the elder Professor Brand and Dr. Mann, who are willing to sacrifice billions of lives for the sake of "the mission." The younger Amelia Brand, Cooper, and Murph all are motivated by love. This love is directed toward individuals, but his particular love does not exclude all of humanity. This humanistic vision of love is the driving force for the political vision of the film, which is, like many sci-fi works, a film about saving the entire. Nonetheless, like many American Sci-Fi films, *Interstellar* projects a future in which America remains a "superpower" and is the country most successful in space travel, demonstrating that, in the twenty-first century, when American artists voyage into space in their creative works, they still end up discovering America.

NOTES

1. Williams, "How Steven Spielberg's Interstellar Would Have Been An Entirely Different Movie."
2. Qtd. in Shone, *The Nolan Variations*, 258.
3. Shone, *The Nolan Variations*, 262.
4. Vaz, *Interstellar*, 17.
5. Vaz, *Interstellar*, 71.
6. Vaz, *Interstellar*, 124.
7. Vaz, *Interstellar*, 147.
8. Ibid.
9. Hassler-Forest, *Capitalist Superheroes*, 2.
10. Hassler-Forest, *Capitalist Superheroes*, 3.
11. Hassler-Forest, *Capitalist Superheroes*, 11.
12. Cramer, "Hard Science Fiction," 189.
13. Fisher, *Capitalist Realism*, 18.
14. Žižek, *Welcome to the Desert of the Real!*, 17.
15. Attebey, "The Magazine Era: 1926–1960," 38.
16. Cramer, "Hard Science Fiction," 193.
17. McGowan, *The Fictional Christopher Nolan*, 1.
18. McGowan, *The Fictional Christopher Nolan*, 4–5.
19. McGowan, *The Fictional Christopher Nolan*, 10.
20. McGowan, *The Fictional Christopher Nolan*, 17.

Chapter 7

Recruiting Blackness in Christopher Nolan's *Tenet*

In February 2018, Marvel introduced its first Black-dominated superhero film, *Black Panther*. The film was met with overwhelmingly positive reviews and tremendous financial success. Many critics praised its Afrocentric casting.[1] However, at the same time, others questioned whether the film, drawn from a franchise created by someone outside of the Black community, Frank Miller, was an inauthentic commodification of Blackness.[2] Just as other films such as *Thor* sought to market and sell Scandinavian mythology to a diverse, global audience, so too was an African culture packaged and sold across the globe. *Black Panther* was part of a wider push across the United States to fill roles traditionally held by European Americans with African Americans as a means to attempting to redress previous exclusion as well as to market American pop culture to people of color across the globe. Christopher Nolan's 2020 *Tenet* is a just such a film that features a black American actor, John David Washington, as the mysterious "Protagonist," who travels across the globe in order to prevent global destruction. However, while Washington's Protagonist is a stoic and cool black James Bond, he ultimately takes the role (as do many of Christopher Nolan's characters) of a servant of the American Empire, battling its enemies and reverencing its institutions.

Tenet appears as a watershed film for the black community, highlighting the increasing prominence of African and especially historic black American population. Some have argued that Washington's role is the not so subtly depicted first black James Bond.[3] The film is replete with seemingly innumerable Bond tropes, which, for the past sixty years, has served as one of the principal archetypes for the postmodern male. *Tenet*, instead of featuring an Irish, Scottish, or English male, features a well-dressed and intelligent wise-cracking historic black American male who charms a beautiful Englishwoman while trying to stop a Ukrainian arms dealer named Andrei Sator (Kenneth Branagh), who is working with people in the future in order to try to stop climate change from severely damaging the earth. *Tenet* is filled with fake deaths, gorgeous (and grim) European landscapes, car chases, fights, and the "Bond girl" Kat Sator (Elizabeth Debicki). The film also, to the frustration of some critics and many viewers, features several "reversed" or "backwards" fight scenes in which the "future" and the "past" collide. On one level, John David Washington's rol is a suave, sophisticated, intelligent, and compassionate hero who battles criminal thugs and ends up, like James Bond, Jason Bourne, and Jack Ryan, saving the world. Indeed, at the end of the film, it is strongly suggested that Washington's Protagonist is himself the head of *Tenet*.

On the other hand, the film is about how a Black man sacrifices himself for the American intelligence community and what former president Dwight Eisenhower called "the military industrial complex." Black representation on film has always been about the tension between financial solvency and racial figuring. As Ed Guerro argues in *Framing Blackness*, film, especially from the 1980s forward, has been centered around moneymaking as opposed to cultural communication: "Instead of efforts to construct a truly universal system of communication that build egalitarian understandings between diverse groups and cultures, what we have seen arise in commercial cinema is a monopolistic, capital-intensive film business."[4] However, as Guerro further notes, it is not simply money that drives moviemaking. Rather, movies serve to uphold an ideological power structure in which blackness is framed, dominated and controlled, and "in almost every instance, the representation of black people on the commercial screen has amounted to one grand, multifaceted illusion. For blacks have been subordinated, marginalized, positioned, and devalued in every possible manner to glorify and relentlessly hold in place the white-dominated symbolic order and racial hierarchy of American society."[5] Guerro's point here is correct. However, his argument must be combined with a classist reading in which all symbolism and identity—whether Indigenous, African, Asian, or European—is subordinated to the logic of capital and the reigning power structure.

This power structure has traditionally subordinated black Americans but will readily provide the illusion of black cultural achievement if it has a pacifying effect on the black community or directs black anger toward a structure other than the center of power. In *Tenet* the black community (as well as the wider global community) is offered an illusory vision of power and prestige that can come to those few people willing and able to dedicate their lives to the perpetuation of the American capitalist system. Guerro further argues for the combined effects of "Hollywood's ideology of racial domination and difference that constructs black people as *other* and subordinate, while it naturalizes white privilege as the invisible but sovereign 'norm.' . . . " as well as "Hollywood's fiscal strategies and shifting economic fortunes, which dictate that the production of narrative cinema is a capital-intensive business and, above all else, must return enormous sums of money from the box office. . . . "[6] Hollywood traditionally has attempted to lure black people in to watch their films while, at the same time, conditioning and training black folks to be subordinates. This is entirely true for *Tenet*.

Tenet is, from start to finish, an endorsement of Black service to America. After a confusing opening scene in which he foils a terrorist attack on the Kiev Opera, the Protagonist eats what he thinks is a "suicide pill" offered by a fellow special forces figure (*Tenet* 2020). He thus appears to commit suicide as opposed to revealing information about his friends. This seems like a noble gesture, but we later learn when he awakens on a ship that it was a "test" as part of recruiting him as a member of Tenet. They man who tells him that it is a test is simply called "Fay" in the script and is played by Martin Donovan. Although raised Irish Catholic, Donovan effects a very Anglo-Saxon CIA figure. The scenes in which he tutors the Protagonist have been played out in innumerable spy and thriller films. There is the naïve recruit, who may come from an older Anglo-Saxon family, or be among the ethnic Catholics, or perhaps even a white southerner who is recruited into the shadowy world of espionage or deep politics. Certainly, characters played by Denzel Washington and Will Smith have been in this situation before, but while (especially with Smith's characters), there is an element of humor involved, the Protagonist plays a brooding and nihilistic character often given to white actors.

We even learn that his team was, in fact, killed. The mysterious Fay tells him that the team was killed and praises him. While others may have talked, he did not and, as Fay tells him, "You chose to die instead of giving up your colleagues" (*Tenet* 2020). When they are on the deck of the boat, Fay tells the Protagonist, "We all believe we'd run into the burning building, but until we feel that heat . . . we can never know. You do" (*Tenet* 2020). This point is critical for the Protagonist's character development and his existential growth. He has literally died for his friends (as well as the United States). Having realized that he has been duped into working for the United States, the Protagonist offers his resignation, but, in order to manipulate and recruit him for a new mission, Fay tells him, "You don't work for us—you're dead" (*Tenet* 2020). The "us" here is the Central Intelligence Agency. Fay further explains, "Your duty transcends national interests. This is about survival" (*Tenet* 2020). When the Protagonist asks whose survival, Fay cryptically responds: "Everyone's. There's a cold war. Cold as ice. To even know its true nature is to lose." This language is very cryptic, and we know that Christopher Nolan, director of *Memento* and *Inception*, thoroughly enjoys the leaving plot holes in a film intentionally to puzzle viewers. In the film, the new Cold War very much parallels the real-world Cold War 2.0 fought between the United States and Russia; indeed, the bulk of the villains in the movie are apparently Russians or at least Eastern Europeans. The heroes, in contrast, are Americans, Englishmen and women, Indians, and those people of color, such as the Protagonist, recruited by the United States in service of American interests. It is important to note, as Ed Guerro does about many other "black" films, that *Tenet* is a film about a Black man, but it is a film directed and produced by other ethnicities, for Black folks have "little institutional control over the production of their screen images."[7] In *Tenet* Fay further explains to the Protagonist that he can only give him a clue that will help navigate his way through his mission: "This is knowledge divided—all I have for you is a gesture— . . . —in combination with a word—'tenet.' Use it carefully, it'll open the right doors, but some of the wrong ones, too" (*Tenet* 2020). This adds an aura of mystery to the film. Neither we nor John David Washington's the Protagonist is given the name of the system he serves, but it is clearly the American-dominated West. Ultimately, Nolan perhaps intentionally leaves the reader with a lot of knowledge divided in the film, and like the "spinning top" scene in *Inception*, may not have an answer for exactly who John David Washington's Protagonist serves.

We are given further clues in the Protagonist's encounter with the physicist Barbara (Clémence Poesy). The Protagonist attempts to find out more about his mission by telling Barbara, "Well to do what I do, I need some idea of the threat we face" (*Tenet* 2020). Barbara explains, "As a understand it, we're trying to prevent World War Three" (*Tenet* 2020). Throughout the twentieth century, the potential for World War Three was a showdown between the United States and the Soviet Union via some sort of nuclear war. The Protagonist assumes as much when he asks, "Nuclear holocaust?" (*Tenet* 2020). Barbara responds, "No. Something worse" and proceeds to demonstrate what is happening via the inverted bullet (*Tenet* 2020). She explains about the bullet, "It's inverted—its entropy runs backwards. So, to our eyes, its movement is reversed. We think it's a type of inverse radiation, triggered by nuclear fission" (*Tenet* 2020). The language here is exceptionally convoluted and has inspired derision from audiences and critics alike. Barbara informs the Protagonist (and the audience) that these bullets are coming from "the future" and are among the "detritus of a coming war" (*Tenet* 2020). Throughout this scene, there is not flirting or romance; they are both dedicated professionals. She does school him in advanced physics preparing him for his service. As the plot unravels, John David Washington's Protagonist becomes a vehicle for recruitment of the increasingly diverse audience to fight Cold War 2.0.

When we are introduced to Mumbai, we see shots of "postmodern" high rises and then we see the Protagonist thrust amid a crowded market overflowing with commodities. This is the world of late or postmillennial capitalism. He is stranger in the Bombay Yacht Club, which is populated by Indian and

Anglo-Saxon elites. He meets the British intelligence agent Neil (Robert Pattinson) who has done his homework on the Protagonist (he knows the Protagonist likes Diet Coke). He further will guide the Protagonist to find the Indian arms dealer. While it may seem like India, Britain, and America are allied together as the plot unfolds, America ultimately plays the dominate role in the relationships. This dominance is displayed in the way in which the Protagonist utilizes various Indian characters. Neil and the Protagonist scale the wall of the Indian arms dealer (a sort of "border crossing") and overwhelm his security. After he accosts him, the Protagonist takes control, telling Sanjay, Priya's husband and supposed arms dealer: "You're an arms dealer, friend. This may be the easiest trigger I've had to pull" (*Tenet* 2020). This is an ironic act as the United States has itself shipped arms around the world fomenting revolutions. However, in the logic of the film, the CIA is a good arms dealer while its competitors are bad. American intelligence in this scene is further superior to British intelligence, for the Protagonist asks Priya if it is "safe to involve British intelligence" (*Tenet* 2020). It is Americans who are at the top. They further outfox the bungling Indian police as the Protagonist and Neil escape into the streets of Mumbai. Like Batman accosting Lau in Hong Kong in *The Dark Knight*, the representative of American power can cross borders and enforce its will.

There is, however, a new racial element in *Tenet* that is not present in the *Dark Knight* trilogy. With the exception of the scenes shot in Mumbai, throughout the film, John David Washington is a black man awash in a sea of whiteness. The opening scene in an entirely ethnically European opera in Kiev, a country with an extremely small African population. The airport scenes take place in Oslo, Norway, a Scandinavian country with a relatively small nonwhite population. The film further takes the viewer to the Amalfi Coast as well as Estonia. Curiously, in these scenes, the Protagonist's Blackness is entirely absent. He is ironically both like and unlike the alien of the science fiction, who often serves as figure for the ethnic other. As Elisabeth Anne Leonard notes, up until the early twenty-first century, sci-fi largely ignored the issue of race.[8] She further notes, that "the majority of sf deals with racial tension by ignoring it."[9] Other works, Leonard argues, make an "attempt to deal with racial issues by imagining a world where they are non-issues, where colour blindness is the norm."[10] This may be what Nolan is doing in *Tenet*, or the director may be ignoring John David Washington's blackness in the plot of the film while marketing the same blackness to the viewer. The Protagonist is profoundly alone and alienated from the world around him, but his blackness is never recognized or acknowledged. He is alone as man but not as a black man. He seems to fit in completely; there is no racial tension or commentary on race—either serious or comical. The Protagonist's isolation in the Windmill emphasizes his loneliness but not his blackness. He opens a duffle bag with a weapon sent to him by the CIA, which emphasizes the agencies ownership over him. He is further given a suicide pill, which we assume is a real one and not a "test" one like the previous one. His life is thus dedicated to service of the CIA. He is further training in modified military style. We learn that he had "basic training" as he reveals to Neil in the Bombay Yacht Club (*Tenet* 2020). He thus is ex-military. There is the sense that he is getting ready for his mission. He seamlessly boards a ship in the North Atlantic and gets into a car. There is one white man who briefly looks at him. There is no sense that this is a Black American man in the North Sea. As the scientist Barbara tells him when meeting in an anonymous Northern European country, "No small talk. Nothing that could reveal who we are what we do" (*Tenet* 2020). Both Barbara, an anonymous European woman and the Protagonist, an anonymous Black man are both in the service of the same network Americentric agencies (CIA, NATO, etc.).

Washington is, throughout these scenes, effectively anonymous. He is simply there as a "CIA agent," or Protagonist. While his strength and intelligence are show cased in the film, and, like James Bond, he is rewarded with adventure and luxury items, he nonetheless remains in the service of the American system. Moreover, granting Washington's Protagonist some power and agency does not necessarily represent a radical step in black culture, for, as Ed Guerro writes, "popular cinema is an integral part of the commodity system itself, vulnerable to economic ups and downs and the twists of right and left cycles."[11] Thus, this power given to the Protagonist is only illusory, and, in *Tenet*, it is power meant to be placed back in the service of American global power. It is further curious that the Protagonist is almost the lone black man in the film, thus keeping in line with what Ed Guerro calls "Hollywood's ongoing repression or containment of the collective."[12] John David Washington is thus another example of "the narrative isolation of the black star," which, like all Hollywood stars, serve as "supreme icons and incarnations of the rootless, decultured 'individual' in industrial consumer society."[13] Moreover, there are no Eddie Murphy or Chris Rock-esque jokes or Richard Pryor comments to defuse to the tension, which at the same time surprisingly does not exist. Like Eddie Murphy before him, John David Washington is in "white milieus" and "white environments and narratives" but does not bring the black humor and wit of Murphy.[14]

There are a few points in the film, however, at which the Protagonist's blackness is highlighted. When he first goes to the members club in England to see Sir Michael Crosby. The host abruptly stops the Protagonist with some degree of racial tension. However, the conflict is framed in the scene more in terms of class than race. When the Protagonist announces that he is "Mr. Crosby's lunch," the Steward remarks, "I presume you mean Sir Michael Crosby's lunch?" (*Tenet* 2020). The "owning" of an Englishman over the question of titles is a standard debate between Americans and the British. However, the debate over titles is not historically a conflict between black America and England; the same testy interchange has occurred between white American and British actors in a host of films. There is a primarily class friction between the host and the Protagonist as well as between Sir Michael Crosby. Noticing his inferior suit choice, Crosby states, "Look, no offence, but this is a world where someone claiming to be a billionaire . . . Brooks Brothers won't cut it" (*Tenet* 2020). The Protagonist responds, "I'm assuming I have a budget" (*Tenet* 2020). Crosby reaches for the incredible and invincible Anglo-American power, the power of credit, tossing the Protagonist a credit card and saying, "Save the world, then we'll balance the books" (*Tenet* 2020). Crosby asks, "Can I recommend a tailor?" (*Tenet* 2020). The Protagonist pluckily responds, "I'll manage. You British don't have a monopoly on snobbery, you know" (*Tenet* 2020). Crosby ends the conversation with "Not a monopoly. More of a controlling interest." All this language in such an opulent scene (preceded by an opulent scene in Mumbai) is indicative of the Anglo-American world order that the Protagonist serves. The Protagonist even adds the "Sir" to Michael Crosby at the end of the lunch as a sign of respect and deference (*Tenet* 2020).

However, these scenes could just as easily work with a white American actor riling the people from whom his ancestor's rebelled. The members club is weirdly an amalgamation of the bourgeois values of Sidney Poitier films joined with the decadence of blaxploitation. It is a panoply of both wealth and good manners that are enjoyed by the global elite and which can be granted to those members of the black community who dedicate themselves to the Anglo-American system that supports it. Like Eddie Murphy in *Trading Places*, the Protagonist is "integrated into the capitalist class" and "has fully internalized their values."[15] It is further curious that Crosby and the Protagonist talk about a "fake" painting. After looking in a shopping bag, the Protagonist announces, "You're carrying a Goya in a Harrods bag?" (*Tenet* 2020). Crosby says, "It's a fake, by a Spaniard named Arepo. One of two we confiscated from an embezzler in Bern" (*Tenet* 2020). The other one was purchased by Sator. The Protagonist asks, "Does she know it's a forgery?" (*Tenet* 2020). To which Crosby hints that Kat and Arepo are having an affair. The notion of forgery is especially pertinent to a spy novel. It is further pertinent to Sir Michael Crosby's command to the Protagonist to go incognito as a billionaire. However, it is also the Protagonist who is a forged product, a servant of the wealthy Anglo-American elite (who is also, at the same time, saving the world). This scene is followed by that of a wealthy English public school as Kat picks up her son. This is the world of Anglo-American elite that the Protagonist must serve.

In contrast to the diverse and humanistic (but occasionally violent) Anglo-American world order is the nefarious Eastern Europeans. The fact that the Ukraine is the site of conflict is curious especially considering the recent conflict that was, even during the film's production, reaching a crescendo. As some critics have noted, the scene in the Kiev opera house could have been entirely contrived simply to recruit the Protagonist.[16] However, we read the scene as at least somehow sincerely involving Russian terrorists, then what we have is battle between US forces aiding partially corrupted Ukrainian officials to stop a Russian terrorist attack (possibly connected with the Russian government?). If it is all staged then we have a very Christopher Nolan-esque reading of the political events of reality as being largely dramatized show piece concealing the true nature of geopolitics, a reading that the script later confirms when Neil discusses how the people of the world do not realize how close they come to destruction because such events are hidden.

Regardless of whether or not the scene is staged—perhaps the best and very Christopher Nolan-esque answer is that the whole film is "staged" and the Protagonist is not a Black or American subject but in fact simply a human subject living the fantasy of saving the world from climate change—the movie, nonetheless, depicts Eastern Europeans as the enemy in a Cold War 2.0 scenario. Andrei Sator is the exact opposite of the Protagonist. Andrei uses and threatens severe violence against Kat while the Protagonist saves her and gives her a signature kiss on the cheek. Both the West and the East engage in arms trafficking, but the West is redeemed by its ultimately noble goal of saving the world while Adrei Sator is principally concerned with himself. Both the West and the East use violence; however, the East uses more severe violence with Sator beating a man to death with a gold brick while the Protagonist uses kitchen implements to maim his attackers.

The East is further a sick place full of waste and ruin while the West is an opulent and sunny world full of Goya paintings, English public schools, and advanced technology. In their dinner meeting in an English club, Sir Michael Crosby explains to the Protagonist, that Sator had grown up in a "closed" or "secret" city in the Soviet Union. This city is given a mysterious John Lacarré-esque narrative as Sir Michael notes, "In the seventies our people estimated its population at almost 200,000. Unacknowledged to this day. Thought to be abandoned" (*Tenet* 2020). This passage is key, for Sator represents the old Cold War spy narrative. Andrei Sator is a ghost from the past of Soviet incompetence and coverups, which the advanced and humanistic West was monitoring. After the Protagonist questions how it was abandoned, Sir Michael explains that it was "Some kind of accident. After which we think it became a site for underground tests." In a Chernobyl like accident, the incompetent Soviets committed a faux pas in which possibly thousands were killed and then covered it up. This past still haunts as some nuclear mischief is afoot as Sir Michael explains, "Just two weeks ago, same day as the Kiev Opera siege, our satellites detected a detonation in north-west Siberia, about where we think Stalsk-12 was" (*Tenet* 2020). Like a Marvel villain, Sator comes from the Cold War past of nuclear disasters and coverup. As Sir Michael narrates, "Sator emerged from this blank sport on the map with an ambition that eventually led him here, to buy his way into the British establishment" (*Tenet* 2020). There is a reference here to the tug of war between the United States and Russia for influence in England. Sator has married into the British establishment. Moreover, not unlike the American West, Sator is attempting to seize the cultural capital of Europe, as Sir Michael explains, "Like a lot of wealthy criminals, he thinks if he covers his walls with tasteful, expensive things it'll distract from the bloodshed. Judging by the lovely girl he married, there might be something in it" (*Tenet* 2020). As during the first Cold War, the West and East battle over who is the true preserver of culture. As the film progresses, we later learn that Sator as a figure for the East is threatening the very existence of the world just as earlier Soviet leaders had.

After the Protagonist saves Sator's life, they continue to discuss the nuclear event that led to Sator. The Protagonist attempts to explain details of nuclear physics, but Sator responds, "I know what it means. You lecture me about radiation. Andrei Sator, digging plutonium from the rubble of my city as a teenager?" (*Tenet* 2020). After the Protagonist questions where Sator grew up, Sator explains that his "home" was Stalsk-12. He describes the "accident" to which Sir Michael Crosby referred: "One pod of a warhead explored at ground level, scattering the others. They needed people to find the plutonium" (*Tenet* 2020). This story of rags to riches of a Russian oligarch who takes advantage of the incompetence of the Soviet Union very much resembles the ruling clique who gained power over Russia in the '90s and who melted into the Putin regime of the 2000s. As Sator explains, this is how he began his rise to power, "It became my first contract—nobody else even bid. They thought it was a death sentence. . . . But one man's probability of death is another man's possibility for a life. . . . I staked my claim in the new Russia. Even now, my company is the only one to operate in the ruins" (*Tenet* 2020). This language is very careful and telling. Sator's corrupt weapons dealing and cooperation with the future got its start in cleaning up the mess of the Soviet Union. Although Ukrainian, Sator is linked to "the new Russia," which in the mind of the audience is linked with Boris Yeltsin but, more prominently in the twenty-first century, with Vladimir Putin (*Tenet* 2020). The east is a dirty and corrupt, literally toxic place. The West, despite its lies and corruption (which Nolan treats through the figure of Gotham in the *Dark Knight* trilogy), is a place of sunlight and prosperity decorated with art and modernist Scandinavian airports. Later the special forces officers Ives further explains during a briefing in the Tenet camp that Stalsk-12 is "Hidden from the world" and a "city where anything can happen . . . " (*Tenet* 2020). The notion is this was the ground zero for a post–Cold War future. Sator gets in contact with the future to help to destroy the past, and it is up to the Protagonist and the mysterious group Tenet to save the world from the machinations of this representative of Slavdom. Like Jim Brown fighting German National Socialists in 1967's *The Dirty Dozen*, John David Washington is a black man in the service of American military interests on the European continent.

There is some question of the identity of Tenet. It appears to be for most the film a larger British and American operation. We know that the Protagonist worked for the CIA, and there is some sense that this is a similar Western intelligence operation. Neil introduces the British Special Forces character Ives, telling him: "He's one of us—" (*Tenet* 2020). The Protagonist asks, throwing Neil against a wall, "Us?! Who are these guys?" (*Tenet* 2020). Neil responds, "Priya's. Ours" (*Tenet* 2020). We hear, "Lying is standard operating procedure" (*Tenet* 2020). This point is true for both the secret society of Tenet and the secret society of filmmakers and the secret societies of real-world geopolitics. When talking about the Protagonist allegedly giving Sator a piece of the algorithm, the Protagonist states, "What's happened's happened. I get it, now. But it's tough to take things on trust from people speaking half-truths" (*Tenet* 2020). The Protagonist states, "You were part of this before we met. Were you working for Priya?" (*Tenet* 2020). Neil responds, "No" (*Tenet* 2020). However, the Protagonist continues, asking him, "Who recruited you, Neil?" (*Tenet* 2020). Neil responds, "It can't possibly do you any good to know that right now. When this is over, if we're still standing and you still care, you can hear my life story, okay?" (*Tenet* 2020). This is an authorial trick, of course. The Protagonist was recruited by whomever Christopher and Jonathan Nolan write he was recruited by. *Tenet* is a puzzle film, but it is also a "choose your own adventure" puzzle film in which the audience is invited to participate and shape their own futures. During this scene, Kat serves as a figure for the audience who asks, "You need to tell me what's going on" (*Tenet* 2020). The Protagonist responds, "Apparently, Neil here knows more about it than I do" (*Tenet* 2020). Neil as the Englishman serves as the source of information initiating the Protagonist and the viewer into the film's secrets. Neil has the upper hand in this white and Black "buddy drama" in as much as he has more information (even though he is working, ultimately, for the Protagonist himself). As a result, according to the logic of buddy films, Neil is the tutoring racial other, who "could personally teach his wounded, misguided, and emotionally insolvent buddies how to match his emotional competence."[17]

As Neil explains to the wounded Kat what happened, we learn the details of the plot of the algorithm, which has one function, as Neil says: "Inversion.

But not objects or people. The world around us" (*Tenet* 2020). This is a clue to understanding the film. The future wants to destroy the past. It is the same revolutionary ethos as Bane's revolution. Neil further explains, "As they invert the entropy of more and more objects . . . The two directions of time are becoming more intertwined . . . But because the environment's entropy flows in our direction. . . . .. we dominate. They're always swimming upstream" (*Tenet* 2020). When Kat asks what happens if the entropy of the world is inverted, "the entropy of the world" (*Tenet* 2020), Neil responds "end of play" (*Tenet* 2020). When the Protagonist asks him to be "more precise" (*Tenet* 2020), Neil explains, "Our present wiped out, our past obliterated. Everyone and everything who ever lived destroyed instantly. Precise enough?" (*Tenet* 2020). The future is attempting to destroy the past with the help of a villainous Eastern European arms dealer. In this monumental struggle, a Black American is allied with an Englishman and Englishwoman in order to save the world.

Neil tells the Protagonist that he did not warn him that they would be going to the past and that the Protagonist fought against his future self in the vault. He explains, "With things the same, I knew you'd be okay. What's happened's happened. If I'd told you and you acted differently . . . who knows? The policy is to suppress" (*Tenet* 2020). Neil that strangely initiates him further into the fold of Tent. The Protagonist asks, "Whose policy?" (*Tenet* 2020). Neil responds, "Ours, my friend. We're the people saving the world from what might have been . . . " (*Tenet* 2020). This is curious, for perhaps the Protagonist, like the audience, is merely supposed to think of himself as the architect, but, as with *Memento* and *Inception*, it's all an allusion.

When Priya explains how the future Oppenheimer rebels against the future and splits the algorithm into nine sections, we get a vision of the new post-War on Terror multipolar world. Priya explains that the future scientist broke up the algorithm and gave it to the world's nine nuclear powers, as she states, "There are nine nuclear powers. Nine bombs. Nine sets of the most closely guarded materials in the history of the world. The best hiding places possible" (*Tenet* 2020). This is a profound symbol of the new normal of a multipolar. Sator, however, is trying to bring back a unipolar world in which one figure, an Eastern European, has all the power in the world. As Priya explains, "Sator's lifelong mission, financed and guided by the future, has been to find and reassemble the algorithm" (*Tenet* 2020). When the Protagonist asks why the future chose Sator, Priya explains, "The necessary combination of greed and ambition. But mostly, he was in the right place at the right time" (*Tenet* 2020). The Protagonist says, "The collapse of the Soviet Union," while Priya adds, "The most insecure moment in the history of nuclear weapons" (*Tenet* 2020). This is an important point, for in it, we see the projected future for the world at the end of history. Either the West and its allies triumph in a multi-polar world or a villainous East takes control of the future.

Many characters in the film tell the Protagonist that he has to "look at the world in a new way" (*Tenet* 2020). This primarily means that he must see things in nonlinear sense. However, when he reveals he has learned to be able to manipulate Sator with Kat's death, Priya tells him, "You have started looking at the world in a new way" (*Tenet* 2020). This is, as we will see, the initiation of the audience as well. The Protagonist, however, begins to act with his own agency, as he says, "And now it's your turn," warning Priya about executing Kat (*Tenet* 2020). Like Batman taking knowledge from the East, the Protagonist (as a touchstone for the viewers) draws from those around him drawing from their information, but tempering it with liberal humanism, emphasizing justice over what is viewed as unnecessary violence.

Coming to an understanding of the death of Sator, the Protagonist states, "In effect, his death activates the algorithm. He dies, the world ends—no one dares kill him" (*Tenet* 2020). This is a very curious scene, for in it we have a potentially potent symbol. If Sator is the symbol of the reactionary European male world order, his defeat by an English female and a historic black American male is profoundly significant. Kat, however, notes, "No, you've missed the point. He's intending to end his life" (*Tenet* 2020). She further explains, "He's dying. Inoperable pancreatic cancer" (*Tenet* 2020). The protagonist then compliments, "And he's taking the world with him." This places Sator as a profound symbol of the Old World, Western Civilization, premodern masculinity, whiteness, Europe, or a host of other authoritarian symbols. They are allegedly dying and threaten to take the world with them. In response, the future, represented by a black American male (and Neil, a young Britain) must help kill the threatening reactionary menace.

Near the end of the film, Sator undergoes an (almost parodic) apotheosis as the dreaded (Eastern European) reactionary villainous white god in his phone conversation with the Protagonist. Sator describes his relationship with radiation: "My fate was always bound up with radiation. We'd work where no one else would. We made a devil's bargain—money for time. We sold our futures" (*Tenet* 2020). In this scene, Sator becomes something like a supervillain whose powers grew from radiation. He is also the archetypal rival to American capitalism: the oligarch who build his fortune from the ruins of the Soviet Union and whose wealth and power challenges America for global supremacy. The Ukrainian arms dealer's tremendous power—as a potential figure for Russian power in general is a threat to world peace as the Protagonist himself states, "Now you're making the same mistake for the entire world" (*Tenet* 2020). Power in the hands of rivals of the Anglosphere—including the Indian Priya—is a threat to world peace. It can be only in the hands of America and her closest allies. Like the Joker and Bane in the *Dark Knight* trilogy, Sator defends himself by trying to undermine the Protagonist's confidence in his cause. Sator states, "It wasn't a mistake. I made the bargain I could. What was yours? You fight for a cause you barely understand. With people you trust so little you've told them nothing about what you're doing. When I die the world dies with me. And your knowledge dies with you. Buried in the tomb like an anonymous Egyptian builder sealed in the pyramid to keep his secret. . . . " (*Tenet* 2020). Branagh's Sator's nihilism is not as alluring as Bane or the Joker's, but his words are consistent with Nolan's villains' attempts to undermine Nolan's heroes' self-confidence by pointing to legitimate criticism of chinks in the tattered armor of the wider American project. Sator tells him, "Your faith is blind. You're a fanatic" (*Tenet* 2020). These lines have been used—especially in the more recent Daniel Crag iterations—of the James Bond series to demoralizes the (usually white) protagonist who still clings to a tattered vision of the British or American Empires that are in a state of free fall collapse. The Protagonist's response is ultimately: "What's more fanatical than trying to destroy the world?" (*Tenet* 2020). Sator's reply seems better: "I'm not. I'm creating a new one. Somewhere, sometime, a man in a crystalline tower throws a switch and Armageddon is both triggered and avoided. Entropy inverts the same way the magnetic poles have switched times over the millennia. Now time itself switches direction. The same sunshine we've basked in will warm the faces of our descendants generations from now" (*Tenet* 2020). In much-derided passage, Sator explains why the future wants to destroy the past: "Because their oceans rose and their rivers ran dry. Don't you see—? Their world shriveled because of us. They have no choice but to turn back, there's no life ahead of them. And we're responsible. Knowing this, do you still want me to stop?" (*Tenet* 2020). The future is attempting to repair the past by working with a sadistic madman, who himself threatens to destroy the world. The Protagonist retorts, "Yes. Each generation looks out for its own survival" (*Tenet* 2020). Sator responds, "That's exactly what they're doing" (*Tenet* 2020). The Protagonist does not present a convincing rebuttal: "Sure, but not you. You're a traitor. Bringing death to all because you have no life of your own left" (*Tenet* 2020). The Protagonist argues, "You don't believe in God. Or a new future. Or anything outside your own experience" (*Tenet* 2020). The checkmate in this argument is that idea that a new future can be created by the present. Perhaps this is one of the keys to understanding the intellectual core of the film. Sator's future is very much tied to his own will, which is fundamentally selfish and cruel. The Protagonist and the Tenet group fight for an alternative future guided by an Anglo-American system guided by a black American who serves that system.

The future is projected in many different directions, and there is a future that seems to be determined, but it can be changed by the ingenuity of the Protagonist. At this point in history, the triumph of a tolerant and liberal future is to be gained by a historical Black American guiding a very Anglo-American centered secret society to stop a Ukrainian oligarch from destroying the world. Sator is a villain because he is violent sadistic and fundamentally selfish, as he says that he only has his own experience: "That's all any of us knows. The rest is belief, and I don't have it" (*Tenet* 2020). The Protagonist states, "Without it you're not human. You're a madman" (*Tenet* 2020). However, Sator states, "Or a god of sorts" (*Tenet* 2020). Sator is also a threat because he is a foreign base of power. There are others in the film, including the Protagonist, who readily use violence. However, they, like Batman, use violence for allegedly humanistic purposes that serve the wider Anglo-American order. Sator's problem is that he represents the old world of violence, selfishness, and tyranny. Sator thus, like Bane in *The Dark Knight Rises*, must be executed and buried, just as the past must.

The scene in which Kat kills Sator has an odd (white) black widow sense to it that feels as out of place as John David Washington's own American blackness in the film. Kat's revenge is predicted earlier in the film. It is done sadistically not simply to save the world but to provide the most pain and humiliation for him. As Kat says to him, "I can't let you think you've won . . . " (*Tenet* 2020). When he asks her what she is talking about, she responds, I'm not letting you go to your grave thinking we're all coming with you. I can't give you that—" (*Tenet* 2020). She continues, "You're dying alone, Andrei" (*Tenet* 2020). He responds contemptuously, "No, I'm not" (*Tenet* 2020). She says, "Andrei, look in my eyes. Which do you see, despair . . . or anger? What?" (*Tenet* 2020). Sator cannot respond. Kat says, "I'm not the woman who could find love for you even though you'd scarred her on the inside . . . I'm the vengeful bitch you scarred on the outside," and then kills him (*Tenet* 2020). Like the film's presentation of American blackness, this scene as feminist triumph over cruel and aggressive masculinity fails precisely because of its lack of authenticity and sincerity. It further fails as the recruitment of American white femininity in the service of the wider service of American liberalism, which Kathryn Bigelow so famously presented with Jessica Chastain in *Zero Dark Thirty*.

At the end, the British special forces figure (and curiously named) Ives argues that the team should hide the pieces of the algorithm and separately commit suicide: "We hide it, we end our lives, It's the only way to be sure. But as to when . . . Maybe that's every man's decision to make for himself" (*Tenet* 2020). This line, in tangent with the rest of the script, is an invitation to the viewer to shape the future; however, it further contains within it elements of Sator's own self-destructive nihilism. Ives is dedicated to the cause of protecting the present from one possible future. However, he, like Sator and other heroes, anti-heroes, villains in the Nolan-verse pushing his ideas too far, is willing to commit suicide in order to hide information. The fact that it's "every man's decision to make for himself" hints at the heart of Nolan's quasi-libertarian existential credo: reality can and often is shaped for us by others; however, we can shape it ourselves (*Tenet* 2020). Thus, we are all protagonists of the future. Although one future is on its way to being determined—in the film, at least, a future in which the earth is poisoned by industrial pollution, this future is not set in stone. Individuals can take the initiative to repair the future that might be.

At the same time, at the end of the film, Neil recognizes that the Protagonist is principally concerned with Kat, asking the Protagonist if he is going to check on her. The Protagonist states in response: "Of course not. That would be too dangerous" (*Tenet* 2020). Kat serves not simply as the (literal) white goddess or adorned European beauty of the film; she has a great deal of political significance as well. She is a wealthy member of the British aristocracy. She is a mother and is providing the next generation of British aristocrats. Neil then sacrifices himself by going back in to complete the task. The Protagonist calls out to him, "Neil, wait." Neil replies, "We just saved the world—we can't leave anything to chance" (*Tenet* 2020). This is a profound scene that places the future in the hand of subjects. The Protagonist asks him, "But can we change things? If we do it differently . . . ?" (*Tenet* 2020). This is the big question in which the characters as well as the viewers of the film must have. Like Leonard Shelby in Nolan's *Memento* and *Following's* Dominick Cobb, they must have confidence that their actions have meaning.

We finally get the revelation that Neil himself is the Protagonist. The Protagonist asks Neil, "You never did tell me who recruited you" (*Tenet* 2020). Neil answers, "Haven't you guessed by now? You did. Just not when you thought. You have a future in the past. Years ago for me. Years from now for you" (*Tenet* 2020). This scene had been foreshadowed by the Protagonists slow development to and embrace of his identity as the Protagonist of the film. He has slowly gained knowledge as well as strength and convinced. As a figure for the viewer him or herself. He says, that this a temporal pincer, while the Protagonist asks, "Whose?" (*Tenet* 2020). Neil responds "Yours. You're only halfway there I'll see you at the beginning, friend" (*Tenet* 2020). Neil's voice then rings, "We're the people saving the world from what might have been . . . The world will never know what could've happened . . . and even if they did they wouldn't care . . . because no one cares about the bomb that didn't go off . . . " (*Tenet* 2020). There is a sense that like Batman, the silent protector, the Black led but very Anglo-American *Tenet* represents the Western forces of liberalism, which are keeping the reactionary past at bay.

The ending of the film is curious. Kat is walking and notices a suspicious car. In it is Priya and some sort of assassin whom Priya instructs, "Do it before the boy comes out" (*Tenet* 2020). The assassin is quickly killed by the Protagonist who jumps in the back seat, getting the upper hand over Priya.

The Protagonist questions her, "That's your idea of mercy?" (*Tenet* 2020). He further emphasizes that Priya gave him his word, but she responds to him, "And I told you what it would be worth" (*Tenet* 2020). This scene is curious, for the Protagonist is at first acting as the Batman-like defender of humanism. He is watching over Kat, a member of the British aristocracy (a symbol of the Anglo-American "West") who was temporarily seduced by a Ukrainian arms dealer (a symbol of the "East"). Priya tries to justify herself saying, "I have to tie up the loose ends" (*Tenet* 2020). At this point, the scene changes and the mood of the setting radically shifts as the brutal killer. The Protagonist states, "That was never your job" (*Tenet* 2020). Priya seems genuinely confused, asking "Then whose was it?" (*Tenet* 2020). The Protagonist states, "Mine. I realized I wasn't working for you. We've both been working for me . . . I'm the protagonist" (*Tenet* 2020). This is another key to the film, for Nolan here is suggesting that the Protagonist has the power to shift the future and shift reality. We are all directors of our own film. Curiously Priya submits to him, stating, "Then you'd better tie up those loose ends" (*Tenet* 2020). He then kills her saying, "Mission accomplished" (*Tenet* 2020). Like Eddie Murphy in *48 Hours*, the Protagonist upholds "the values of the dominant society" and, like other Black and white buddy cop films, "the black makes a sacrifice to solve problems the white man defines."[18] This mission is accomplished, but the implication in *Tenet*, like that of *The Dark Knight* trilogy's recruitment of Joseph Gordon-Levitt's Robin, is that the war must go on, and this war must be won by the American-led West.

Ultimately, the wider African diaspora as well as the wider world stands at a key juncture in the current era. No longer do we live in the "end of history" or even in Mark Fisher's "capitalism realism" in which American capitalism exercises unlimited full spectrum dominance over the world order. The rise of a host of various extremist movements online and the real world as well as the increasingly influence of various rightist regimes in Latin America, Europe, and Asia as well as the worldwide emergence populist movements within the United States has led to a tumultuous situation. The future is, indeed, very much unwritten.

The increasing presence of African and black people in media across the globe can be viewed as part of a just framing of blackness, but, in the end, it is, on one level, part of a wider desire to recruit the black community in the service of what still remains one of the dominant world systems: American neoliberal late capitalism. The Anglo-American filmmaker Christopher Nolan's works are complex and many layered and do not easily yield to facile categorization. Nolan's *Tenet* is no exception to this statement and, while the film does, in one sense, showcase the first "black James Bond," it also, like the previous James Bonds who utilized English, Irish, and Welsh actors, nonetheless presents them as servants of the (late) British (and American) Empire. Like a host of other ethnicities who have played the role of the "spy," John David Washington's "the Protagonist" is, in *Tenet*, ultimately a servant of empire and power. He must sacrifice his physical and mental health in the service of an Anglo-American or Western European dominated world. Despite its redeeming qualities, *Tenet* is, in the end, a film in which the subaltern still is unable to speak.

NOTES

1. Truitt, "Daring, Diverse 'Black Panther' promises to be Hollywood's latest 'cultural touchstone.'" Wong (Omowale), "The Black Panther and Neo-Colonial Politics in Africa"; Babb, "The Past is Never Past: The Call and Response between Marvel's *Black Panther* and Early Black Speculative Fiction"; Niessen, "Black Panther Transmedia: The Revolution Will Not Be Streamed."
2. Cobb, "'Black Panther' and the Invention of 'Africa.'"
3. Matadeen, "Tenet Basically Gives Hollywood Its First Black James Bond"; Ponniah, "Tenet Was Secretly 2020's James Bond Movie: Every 007 Trope Explored"; Abiona, "*Tenet:* It's Ambitious, Glossy and the Black James Bond We've Been Waiting For."
4. Guerro, *Farming Blackness*, 2.
5. Ibid.
6. Guerro, *Farming Blackness*, 5.
7. Guerro, *Framing Blackness*, 44.
8. Leonard, "Race and Ethnicity in Science Fiction," 253.
9. Leonard, "Race and Ethnicity in Science Fiction," 254.
10. Ibid.
11. Guerro, *Framing Blackness*, 56.
12. Guerro, *Framing Blackness*, 127.
13. Ibid.
14. Guerro, *Framing Blackness*, 128–29.
15. Guerro, *Framing Blackness*, 132.
16. Farnell, "Tenet Opening Scene Explained, 2021.
17. Russworm, *Blackness is Burning*, 51.
18. Guero, *Framing Blackness: The African American Image in Film*, 131.

Conclusion

The Shining Forth of Truth in Christopher Nolan's Insomnia

Largely known for his blockbusters such as the *Dark Knight* trilogy and *Dunkirk*, Christopher Nolan, in fact, began his movie career as a director of small arthouse films, as well as one "medium budget" neo-noir. Nolan's 2002 *Insomnia* is usually forgotten by critics and viewers (outside of diehard Nolan or film noir fans) as well. This may seem odd, for the film starred three titans of contemporary cinema: Al Pacino, Robin Williams, and Hillary Swank, who herself would become one of the most important actresses of the twenty-first century. The film is widely considered excellent (it has a 92 percent fresh rating on Rotten Tomatoes). It is further is a unique twist on the noir genre: it is set during summer in Alaska when the sun is constantly out. J. L. A. Garcia, in one of the few academic articles on *Insomnia,* sees this light as an essential element of the moral fabric of the film, arguing notes that a "bright glare" appears throughout the film, "which might eventually facilitate vision but at first only blinds and dizzies both the characters and us viewers."[1] McGowan notes that *Insomnia,* "the exploration of the lie occurs within a summertime artic setting that allows for no darkness."[2] This is ironic because most of Western philosophy has associated truth with light.[3] However, this is precisely Nolan's point. As McGowan notes, the film seems to suggest "the truth will always manifest itself."[4]

There are a number of very Nolan-esque elements to the film, including the papering over of a painful truth with a seemingly necessary lie, the question of whether or not certain characters that torment the protagonist are "real," and a meta-commentary on filmmaking itself. On the other hand, the film is perhaps Nolan's most derivative work. *Insomnia* is a remake of an earlier 1997 Scandinavian film of the same name starring Stellan Skarsgård and directed by Erik Skjoldbjærg. The original script for Nolan's remake was also crafted by Hillary Seitz, although Nolan claims to have had a great deal of influence on the script. Nolan himself notes to Tom Shone that the film is one his "personal" films.[5] Indeed, with its upending plot twist, nonlinear structure, and deeply philosophical subtext, *Insomnia* very much bears the marks of Nolan's skillful hand. However, *Insomnia* is perhaps the most atypical of Nolan's films. There is no deep plot twist at the end, the structure is perfectly linear, and despite some insomnia-induced hallucinations does not deal deeply with the issue of the nature of reality and consciousness (although comments from Nolan himself seem to contest this view). In conversation with Tom Shone, Nolan notes that he explained Finch's role to Robin Williams, nothing that "the guy could be unreal' as in, he might not exist" or he "is Dormer's conscience" or the ghosts in Macbeth, "where it's all about the central character's guilt and his self-destructiveness, essentially. Finch just whispers in his ear to point out things he already knows, or should already know.'"[6] Moreover, with its deeply upsetting themes of the murder of children, the film resonates more with other films from the same era. The film ultimately feels and looks like a well-wrought and intelligent Hollywood thriller.

However, what is perhaps most unique about the film is its strong affirmation of the concept of truth in the face of lies and deception. Indeed, the film's plot presents honesty and sincerity as its moral underpinning. There is clearly a shift in the moral tenor from the first film to Nolan's remake. Garcia calls the Nolan remake a "moral drama."[7] McGowan argues that Nolan changes *Insomnia* from its original "unrelenting pessimism" to "what resembles a standard moralistic thriller" that ends in Dormer's "punishment through death."[8] Like all of Nolan's films, there are various lies and degrees of self-deception as well as deception of others—in *Insomnia* this concepted is developed around the question of Will Dormer's reputation. Moreover, there is a great deal of questioning of the relationship between what is written about someone and who that person really is—in *Insomnia*, there is a discrepancy between what is written in police reports, which are themselves used to convict alleged criminals, and what is really true. However, in the end, the truth is revealed, and this truth shines forth with varnish or typical Nolan-esque irony or illusion.

The film begins with detective Will Dormer flying in a plane with his partner Hap. Will is nodding in and out of sleep with flashbacks of what looks like blood leaking through a bandage as well as autopsy photos. Will's Partner Hap says, "There's just nothing down there" (*Insomnia* 2002). This sets up the idea of another "nihilistic" noir film; however, Hap is not quite correct, for there is something, the truth, that seeks to burst through the paper of lies. In this medley of shots and dream sequences in *Insomnia*, the plane is flying over the Columbia glacier near Valdez, Alaska. Glaciers play an important role in *Batman Begins* as well as *Interstellar* as places where the protagonist learns some (usually harsh) truth. In this case, LA police detective Will Dormer is being haunted by a curious and very Nolan-esque truth. As we later learn in the film, the scenes of blood leaking are references to Will putting blood samples of a victim on the clothes of a murder on whom the police do not have enough evidence. Will is further reading from a newspaper mentioning the Internal Affairs investigation by which he is being targeted. For Garcia, the forest at the beginning represents "almost unimaginably lush, verdant forest—hinting at the possibility of an inner peace to match this idyllic glimpse—then plunges into impenetrable fog."[9] This point is key to understanding the film, for Will's own internal affairs are themselves torturing him. Garcia notes that "the moral struggle" that "occurs is an internal affair, something within the agent's soul, not a matter of results in the external world—not even the number of lives lost and saved."[10] There is a truth that needs to be revealed and which is torturing Will. At one point, his partner Hap says, "Cheer up, will ya?" (*Insomnia* 2002). Whereas, Dormer responds, "Tell that to her partner," showing a picture of Kay's corpse (*Insomnia* 2002). This scene demonstrates Dormer's seriousness as well as somber, noirish character of the film. The pilot says, "Better hang on, guys. It's going to get rough again" (*Insomnia* 2002). This is literally a reference to the plane, but it is a reference to another tough crime they will have to face. The town is called "Nightmute," which as critics have noted, is a little bit too "on the nose," but that as J. L. A. Garcia notes it is in silence paradoxically that the truth is uncovered. This opening scene is meant to be deceptive, ultimately tricking the viewer into thinking that the blood spots are associated with the murder currently about to be investigated. There is an intimate connection in the film between what we learn is the Dobbs case and the Connell case, and we can assume that the Connell case, "which acts as the second trauma effectively reviving the effect of the earlier memory of Dormer's actions in the previous case."[11]

Another key element of the film is Dormer's (and many others' appearance vs. the complexity of their inner lives). The naïve rookie (and very wholesome Rocky Mountain-esque) Alaskan cop, Ellie, who picks up Dormer and Hap from the plane landing sight, says about meeting the harden LA detective, "It's so incredible to be working with you, detective Dormer. I've followed all of your cases" (*Insomnia* 2002). Dormer's exterior is defined by his reputation, which is manifested in his cases. These cases (in the largely semi-digital) are typed and recorded on paper. Ellie, near the beginning of the film, provides a list of the famous cases on which Will has worked: "I've followed all your cases, Theodore Dineli, Frank and Casey Prud'homme, the Port Angeles shootings, and especially the Leland Street Murders. That was my case study at the Academy" (*Insomnia* 2002). Ellie has a (literal) textbook examination of the facts of Will Dormer's life and work. However, as the film unfolds, we learn there is more to the matter. Many (perhaps all?) of these cases were solved with the help of a variety of illegal methods, including planting evidence.

This is another key image in the film: the contrast between word or deed or the stories that people tell about themselves or others. The point is that Dormer is a good character on the outside, but he is complex. There is a hidden truth to him behind the truth of his moral goodness and skill as a detective. This is point is further emphasized during the "halibut" dinner between Hap and Dormer at their hotel in which Hap confesses that he will make a deal, which will likely bring down Dormer. In this scene, Dormer's (perhaps reckless) selflessness and commitment to duty is challenged by Hap's devotion to his family. Although aware of Dormer's missteps as a cop (as Dormer is of Hap's "shaking down drug dealers"), Hap views Dormer as a "hero" with a solid reputation (*Insomnia* 2002). Dormer responds that this reputation is his "problem" (*Insomnia* 2002). Hap refers to Dormer as being "clean," but Dormer responds, "I'm a good cop, yeah . . . " (*Insomnia* 2002). This point is that Dormer is not clean or immaculate but rather he has some dirt on him even though he envisions himself as being a good cop. Dormer explains that "There's always something they could use to get at your credibility" (*Insomnia* 2002). This point is key for, in noir, no one (or at least very few people) are innocent. All the cases depended upon Dormer's "word" and "judgement" (*Insomnia* 2002). This word and judgement would be cast into doubt by the fact that Dormer has done some unquestionable things in apprehending criminals. His reputation is thus dependent upon the illusion of cleanliness. Dormer's life is marked by "moral confusion," although his life is marked by "genuine integrity."[12] "You're tainted forever. You don't' get to pick when you tell the truth. Truth is beyond that," Finch tells Dormer (*Insomnia* 2002). Garcia argues that "in fighting for Burr against Finch, Will Dormer is struggling with and for his own self, the two characters representing different aspects of his past, possible futures, and version of his identity" and these two characters, offer him "divergent possible futures."[13] Ellie ironically presents both sides of Dormer when she tells him at a morning after a bad night's sleep, "A good cop can't sleep because a piece of the puzzle's missing, and a bad cop can't sleep because his conscience won't let him" (*Insomnia* 2002). Dormer can't sleep for both reasons. He is a good bad cop or a bad good cop. This contrast is repeated after Dormer violently interrogates Finch. One of the Nightmute PD tells Finch, "He's a good cop" (*Insomnia* 2002). Finch responds, "I'd hate to see the bad cop" (*Insomnia* 2002). Both are right in their description of Dormer who is both good and bad. This sense of Dormer as a flawed hero is in stark contrast to Nightmute's chief of police's statement to Hap and Dormer upon their arrival: "I think you're going to find us a lot more straight forward up here. Good guys. Bad guys. It's simple" (*Insomnia* 2002). It may be that simple for certain figures like Dobbs who is entirely bad and Ellie who is mostly good, but for both Finch and Dormer (and for Christopher Nolan), the truth is not that simple.

This notion of shades or degrees of evil is critical in the film. During the halibut dinner Hap refers to the child murder Dobbs as being "shit." Such a harsh term is applicable to a child murderer and abuser. This is the bottom of the moral standards of the film. Dobbs is unquestionably evil in *Insomnia*, and this wickedness at least lends weight to the idea that Dormer was somewhat justified in tapering with the evidence to get Dobbs convicted. But each person in the film (with the possible exception of the rookie Ellie) is tainted.

Kay's boyfriend Randy is abusive and headstrong. He deserves noirish justice, but he does not deserve to be the patsy for the murder. Moreover, we learn that he lives in a room above his grandfather's, so there is clearly some trauma in Randy's own background. This does not justify Randy's crimes, but it does complicate things further. He is not aware of his own wickedness or at least is not consciously aware. While being interrogated in the empty schoolroom, he says he hasn't done anything wrong. Dormer responds, "You haven't?" This is a classic noirish line in which the notion of pervasive human guilt is addressed. When he is aware of his guilt as well as aware of Dormer's awareness of his guilt, he, like Dormer himself, lashes out in anger. Randy eventually admits—albeit obloquy—to hitting Kay by saying that he tried "pretty hard" to get the information out of her (*Insomnia* 2002). This admission produces somewhat of a cathartic experience for Randy as he (at least temporarily) has a look of relief on his face—his defiance and anger will later return. The key point is that Randy, like virtually every other character in the film, is guilty of something. The degree to which he should be punished is difficult to determine especially when that punishment is being affected by police who are themselves very imperfect. Ellie herself is being set up in typical noir fashion to become some version of a corrupt cop. When the chief says that Ellie "loves the job" after Dormer calls her a "nice kid," there is the idea that, as in all, noir films, she will no longer be a nice kid after a few cases, and her love for the job will turn into a combination of hatred and obsession (*Insomnia* 2002).

On one level, all of the corruption is hidden under the belief that the ends justify the means and the idea of the "noble lie" that Nolan will explore in other films such as *Interstellar* and the *Dark Knight* trilogy. This point is emphasized by Chief Nyback in the scene after they discover Kay Connelly's bag. Will is worried about pulling a trick on the Kay Connelly suspect by placing her bag where they found it and announcing that the bag is missing. Chief Nyback assures him: "Someone out there just beat a 17-year-old girl to death. Your job is to find them. You're a cop, not a lawyer" (*Insomnia* 2002).

He further tells him not to let Internal Affairs castrate him. Dormer's job is to find bad guys. He employs irregular methods and does not do it "by the book" (*Insomnia* 2002). He is justified in doing so as a policeman, but he cannot hide the truth that he has committed crimes and done immoral things, the last being the accident murder of Hap. There further an incredible violence in Dormer, which is revealed in Dormer's outbursts. It is further noted in Finch's comment after Dormer rages at him, "I thought you wanted to kill me in there" (*Insomnia* 2002). To which Dormer responds, "I did" (*Insomnia* 2002). Just as Dormer appears to lust (albeit briefly) after Tanya Francke and is possibly projecting that lust onto Finch during the interrogation scene (even though, of course, Finch grotesquely lusted after Kay Connell), so too does he have the same homicidal impulses as the men he arrests. The difference is that does not act on them. He has them under control (most of the time). He is not the same "excrement" as the worst villains in the film. However, Finch himself, because of his intelligence and cleverness, also, at least on one level, evades an easy categorization.

Despite his apparently complexity, Walter Finch is clearly the villain of the film. He brutally murders a seventeen-year-old girl whom he was apparently grooming and for him he had an odd attraction. However, this murder, until the end of the film, has yet to be brought to life. Walter Finch is in the eyes of the world a lonely novelist who escaped to Alaska. As he says, "There's no evidence that I killed Kay" (*Insomnia* 2002). There is no report or case on him yet. He says on the ferry a second time, "I'm not who you think I am" (*Insomnia* 2002). The notion here is that Dormer simply thinks that Finch is simply a scumbag criminal who murdered an underage on whom he had a disturbing crush. Finch has more in him than mere violence and lust. He does attempt to rationalize his lust when he tells Dormer what happened over the course of a phone call. Finch may have some truth to what he is saying to Walter, although, on the other hand, Dormer's description of him is also correct: "Lousy writer. Lonely freak. Murderer. No?" (*Insomnia* 2002). We don't know how "good" Finch's novels are, but he is a lonely freak as well as murder. Although, in a certain sense, Dormer is a lonely freak too as well as a murderer. Finch is, in a certain sense, and underdeveloped Dormer. He wanted to be a cop and writes detective novels. Both men have killed and view themselves as superior to others, as Finch notes, the local Alaskan cops. Garcia notes that Finch's applies the "procedures of professional inquiry to solve murder, though only those of his own fictional invention."[14] Finch also thinks that his knowledge of fictional killings makes able to "perceive the deeper affinity between those who commit crimes, even murders, and those who do not."[15]

Finch attempts to convince Dormer of their alleged similarities, depicting Dormer and him as having some secret inside knowledge because of both of them having killed someone. He tells Dormer, "Killing changes you. You know that. It's not guilt. I never meant to do it. It's like awareness" (*Insomnia* 2002). Finch is sentimental and attempts to rationalize and justify his feelings to Dormer, whom he considers to be a kindred spirit. Dormer, however, responds with hard-headed honesty: "You trying to impress me, Finch? Because you got the wrong guy. Killing that girl made you feel special" (*Insomnia* 2002). He is very likely right in noting that Finch is a sadistic murderer, but Dormer himself very likely has experienced similar emotions in killing criminals. His killing of Hap, however, reveals that he Its because Dormer himself felt special. He says, "But you're not. You're the same distorted, pathetic freak I've been dealing with thirty years" (*Insomnia* 2002). This is partially true and partially not true of Dormer himself.

Moreover, Dormer's suggestion during the interrogation scene at the police station that Finch wanting to have sex with Kay but then regretting not having done it perhaps reflects the slightly flirtatious behavior that Dormer displays toward Kay's friend Tanya. Dormer glances at Tanya when they are driving and touches her hair when they are at the dump where Kay's body is found. This behavior is done to get information from Tanya, but it also does not mean that Dormer did not have some of the same thoughts that affected Finch. Indeed, when Dormer tells Finch, "You're about as mysterious to me as a blocked toilet is to a plumber," he is revealing that he understands much of what Finch is feeling (*Insomnia* 2002). The difference is that Dormer chooses to do good and (mostly) adverts choosing evil. Finch tells Dormer: "Motivations are everything, Will" (*Insomnia* 2002). Finch's motivations may be complex, but he is willing to commit horrendous acts of evil.

Finch tries to justify his actions to Dormer and tries to equate their killings, telling Dormer, "We're in the same situation, here" (*Insomnia* 2002). Finch explains to Dormer, "You didn't mean to kill, Hap any more than I meant to kill Kate" (*Insomnia* 2002). This is not true as Dormer's act was done in a split-second while Finch's was an extended act of violent rage. Finch further attempts to shift the blame by describing Kay's death as a seeming accident: "I didn't murder her. I killed her. It just ended up that way" (*Insomnia* 2002). Finch's refusal to take responsibility for what he did is another key difference between Dormer and him. Dormer eventually reveals the truth. However, according to McGowan, in *Insomnia* "the lie provides the key to arriving at truth."[16] McGowan argues that the message of *Insomnia* is not the relativization of truth but "a reformulation of the relationship between the lie and truth."[17] *Insomnia* achieves these revelations, McGowan argues, by "foregrounding the necessary lie throughout but ending with the revelation of truth. . . . "[18] McGowan further explains that in *Insomnia*, "One can never escape deception because it forms the basis of our inquiry into truth. The recognition of the priority of the lie allows us to reimagine truth in the form of fiction."[19] Yet, this truth can only merge through the lie Dormer fabricates after shooting Hap.[20] However, the ending is not fiction so much as it is the revelation of truth through debasement and deconstruction of the self. While driving with Ellie in the morning, Dormer says, "You know small lies. Small mistakes. People give themselves away same away in misdemeanors as they do in murder cases. It's just human nature" (*Insomnia* 2002). Dormer himself has made some small mistakes himself. Who Finch is, is revealed in Dormer's comment that Kay is the first of many murders. Finch had "crossed the line, and he didn't even blink" (*Insomnia* 2002). Dormer crossed the line too, but his crossing did not produce a murderer like Finch; it produced a dirty cop. According to McGowan, the film depicts "the necessary badness of the good cop."[21]

Bodies—both living and dead—are also sites of truth in the film. Although he has the coroner's report, Dormer wants to see the body of Kay Connelly for himself. The mustached Alaskan cop (who appears skeptical of the outsider Dormer) Dugger offers just the report, but Dormer wants to also see the body, which reveals the truth of what happened, noting various modifications that Finch made to the corpse. Dugger says, "the body gave us nothing" (*Insomnia* 2002). Dormer responds, "Oh, she gave us plenty" (*Insomnia* 2002). It is important that he uses the third-person feminine pronoun she. Much of the film—like much of Nolan's films—is focused on the solidity of the material world and hard data facts as well as how these facts can be manipulated to obscure the truth. Detective Dormer has a scare on his neck. She asks him, "That's where Ronald Langley cut you in the basement of his father's house on 325 Leland, isn't it?" (*Insomnia* 2002). Once again, trauma to the body gives signs of truth. It is not the full truth (there is probably more to the story).

Contrary to Nolan films like *Memento* and *Inception*, *Insomnia* is not structured upon a never ended series of lies. The truth is that Will Dormer is a good cop who used illegal means to put away criminals who were guilty of horrendous evil. The truth of the matter is, like Guy Haines in Hitchcock's 1951 *Strangers on a Train*, on some level, Dormer wanted to kill his partner Hap, but he also would not deliberately and methodically have killed him. The murder of Hap was very likely an (accident) even if Will wanted to kill him. Will is thus not innocent of the desire for murder or innocent of committing crimes to punish criminals, but he is not as guilty as the criminals whom he put away. Finch, however, takes ten minutes to kill Kay. Clearly, Finch's self-defense has some merit. He is clearly a mentally ill man and had some bizarre attraction to the girl. However, what distinguishes Dormer from Finch is his desire and ability to the right thing as well as his refusal to do the wrong thing. Garcia importantly notes that it is Dormer's final attempt to protect Ellie from Finch as opposed to vice versa that "seals his fate and secures him a kind of redemption. . . . "[22] Ellie's process is one of disillusionment, and "Dormer must decide whether to try to protect her and again become worthy of her respect. . . . "[23] Garcia argues, "It is the fact that Dormer can still save himself, can still 'come back,' that provides the film its central ethical drama. At the end of the film, according to Garcia, Dormer receives "long delayed rest and peace" after undergoing an "involuntary" purgatory.[24] There is no question that Dormer suffers incredibly throughout the film, and this suffering increases after the (very likely) accidently kills Hap. In the end, he suffers attempting to hide a truth with a lie.

It is difficult (and perhaps impossible and even unnecessary) for critics to step outside their own *weltanschauung*. Clearly, a believer in real ontology such as a Christian could see the film as affirming the transcendence and permanence of the truth (this is exactly what J. L. A. Garcia does in his analysis). However, this is exactly what the film does perhaps more so than any other Christopher Nolan film. In *Insomnia*, the truth is something bigger than delusion and doubt and lies. It is also something bigger than all too human perception. In *Insomnia* the truth is something supra-human. It is something above and beyond human control and something to which humans must acquiesce. Will says, "let me sleep" (*Insomnia* 2002). Ellie tells him, "Nobody needs to know. You didn't mean to do it, and I know it even if you don't" (*Insomnia* 2002). Will tells her "don't lose your way" (*Insomnia* 2002). The implication here, contrary to the bulk of Nolan's films, is that there is a right and wrong way. There is a truth and this truth manifests itself in humble self-abnegation.

Most of Nolan's films deal with the notion of the "noble lie" or the fiction necessary to maintain dwelling in the world. This lie takes many forms. Some figures like *Memento*'s Leonard Shelby lie to themselves in order to escape from the monotony of their all too comfortably life. Leonard had achieved the apex of consumer life as a successful insurance fraud investigator living in late 1990s/early 2000s California. This life enables Leonard as an affluent and good-looking male the time, education and leisure to create his own fantasy in which he brutally murders criminals. This is the central paradox of *Memento* as well as much of noir: prosperity leads to unhappiness and boredom. This prosperity in Nolan's vision is fundamentally a good.

The *Dark Knight* trilogy further deals with the problem of the noble lie. Bruce Wayne becoming Batman is the combination of two lies and two realities. Batman is a lie, a mask that Bruce Wayne wears, but Batman is also the truth of who Bruce Wayne is. He is a powerful and skilled fighter who sacrifices himself for the sake of Gotham (which serves as a vision of New York and America). Bruce Wayne the playboy is an act as well, but this spoiled and clueless playboy is, in a certain sense, part of who he is. Bruce Wayne, Jim

Gordon, Rachel Dawes, and Harvey Dent all believe that Gotham is fighting for, and, in as much as Gotham is an image of America, it is, for Christopher Nolan, worth fighting for. Despite its imperfections, Gotham as a symbol of American liberalism is worth fighting (and lying for). It is true that the "truth" erupts several times throughout the *Dark Knight* trilogy. Batman and Gordon's attempt to shield Harvey Dent from blame in *The Dark Knight* is upended in *The Dark Knight Rises* by Bane. However, the movie series ends with several lies. There is the lie that "Batman" died saving the city. There is further the lie of the "happily after scene" between Selena Kyle and Bruce Wayne, two deeply traumatized individuals who dress up and costumes and fight criminals, who abscond to Florence. Nonetheless, the entire system that provides such a lavish (if fictious) happily ever after is depicted approvingly throughout Nolan's work.

Inception is a film full of interminable lies. It is about the comforting lies that foment reconciliation in families. Moreover, like *Memento*, it is about the lies and fantasies with which we fill our lives in order to be happy. Cobb (probably) does not return to his real kids at the end of the film, but the key point is that he thinks he does. Fantasy is just as real or more real than reality. *Inception* is about films and filmmaking, and just as the films Nolan himself produces and directs are made possible by the world of American capitalism, so too is the world of Cobb's inceptions and dreams. The projected future world of *Inception* is a world dominated by (Western) corporations who have the ability to colonize the minds of human subjects. Nolan, himself able to create films popular around the globe and enter the minds of his audience, "incepting" them, does not seem to depict this future world in a negative light.

Interstellar began as a film about a space race between the Chinese and Americans under the direction of Steven Spielberg. However, in the hands of Christopher Nolan, it became the story of the triumph of love between a father and his daughter as well as story about how a new kinder, gentler America could emerge during the Obama era in which the rougher Cold War and War on Terror version of the United States would be shed for a more tolerate and humanist vision of space. Love ultimately transcends space and time and Cooper returns to his daughter with whom he saves. The film only indirectly deals with the concept of the lie in as much as what Cooper and Murph achieve is done with the help of a project fantasy of highly evolved humans who travel backward in time to save the human race. Humankind led by an American family thus triumphs over disaster with fantasy. This does not make the love between Murph and Cooper any less real, but the film frames their familial love as the "engine" that will drive the new era of space exploration, and this new era of space exploration will be led by the United States.

Tenet presents one of the ultimate wish fulfillment fantasy of the twentieth century retooled for the twenty-first century: the James Bond life.

However, here it is retooled for the twenty-fist century with a historic Black American in the title role. While Nolan's casting was part of the wider post–George Floyd attempt to replace traditionally white characters with people of color, *Tenet* fails to present a convincing story in as much as John David Washington's blackness is completely silent throughout the film. He moves effortless throughout Europe as simply "some guy" who blends in, in nearly entirely white environments. The entire film reads as a recruitment film for the CIA or Western intelligence in general in which the tolerant American dominated West faces off against a violent and totalitarian (European) East headed by the Ukrainian arms dealer Sator. The ultimate message is the new global subject viewing the film can likewise serve as the "protagonist" in supporting the American-dominated West in its struggle against the "East" for control of the future.

Insomnia is different in as much as the "protagonist" dies at the end of film. It is in his death that the truth can finally be revealed. This perhaps is Nolan's message that only upon death will lies and deception cease or that lies are essential for human functioning. Regardless, the truth does come out and Ellie is directed toward the right path. The big question is then: what does Christopher Nolan believe? We don't quite know that answer, but using the notion of attunement from Heidegger we can answer the question of what his movies suggest is the most approximate truth for how politics should work. Throughout his work, Nolan presents the attractiveness of totalitarian or pre-liberal "Old World" political systems. Whether in the *Dark Night* trilogy or in the form of a "stiff upper lip" Anglo-Saxon/Germanic aggressive will to power nationalist liberalism as found in characters such as Dr. Mann, Nolan demonstrates that these systems are fundamentally too brutal and cruel to survive. In his films, Nolan prizes the self-sacrificing hero whose is ultimately humane and generous as opposed domineering and cruel.

This hero is motivated by love of family and country and is often overwhelmed by trauma obsession and grief. This hero makes mistakes and is deeply flawed and, in many ways, resembles the villain against (in Nolan it is usually "he") he is fighting. At the same time, this hero is driven by a love for female and some higher ideal. In Nolan's film, this higher ideal manifest itself in an (Anglo-)American patriotism. This patriotism is not unqualified or with criticism of American liberalism's flaws. However, Nolan quite clearly sees this Anglo-American liberalism as the best of many deeply flawed systems.

It is easy to take aim at the many injustices and faults of the Anglo-American order. Indeed, outside of Germany (and perhaps France), no two countries have come under the deconstructive gaze more than the United States and Great Britain. At the same time, there are numerous works arguing for the inherent goodness of the United States and Britain—with some even arguing in support of the British Empire. As Christopher Nolan explores in his films, much of our understanding of reality is clouded by illusion and fantasy, and much of the time this illusion and fantasy is at least subconsciously willed by us. It is difficult to see the truth shinning forth, but as illustrated in *Insomnia*, the truth does find its way forth, and provides, for many, freedom.

NOTES

1. Garcia, "White Nights of the Soul," 96.
2. McGowan, *The Fictional Christopher Nolan*, 69.
3. Ibid.
4. McGowan, *The Fictional Christopher Nolan*, 79.
5. Shone, *The Nolan Variations*, 109–10.
6. Shone, *the Nolan Variations*, 112.
7. Garcia, "White Nights of the Soul, 86–87.
8. McGowan, *The Fictional Christopher Nolan*, 68.
9. Garcia, "White Nights of the Soul," 95–96.
10. Garcia, "White Nights of the Soul," 102.
11. Joy, "Revisiting the Scene of the Crime," 137.
12. Garcia, "White Nights of the Soul," 106.
13. Garcia, "White Nights of the Soul," 86–87.
14. Garcia, "White Nights of the Soul," 90–91.
15. Ibid.
16. McGowan, *The Fictional Christopher Nolan*, 82.
17. McGowan, *The Fictional Christopher Nolan*, 85.
18. Ibid.
19. Ibid.
20. McGowan, *The Fictional Christopher Nolan*, 79.
21. McGowan, *The Fictional Christopher Nolan*, 71.
22. Garcia, "White Nights of the Soul," 91.
23. Garcia, "White Nights of the Soul," 92.
24. Garcia, "White Nights of the Soul," 100.

References

Abiona, Ore. "*Tenet:* It's Ambitious, Glossy and the Black James Bond We've Been Waiting For." *The Root*, September 2, 2020, https://www.theroot.com/tenet-it-s-ambitious-glossy-and-the-black-james-bond-1844926933.

Alpert, Robert. "Dominant tendencies of 80s Hollywood revisited thirty years later." *Cineaction* 98 (2016), https://link.gale.com/apps/doc/A456344440/AONE?u=googlescholar&sid=googleScholar&xid=42d74dd9.

Attebery, "The magazine era: 1926–1960." James and Mendlesohn, 32–47.

Auxier, Randall E. "Once Upon a Time." Botz-Bornstein, 129–47.

Babb, Valerie "The Past is Never Past: The Call and Response between Marvel's *Black Panther* and Early Black Speculative Fiction." *African American Review*, 53, no. 2 (2020): pp. 95–109.

Boyd-Barrett, Oliver David Herrera, and Jim Baumann, *Hollywood and the CIA: Cinema, Defense, and Subversion*. New York: Routledge, 2011.

Blessing, Kimberly. "Mal-Placed Regret." Botz-Bornstein, 295–309.

Bordoloi, Mridul. "Re-packaging Disaster Post 9/11 and Christopher Nolan's *The Dark Knight* Trilogy." *Journal of Creative Communications* 7, no. 1 (2012): 87–100.

Bordwell, David. *The Way Hollywood Tells It*. Berkeley: University of California Press, 2007.

Boscaljon, Daniel. "The Flip Side of Justice: The Two-Face Spirit of *The Dark Knight*." *Iowa Journal of Cultural Studies*, vol. 14, no. 1 (2013): pp. 44–65.

Botz-Bornstein, Thorsten ed. *Inception and Philosophy: Ideas to Die For*. Chicago: Opencourt, 2011.

Bragues, George. "Memory and Morals in Memento." *Film-Philosophy* 12, no. 2 (2008): 62–80.

Brooker, Will. *Hunting the Dark Knight: Twenty-First Century Batman*. London: I.B. Tauris, 2012.

Brophy, Matthew. "Shared Dreams in Virtual Worlds." Botz-Bornstein, 189–202.

Burke, Liam. *The Comic Book Film Adaptation: Exploring Modern Hollywood's Leading Genre*. Jackson: University of Mississippi Press, 2015.

Carter, David. *Constellations: Inception*. Leighton: Auteur, 2019.

Chan, Albert J. "Honor and Redemption in Corporate Espionage." Johnson, 166–74.

"Christopher Nolan: 'Dark Knight Rises Isn't Political.' Interview with Christopher Nolan." *Rolling Stone*. Warner Media. July 20, 2012. Web. December 1, 2013.

Clarke, Melissa. "The Space-Time Image: The Case of Bergson, Deleuze, and Memento." *The Journal of Speculative Philosophy* 16, no. 3 (2002): 167–81.

Cobb, Jelani "'Black Panther' and the Invention of 'Africa.'" *The New Yorker*, February 18, 2018, https://www.newyorker.com/news/daily-comment/black-panther-and-the-invention-of-africa.

Cortiel, Jeanne, and Laura Oehme. "The Dark Knight's Dystopian Vision: Batman, Risk, and American National Identity." *European Journal of American Studies*, 10, no. 2 (2015). https://journals.openedition.org/ejas/10916.

Cramer, Kathryn. "Hard science fiction," James and Mendlesohn, 197–208.

"The Dark Knight—Christina Bale and Christopher Nolan interview." *Indie London*, http://www.indielondon.co.uk/Film-Review/the-dark-knight-christian-bale-and-christopher-nolan-interview.

Deakin, Peter. "Men in Crisis: Christopher Nolan, Untruths, and Fictionalising Masculinity." *The Cinema of Christopher Nolan: Imagining the Impossible*, edited by Jacqueline Furby and Stuart Joy, New York: Columbia University Press, 2015. pp. 85–98.

Dhaliwal, Nirpal. "How movies embraced Hinduism (without you even noticing)." *The Guardian*, December 25, 2014, https://www.theguardian.com/film/2014/dec/25/movies-embraced-hinduism.

Douthat, Ross. "The Politics of 'The Dark Knight Rises.'" *NYTimes.com*, July 23, 2012. Web. December 1, 2013.

Eco, Umberto. "The Myth of Superman." *Diacritics*, vol. 2, no. 1 (1972): pp. 14–22.

Farnell, Chris. "Tenet Opening Opera Scene Explained." *Den of Geek* May 1, 2021, https://www.denofgeek.com/movies/tenet-opening-scene-opera-explained/.

Fisher, Mark. *Capitalist Realism: Is There No Alternative?* Winchester: Zero Books, 2009.

Fisher, Mark. *Ghosts of My Life: Writings on Depression, Hauntology and Lost Futures*. Zero Books, 2014.

Fisher, Mark "How to kill a zombie: strategizing the end of neoliberalism." *Open Democracy*, July 18, 2013, https://www.opendemocracy.net/en/how-to-kill-zombie-strategizing-end-of-neoliberalism/.

Fisher, Mark, and Rob White. "The Politics of 'The Dark Knight Rises': A Discussion." *Film Quarterly*. UC Berkeley P. September 28, 2012. Web. December 1, 2013.

Floury, Nicolas. "Dreams, Mourning, and Desire." Botz-Bornstein, 233–42.

Forbes, Daniel. "You're Just a Shade." Botz-Bornstein, 313–14.

Fradley, Martin. "What Do You Believe In? Film Scholarship and the Cultural Politics of the Dark Knight Franchise," *Film Quarterly* 66, no. 3 (2013): 15–27.

Frank. Michael C. "Alien Terrorists: Public Discourse on 9/11 and the American Science Fiction Film." in Philip Hammond, ed. *Screens of Terror: Representations of War and Terrorism in Film and Television Since 9/11*. Suffolk: Arima, 2011, pp. 149–69.

Fukuyama, Francis. "The End of History." *The National Interest* no. 16 (1989): pp. 3–18.

Fukuyama, Francis. *The End of History and the Last Man*. New York: Free Press, 2006.

Furby, Jacqueline, and Stuart Joy, editors. *The Cinema of Christopher Nolan: Imagining the Impossible*, New York: Columbia University Press, 2015.

Gallego, Carlos. "Coordinating Contemporaneity: (Post)Modernity, 9/11, and the Dialectical Imagery of *Memento*." *Cultural Critique* 75 (2010): 31–64.

Gargett, Adrian. "Nolan's Memento, Memory, and Recognition." *Comparative Literature and Culture* 4, no. 3 (2002). http://dx.doi.org/10.7771/1481-4374-1163.

Garvin, Joseph. "Right and Wrong in Dreams," Botz-Bornstein, 109–16.

Gaut, Berys. "Telling Stories: Narration, Emotion, and Insight in Memento." *Narrative, Emotion, and Insight*, edited by Noel Carroll and John Gibson. University Park: Penn State University Press, 2011. 23–44.

Gearhart, Grant. "Suiting Up the Hero: Legacies of Medieval and Renaissance Armor and Identity in Christopher Nolan's *Batman Begins*." *The Journal of Popular Culture* 50, no. 4 (2017): 665–84.

Geary, Daniel, Camilla Schofield, and Jennifer Sutton, editors. *Global White Nationalism: From Apartheid to Trump*, Manchester: Manchester University Press, 2020.

Goh, Robbie B. H. "Myths of Reversal: Backwards Narratives, Normative Schizophrenia, and the Culture of Casual Agnosticism." *Social Semiotics* 18, no. 1 (2008): 61–77.

Grossman, Julie. *Rethinking the Femme Fatale in Film Noir: Ready for Her Close-Up*. New York: Palgrave Macmillan, 2009.

Hajjar, Lisa. "From the Manchurian Candidate to Zero Dark Thirty: Reading the CIA's History of Torture through Hollywood Thrillers." *Film & History* vol. 47, no. 2 (2017): 41–54.

Hassler-Forest, Dan. *Capitalist Superheroes: Caped Crusaders in the Neoliberal Age*. Winchester: Zero Books, 2012.

Hastings, Michael. *The Operators: The Wild and Terrifying Inside Story of America's War in Afghanistan*. New York: Penguin, 2012.

Haynes, Jeffrey. *Trump and the Politics of Neo-Nationalism: The Christian Right and Secular nationalism in America*. London: Routledge, 2021.

Hesselberth, Pepita, and Laura Schuster. "Into the Mind and Out to the World: Memory Anxiety in the Mind-Game Film." *Mind the Screen: Media Concepts according to Thomas Elsaesser*, edited by Jaap Kooijman et al. Amsterdam: Amsterdam University Press, 2008. pp. 96–111.

Horton, Owen R. "Origin Stories: Rebooting Masculinity in Superhero Films After 9/11." *Human: Journal of Literature & Culture* no. 5 (2016): 72–85.

Husson, Valentin. ""Building and Dwelling in Inception." Johnson, 269–78.

Ip, John. "The Dark Knights War on Terrorism." *Ohio State journal of Criminal Law* 9, no. 1 (2011): 209–24.

Jackson, Tony E. "'Graphism' and Story-Time in Memento." *Mosaic* 40, no. 3 (2007): 51–66.

James, Edward, and Farah Mendlesohn, eds. *The Cambridge Companion to Science Fiction*. Cambridge: Cambridge University Press, 2003.

Jameson, Frederic. *Postmodernism: Or, the Cultural Logic of Late Capitalism*. Chapel Hill, NC: Duke University Press, 1981.

Jeffords, Susan. *Hard Bodies: Hollywood Masculinity in the Reagan Era*. New Brunswick, NJ: Rutgers University Press, 1994.

Jesser, Jody Duncan, and Janine Pourroy. *The Art and Making of* The Dark Knight *Trilogy*. New York: ABRAMS, 2012.

Johnson, Chalmers. *Blowback: The Costs and Consequences of American Empire*. New York: Henry Holt, 2001.

Johnson, David Kyle, ed. *Inception and Philosophy: Because Its Never Just a Dream*. New York: Wiley, 2011.

Johnson, Vilja "'It's What You Do that Defines You': Christopher Nolan's Batman as Moral Philosopher." *The Journal of Popular Culture* 47, no. 5 (2014): pp. 952–67.

Joy, Stuart. *The Traumatic Screen: The Films of Christopher Nolan*. Bristol: Intellect, 2020.

Kania, Andrew, editor. *Philosophers on Film: Memento*. New York: Routledge, 2009.

Klavan, Andrew. "What Bush and Batman Have in Common." *The Wall Street Journal*, July 25, 2008. http://www.wsj.com/articles / SB121694247.343482821=

Klein, Naomi. *The Shock Doctrine: The Rise of Disaster Capitalism*. New York: Henry Holt, 2007.

Laderman, Scott, and Tim Gruenewald, ed. *Imperial Benevolence: U.S. Foreign Policy and Popular Culture since 9/11*. Berkeley: University of California Press, 2018.

Leonard, Elisabeth Anne. "Race and Ethnicity in Science Fiction." James and Mendlesohn, 253–263.

Lyons, Diran. "Vengeance, the Powers of the False, and the Time-Image in Christopher Nolan's Memento: A Note on Ressentiment at the Beginning of the New Millennium." *Angelaki*, 2, no. 1 (2006): pp. 127–35.

Lyotard, Jean-Frangois. *The Postmodern Condition: A Report on Knowledge*. Translated by Geoff Bennington and Brian Massumi. Minneapolis: University of Minnesota Press, 1984.

Margulies, Joseph. *What Changed When Everything Changed: 9/11 and the Making of National Identity*. New Haven, CT: Yale University Press, 2013.

Matadeen, Renaldo. "Tenet Basically Gives Hollywood Its First Black James Bond." *CBR.com*, September 12, 2020, https://www.cbr.com/tenet-hollywood-first-black-james-bond/.

McSweeney, Terrence. *The "War on Terror" and American Film: 9/11 Frames per Second.* Edinburgh: Edinburgh University Press, 2014.

McGinley, Rhys. "10 Unpopular Opinions About Christopher Nolan Movies (According to Reddit)." *ScreenRant*, July 22, 2021, https://screenrant.com/christopher-nolan-movies-unpopular-opinions-reddit/

McGowan, Todd. *The Fictional Christopher Nolan*. Austin: University of Texas Press, 2012.

McGowan, Todd. "Memento and the Desire Not to Know." *The Fictional Christopher Nolan*. Austin: University of Texas Press, 2012. pp. 39–66.

Molloy, Claire. *Memento*. Edinburgh: Edinburgh University Press, 2010.

Mottram, James. *The Making of Memento*. New York: Faber and Faber, 2002.

Ney, Jason. "Dark Roots: Christopher Nolan and Noir." *Noir City*, 2013, 61–67, *Film Noir Foundation*, http://filmnoirfoundation.org/noircitymag/Dark-Roots.pdf

Niessen, Niels. "Black Panther Transmedia: The Revolution Will Not Be Streamed." *JCMS: Journal of Cinema and Media Studies*, 60, no. 5 (2020–2021): pp. 1–30.

Nolan, Christopher, dir. *Batman Begins*. 2005; Burbank, CA: Warner Bros.

Nolan, Christopher, dir. *The Dark Knight*. 2008; Burbank, CA: Warner Bros.

Nolan Christopher, dir. *The Dark Knight Rises*. 2012; Burbank, CA: Warner Bros.

Nolan, Christopher, dir. *Inception*. 2010; Burbank, CA: Warner Bros.

Nolan, Christopher, dir. *Interstellar*. 2014; Los Angeles, CA: Paramount.

Nolan Christopher, dir. *Memento*. 2000; Burbank, CA: Warner Bros.

Nolan, Christopher, dir. *Tenet*. 2020; Burbank, CA: Warner Bros.

Novak, Philip. "It's Like Waking": Making Meaning in and of Christopher Nolan's *Memento*." *Journal of Film and Video* 71, no. 4 (2019): pp. 195–226.

Parker, Jo Alyson. "Remembering the Future: Memento, the Reverse of Time's Arrow, and the Defects of Memory." *KronoScope* 4, no. 2 (2004): pp. 239–57.

Parker, Tracy K. '"Do I Lie to Myself to Be Flappy?': Self-Help Culture and Fragmentation in Postmodern Film." *Interdisciplinary Literary Studies* 10, no. 1 (2008): 1—15.

Podhoretz, John. "Evil Undone: The Moral Clarity of Christopher Nolan's Batman Series." *The Weekly Standard* 17.32, July 30, 2012. Web. December 1, 2013.

Ponniah, Gabriel. "Tenet Was Secretly 2020's James Bond Movie: Every 007 Trope Explored." *Screen Rant*, December 19, 2020, https://screenrant.com/tenet-bond-tropes-explained-007

Posner, Sarah. *Unholy: How White Christian Nationalists Powered the Trump Presidency, and the Devasting Legacy They Left Behind*. New York: Random House, 2021.

Ramji, Rubina. "From Navy Seals to The Siege: Getting to Know the Muslim Terrorist, Hollywood Style." *Journal of Religion & Film* 9, no. 2 (2005): 1–40.

Russell, Patrick Kent. "Christopher Nolan's *The Dark Knight* Trilogy as a Noir View of American Social Tensions." *Interdisciplinary Humanities* 33, no. 1 (2016): 171–86.

Said, Edward. *Orientalism*. New York: Vintage, 1979.

Sanger, David. *Confront and Conceal: Obama's Secret Wars and Surprising Use of American Poet*. New York: Crown, 2013.

Serdouk, Ali. "Hollywood, American Politics, and Terrorism: When Art Turns into a Political Tool." *Arab Studies Quarterly* vol. 43, no. 1 (2021): pp. 26–37.

Shone, Tom. *The Nolan Variation's: The Movies, Mysteries, and Marvels of Christopher Nolan*. New York: Alfred A. Knopf, 2020.

Shores, Tyler. "Paradox, Dreams and Strange Loops in Inception." Johnson, 326–37.

Sibielski, Rosalind. "Postmodern Narrative or Narrative of the Postmodern? History, Identity, and the Failure of Rationality as an Ordering Principle in Memento." *Literature and Psychology* 49, no. 4 (2004): pp. 82–100.

Sisco, Claire King, *Washed in Blood: Male Sacrifice, Trauma, and the Cinema.* Brunswick, NJ: Rutgers University Press, 2012.

Spicer, Andrew. "Problems of Memory and Identity in Neo-Noir's Existential Antihero." The Philosophy of Neo-Noir, edited by Mark T. Conrad. Lexington: University of Kentucky Press, 2007. pp. 47–63.

Spivak, Gayatri Chakravorty. "Can the Subaltern Speak?" *Marxism and the Interpretation of Culture*, edited by Cary Nelson and Lawrence Grossberg. Champaign: University of Illinois Press, 1988. pp. 271–316.

Treat, Shaun. "How America Learned to Stop Worrying and Cynically ENJOY! The Post-9/11 Superhero Zeitgeist." *Communication and Critical/ Cultural Studies* 6, no. 4 (2009): 103–109.

Truitt, Brian "Daring, Diverse 'Black Panther' promises to be Hollywood's latest 'cultural touchstone.'" *USA Today*, January 29, 2018, https://www.usatoday.com/story/life/movies/2018/01/29/marvel-black-panther-superhero-diversity-cultural-touchstone-event/1071858001/

Tuck, Greg. "When more is less: CGI, spectacle and the capitalist sublime." *Science Fiction Film and Television* 1, no. 2 (2008): pp. 249–73.

Varisco, Daniel Martin. *Reading Orientalism: Said and the Unsaid.* Seattle: University of Washington Press, 2017.

Vaz, Mark Cotta. *Interstellar: Beyond Time and Space, Inside Christopher Nolan's Sci-Fi Epic*. Boston, MA: Running Press, 2014.

Vukovic, Kresimir, and Rajko Petkovic. "Legendary Caesar and the Architect Ariadne: Narrative, Myth and Psychology in Christopher Nolan's *Batman Begins*, *The Dark Knight* and *Inception*." *PSYART: A Hyperlink Journal for the Psychological Study of the Art* (2013), https://search.ebscohost.com/login.aspx?direct=true&AuthType=ip,shib&db=mlf&AN=EIS95399247&site=eds-live&scope=site&custid=gsw1.

Waddell, Nathan. "Christopher Nolan's *The Dark Knight*: An Unacknowledged Adaption of Joseph Conrad's *The Secret Agent*?" *Adaption*, 6, no. 1 (2012): pp. 43–59.

Weese, Katherine. "(Mis)Reading Natalie: The Viewer's Cognitive Processes and the Unreadable in Christopher Nolan's Memento." *StoryWorlds: A journal of Narrative Studies* 7, no. 1 (2015): 101–27.

Williams, Jordan. "How Steven Spielberg's *Interstellar Would Have Been an Entirely Different Movie*." *Screen Rant*, May 8, 2021, https://screenrant.com/steven-spielberg-interstellar-direct-pass-different-movie-how/.

Willmetts, Simon. *In Secrecy's Shadow: The OSS and CIA in Hollywood Cinema, 1941–1979.* Edinburgh: Edinburgh University Press, 2016.

Winchur, Drew. "Ideology in Christopher Nolan's Inception." *Cineaction* 88 (2012): 44–47.

Winterhalter, Benjamin. "The Politics of the Inner: Why *The Dark Knight Rises* is Not a Conservative Allegory." *The Journal of Popular Culture* 48, no. 5 (2015): 1030–47.

Wong (Omowale), Dwayne. "The Black Panther and Neo-Colonial Politics in Africa." *HuffPost*,
January 14, 2018, https://www.huffpost.com/entry/the-black-panther-and-neo-colonial-politics-in-africa_b_5a5be4c7e4b003efadb6af33.
Wood, Robin. *Hollywood from Vietnam to Reagan . . . and Beyond.* New York: Columbia University Press, 1986.
Yeo, Dennis. "The Mindfreak: Monstrous Memory in McGrath's The Grotesque (1989) and Nolan's Memento (2000)." *Irish Journal of Gothic and Horror Studies* 13 (2014): 77–93.
Žižek, Slavoj. *Living in the End Times*. London: Verso Books, 2010.
Žižek, Slavoj. "The Politics of Batman." *New Statesman*, August 23, 2012, http://www.newstatesman.com/culture/culture/2012/08/slavoj-%C5%BEi%C5%BEek-politics-batman.
Žižek, Slavoj. *Surplus-Enjoyment: A Guide for the Non-Perplexed*. London: Bloomsbury, 2022.
Žižek, Slavoj. *Welcome to the Desert of the Real*. London: Verso Books, 2002.

Index

About the Author

Jesse Russell is associate professor of English at Georgia Southwestern State University. His work has appeared in *Texas Studies in Literature and Language*; *New Blackfriars*; *European Journal of American Studies*; *International Journal of Jungian Studies*; *Renaissance Papers*; *Religion and the Arts*; *Politics and Religion*; *Cahiers Élisabéthains*; *Politics, Religion, and Ideology*; *Literature and Theology*; *Political Theology*; *Reinardus*; and *Explorations in Renaissance Culture*. He is also a long-distance runner and a volunteer fire fighter.